STRANGERS IN THE ARCHIVE

Victorian Literature and Culture Series

STRANGERS IN THE ARCHIVE

Literary Evidence and London's East End

Heidi Kaufman

University of Virginia Press • *Charlottesville and London*

University of Virginia Press

Printed in the United States of America on acid-free paper

First published 2022

9 8 7 6 5 4 3 2 1

Library of Congress Cataloging-in-Publication Data

Names: Kaufman, Heidi, author.
Title: Strangers in the archive : literary evidence and London's East End / Heidi Kaufman.
Other titles: Literary evidence and London's East End
Description: Charlottesville : University of Virginia Press, 2022. | Series: Victorian literature and culture series | Includes bibliographical references and index.
Identifiers: LCCN 2022007574 (print) | LCCN 2022007575 (ebook) | ISBN 9780813947372 (hardcover) | ISBN 9780813947389 (ebook)
Subjects: LCSH: East End (London, England)—Archival resources. | East End (London, England)—In literature. | Polack, Maria, 1787–1849. Fiction without romance, or, The locket watch. | East End (London, England)—Social conditions—19th century.
Classification: LCC DA685.E1 K38 2022 (print) | LCC DA685.E1 (ebook) | DDC 820.9/3584215—dc23/eng/20220429
LC record available at https://lccn.loc.gov/2022007574
LC ebook record available at https://lccn.loc.gov/2022007575

Cover art: *A Plan of the Cities of London and Westminster, and Borough of Southwark; with the Contiguous Buildings; from an Actual Survey, Taken by John Rocque, Land-Surveyor, and Engraved by John Pine* (London: John Pine & John Tinney, 1746). (Wikimedia/Library of Congress, Geography and Map Division, G5754.L7 1746.R6)

Archival silences, however they occur, have a potentially disastrous impact on the marginalized groups.

—Rodney G. S. Carter, "Of Things Said and Unsaid: Power, Archival Silences, and Power in Silence"

CONTENTS

ILLUSTRATIONS

ACKNOWLEDGMENTS

THIS PROJECT has benefited from the support of several organizations. I would like to thank the following for their generosity: the Bibliographical Society of America, the Hadassah-Brandeis Institute, the University of Oregon Libraries for a Digital Scholarship Center faculty grant, the College of Arts and Sciences at the University of Oregon for a Web Services development grant, and the Oregon Humanities Center for a Coleman-Guitteau Teaching Professorship Award. For their willingness to reproduce previously published work, I'd like to thank Taylor & Francis, the British Library, and Pearl Binder's three children.

The University of Virginia Press has been a paragon of professionalism and encouragement. I offer my most sincere thanks to Eric Brandt for his advocacy and care in shepherding this book through the review process. I am also very grateful for the anonymous readers and editors whose thoughtful suggestions made this a much better book. The series editors in particular exhibited an extraordinary level of care that has been invaluable to the revision process. I'd also like to thank Helen Chandler for her expert assistance with logistics and Colleen Romick Clark for her careful editing work.

The idea for this book emerged over time through discussions with students, colleagues, friends, and family. I treasure very early conversations with Amanda Wlock, whose inspiring curiosity and research interests helped me to see *Fiction without Romance* with fresh eyes. Since then, numerous students have shared their skills in research, transcription, data curation, digital recordings, recitations, and mapmaking. I wish to thank the following students in particular for their contributions to the East End Digital Library and research for this book: Nathan M. Asman, Joey Brundan, Ainsley Davis, Vharath Kumar, Greg LaLuna, Mai-Ling Maas, Katie Puzzullo Marchesiello, Suwan Phommachanh, Kenneth Wallach, Joey Walters, and Paige York. It's been a privilege to work with graduate students whose rigor and curiosity have pushed my thinking about digital humanities and archives: Caela Fenton, Courtney Floyd, Matt Hannah, Kate Huber, Maddie Pfleuger, Valérie Simon, Alexander Steele, Czander Tan, Sarah Wyer, and Dewi Yokelson. The East End Digital Library benefited enormously from the creative expertise of the following people who helped with site development and design inspiration: Anneliese

Dehner, Franny Gaede, Azle Malinao-Alvarez, Daniel Mundra, Jennifer R. O'Neal, Cameron Seright, Sarah Seymore, Julia Simic, Randy Sullivan, and Kate Thornhill. I'd also like to thank R. Benjamin Gorham, Research Data and GIS Specialist at Case Western Reserve University, for his expert assistance with Gephi.

The creation of the Lyon Archive and chapter 3 would not have been possible without the generosity of the Lyon family. Naomi Cream, Annabel Foster-Davis, and Diane Lyon Wead opened up their family archive to a stranger. It has been a rare and unexpected treat to learn from their stories and family history. Friends and colleagues in Jamaica have sustained my curiosity, facilitated research opportunities, and responded to my many questions with patience and kindness. I offer my most sincere gratitude to Cleveland DaCosta, Marina Delfos, Ainsley Henriques, and James Robertson.

Researchers in Devon offered their time and expertise to solve the riddle of locations in *Fiction without Romance*. Special thanks to Helen Fry, the late Ray Girvan, George Hampshire, Melissa Hardie-Budden, Nigel Hyman, Julia Neville, Phillippe Planel, and Tess Walker. In the final days of writing this book, key revelations emerged from Nicholas Hatton's exemplary sleuthing skills. I'm extraordinarily grateful for his help tracking down details about the lives of Elisabeth and Maria Polack. I'm also very grateful for advice and support from Malcolm Dick and Justine Pick at the University of Birmingham. Trips to UK repositories have been a centerpiece of this project. Research would have been impossible without support from archivists and librarians. Their scholarly acumen and expertise shaped my thinking in crucial ways. I'm especially grateful to librarians and archivists at the London Metropolitan Archives, the British Library, and the University of Southampton's Hartley Library. Melvyn Hartog and Leonard Shear from the United Synagogue assisted with questions during visits to Brady Street Cemetery, and I'm grateful for the time they spent answering questions and facilitating access to the cemetery. Charles Tucker, archivist of the London Beth Din, was exceptionally helpful in addressing early questions about the Polack family. I would also like to thank Louis Berk, whose photographs and friendship were a source of inspiration through the writing of this book. An early conversation with Ariel Sabar changed everything about my approach to the elusive Maria Polack and her East End community. I'm grateful for his suggestion to tell the story a different way.

Colleagues and friends have sustained me during the research and writing of this book. In obvious and subtle ways, they have given me the courage to take risks and to have faith in the process of finding my way through the maze of archival silences and echoes. I offer heartfelt thanks for their encouragement and friendship: Elizabeth Andersen, Liz Bohls, Joey Brown, Katy Brundan, Sarah Casteel, Steve Fickas, Karen Ford, Rachel Frankel, Gantt Gurley, David Hanson, Stephanie LeMenager, Toni Mucker, Toni Pitock, Elizabeth Raisanen, Meri-Jane Rochelson, Michael Scrivener, Helen Southworth, Sheila Spector, Marlene Tromp, Megan Ward, Jo Weaver, Karen Weisman, Sharon A. Weltman, and Mary Wood.

Family members have been steady supporters of this project for many years, providing curiosity and humor as they listened to strange stories of cemeteries and dusty archives. I cannot thank them enough for their love and encouragement. It has been a special privilege to share this project with my husband, David Schwartz, the only one on the planet whose archive fever rivals my own. I dedicate this book to him with my deepest gratitude for listening to me tell thousands of archive stories thousands of times and for his conviction—after all these years—that the lost pages of Polack's life will someday surface.

STRANGERS IN THE ARCHIVE

INTRODUCTION

Visuality and the Archive

On the morning of September 8, 1888, the *Illustrated London News* reported the first of many articles about the gruesome Whitechapel murderer, the figure who came to be known as "Jack the Ripper." According to the journalist,

> At a quarter to four on Friday morning Police-constable Neil was on his beat in Buck's-row, Thomas-street, Whitechapel, when his attention was attracted to the body of a woman lying on the pavement close to the door of the stable-yard in connection with Essex Wharf. Buck's-row, like many other miser thoroughfares in this and similar neighbourhoods, is not overburdened with gas lamps, and in the dim light the constable at first thought that the woman had fallen down in a drunken stupor and was sleeping off the effects of a night's debauch. With the aid of the light from his bullseye lantern Neil at once perceived that the woman had been the victim of some horrible outrage.[1]

The above passage includes details that came to define both the Victorian press's coverage of the murders and the East End locations where they occurred. The writer begins with a lurid description of Whitechapel, which by 1888 had a reputation as one of the most economically depressed districts in London. The docks, built in the early nineteenth century, brought shipping industry to the East End, thereby constructing its identity as a place where sailors and newly arrived immigrants made a home for themselves. In response, nineteenth-century writers and the periodical press habitually imagined the East End as both a place of foreigners and a foreign place.[2] Accounts of this region typically emphasized the East End's poverty, menacing aliens, prostitutes, and dark, labyrinthine streets. Significantly, in the above passage Police Constable Neil initially misreads the scene, assuming the body to be that of a woman passed out from drink. The bullseye lantern remedies his flawed conclusion. In this corrective process, however, the lantern throws the rest of the space into obscurity. Readers learn only about what falls within the margins of the lantern's stream of light—the murder victim—while the rest of the East End is cast in darkness, as if it didn't exist.

The choice of the *Illustrated London News* to depict a policeman holding up a bullseye lantern constructs the scene through Neil's gaze. Tim Barringer has read this kind of visuality as an assertion of an authoritative viewing position or "a regime of looking that is associated with a dominant ideology."[3] Neil's visuality is thus a projection constituted both by his authority as the police constable and by the lantern, the technology that presumably facilitates knowledge of the objects on which he shines the light. Yet the system of illumination doesn't simply guide the audience's eye; it determines the scope of our vision. In aligning readers with the police constable's visuality, the bullseye lantern engages in a curation process, creating the conditions of possibility for what we *can* see by delineating what will be made visible or hidden.

Neil was not alone in using a bullseye lantern to read the East End streets. A few years earlier Gustave Doré created an image of Whitechapel homelessness in his illustration "The Bull's-eye" (fig. 1). Set in precisely the location where the Whitechapel murders would take place a few years later, Doré's illustration depicts an East End family ambushed by the policeman's lamp. The beam of light exposes a family dressed in tattered clothes and barefoot as they are scrutinized by suspicious onlookers. But the precise prompting for the lantern remains unknown. The onlookers in this scene see only what the policeman deems significant, what *he* believes will be clarified by turning his penetrating lamp on his chosen target.

Instead of objectifying East Enders, like the image from the *Illustrated London News,* Doré's illustration makes an object of those who look. In Doré's account, the East End is constructed as a place where onlookers glare suspiciously at those deemed dangerous under the penetrating light of the bullseye lantern. It is perhaps understandable that bullseye lamps became so prominent in depictions of the late nineteenth-century East End. For it was in this period when a significant portion of its population was starving, a serial murderer was on the loose, and religious or racial persecution in other nations mobilized a steady flow of people to the East End, which in turn led to a rise of anti-Semitism, xenophobia, and racism.[4] Images of bullseye lamps in the periodical press reinforced the perception that a growing population of people imagined to be foreign and threatening needed to be watched.

My interest in the nineteenth-century East End began while researching Maria Polack, a resident of the East End and, according to Cecil Roth, the first English Jew to publish a novel, titled curiously *Fiction without*

FIG. 1. "The Bull's-eye," by Gustave Doré, from *London: A Pilgrimage* (1872)

Romance, or The Locket-Watch (1830).[5] Nothing I had read prepared me for the existence of a writer from Whitechapel—not Charles Dickens's depictions of the docklands in *Our Mutual Friend* or Henry Mayhew's presentation of shoeless street children subsisting on watercress sales in *London Labour and the London Poor;* not even George Eliot's eponymous hero, Daniel Deronda, encountering a foreign cultural universe in his forays into Whitechapel. In all of these accounts, the East End is portrayed as a site of abjection, a dangerous place where characters face hordes of uneducated or dangerous foreigners. Even today such narratives continue to dominate our perception of the nineteenth-century East End. A *Los Angeles Times* article about the 2012 Olympics offered the following description of this infamous region:

> This once was a grimy industrial zone where factories brewed ale and belched smoke, where 17th century French Huguenot immigrants were followed by 19th century Irishmen and Jews from throughout Europe, who were followed by 20th century Bengali immigrants, whose curry shops remain. . . . The East End wasn't just poor and dangerous in the bad old days; it was inspirationally poor and dangerous. Ikey Solomon, the 19th century criminal who inspired Charles Dickens' Fagin, had his shop

> here on Bell Lane. The unfortunate Joseph Merrick was displayed as the Elephant Man on Whitechapel Road and died after years in residence at the London Hospital on the same thoroughfare. Jack the Ripper stalked victims here and is said to have patronized the Ten Bells pub, still in business at 84 Commercial St. opposite the Old Spitalfields Market.[6]

Such descriptions deserve our attention not just because they are reductive and misleading, but because they point to the persistence of a pernicious Victorian narrative of East End danger.

In my early readings of *Fiction without Romance*, I was puzzled by Polack's allusions to London literary and theatre culture. How could an East Ender—poor, dirty, and likely a barefoot criminal—have written a novel integrating so many cultural interests on topics as far ranging as female education, romance, music, comparative religion, charity, theatre, anti-Semitism, and courtship rituals? And how could an East End writer in this period have gained access to printers and publishers, or to the books and theatre performances mentioned on the pages of her novel? Lending libraries and theatre tickets cost money, more money than starving people could afford. I struggled to accommodate my understanding of the East End life I'd studied on the pages of nineteenth-century periodicals and novels alongside the existence of *Fiction without Romance*. In an attempt to make sense of such inconsistencies, I made my way to archives containing evidence of nineteenth-century East End cultural life. When I began this project, I had assumed incorrectly that Maria Polack must have been an exceptional East Ender to have written as early as 1830, long before more famous East End authors, such as Arthur Morrison and Israel Zangwill, published successful fiction in the 1880s and 1890s. My initial forays into archives suggested that nineteenth-century East Enders had a vibrant cultural history as writers, printers, musicians, painters, actors, teachers, and philanthropists. Admittedly, most of their work hadn't been published, but archival records preserved traces of creative and intellectual industry that directly challenged infamous portraits of the East End found in the popular press. Why, I wondered, do depictions of this important region of London remain mired in sensational stories of crime and filth at the expense of narratives of artistic culture and intellectual life? Or more to the point of this study, how might we read archival evidence of East End cultural and intellectual production against sensational and well-known narratives of East End depravity?

This study argues that in spite of their poverty or hardships, many nineteenth-century residents of the East End were intellectually curious, artistically productive, and eager to redress economic or social hardships of fellow community members. Yet their voices are mostly absent from the historiography of the East End. Scholarship on Victorian London remains primarily focused instead on popular writers—such as Dickens, Mayhew, and Stead, to name just a few—whose work created powerful and enduring social commentary about the locations they visited in their sojourns through East End neighborhoods.[7] Even late-century writers, such as William Booth and Margaret Harkness, suggest that economic and social reform were imported to the East End by outsiders, and thus were not significant concerns among East End residents. Ellen Ross's study of working-class culture from 1870 through the post–World War I era demonstrates that in fact "mothers and their domestic needs were in many ways the key to the order and pattern that the observers began to find in the noisy, bustling streets of the East End." Their role in supporting one another was often overlooked by late-Victorian social reformers.[8]

Strangers in the Archive considers narratives created by insiders, or residents of the East End, that resist well-known stories of depravity produced by visitors. At the same time, I politicize the category of "insiders" by foregrounding the diasporic or marginalized identities of those living in and immigrating to the East End in this period. My goal is not to argue that one perspective or group got the East End "right" in their depictions, but to show how the East End's identity emerged in this period through voices of dissent, dissonance, and resistance, many of which have been occluded by narratives from the periodical press and popular novels that tend to flatten the East End's qualities with images depicting universal poverty and pervasive crime. Such reductive and sensational stereotypes have a tendency to dehumanize the working classes and ethnic and racial minorities living in the East End.

I approach the archives discussed in this study not as neutral, unmediated holding tanks of rare materials, but as politicized spaces with the power to invent and challenge our understanding of East End literary, print, and material cultures. And I pay particular attention to the archive's form and history, as a space whose boundaries, provenance, infrastructure, and selected/saved content work to recover, shape, and sometimes silence East End voices. The first chapter of this study examines the evolution of nineteenth-century published discourse that helped construct the East End as a site in desperate need of social reformers. The subsequent three chapters and conclusion focus on archives that resist these well-known constructions in quiet and sometimes profound ways. Finally, my creation of a digital archive that corresponds with chapters in this study weaves together and highlights archival voices otherwise difficult to access. Together, the book and digital archive demonstrate how physical and digital archives challenge well-known historiographies of the East End, and how the creation of new archives might offer key scholarly interventions in dominant or reductive spatial narratives of Victorian London and literary culture.

The East End and Its Others

By the time the *Illustrated London News* and Doré published their texts, the East End had long been constructed in the periodical press as a cultural wasteland, a ghetto space dominated by ethnic minorities and working-class people in desperate need of redemption by middle-class Christian social reformers.[9] Such narratives were frequently informed by anti-immigration rhetoric. One of the earliest immigrant groups to arrive in large numbers was the French Huguenots, or Protestants who fled seventeenth-century Catholic oppression. They were followed by Sephardim, or Jews originally expelled from the Iberian Peninsula by the Spanish Inquisition and subsequently settled in Amsterdam prior to their migration to London for greater economic and political freedom. By the eighteenth and early nineteenth centuries, lascars from southeast Asia found their way to the East End through work in the shipping industry, while waves of Ashkenazim, or Jews from central and eastern Europe, also began establishing communities. Irish groups followed during and after the famine (1845–49), succeeded by a second generation of Ashkenazim fleeing eastern European and Russian pogroms of the 1880s and beyond. Throughout the nineteenth century, people enslaved or formerly enslaved as well as other Afro-Caribbean individuals made their way to the East End. Additional Caribbean and West Indian groups arrived in larger waves around the turn of the twentieth century and beyond, alongside Chinese, Indian, Pakistani, Malaysian, and African peoples.[10]

Nineteenth-century literary culture commonly evokes these immigration histories with stories and images of dangerous East End foreigners. Dickens's *Oliver Twist* (1837–39) rehearses some of the anxieties that produced the East End and its growing population as a threat. In the following passage the narrator imagines the villainous Fagin leaving his Whitechapel home:

> The Jew stopped for an instant at the corner of the street; and, glancing suspiciously round, crossed the road, and struck off in the direction

> of Spitalfields. . . . The mud lay thick upon the stones: and a black mist hung over the streets; the rain fell sluggishly down: and everything felt cold and clammy to the touch. It seemed just the night when it befitted such a being as the Jew, to be abroad. As he glided stealthily along, creeping beneath the shelter of the walls and doorways, the hideous old man seemed like some loathsome reptile, engendered in the slime and darkness through which he moved: crawling forth, by night, in search of some rich offal for a meal.[11]

Fagin isn't just an alien intruder in this passage; he is a product of his filthy East End environment, "engendered in the slime and darkness through which he moved." He's also a foreign presence and a throwback from an earlier developmental stage of humanity. Dickens provides several names—Jew, hideous old man, and loathsome reptile—which together render Fagin both degenerate and the antithesis of this progress novel's English hero, Oliver Twist. It's noteworthy that Dickens's narrator speaks from a distance, not as an East End insider, but as a viewer gazing into an unfamiliar region of London.

Seven years earlier, the East End Jewish author Maria Polack offered a description of a sukkah near the location where Dickens placed Fagin's Whitechapel home. A sukkah is a holy space created in observance of Sukkot, a Jewish holiday celebrating the harvest. Polack's construction of Jewishness in the following passage offers a striking contrast with Dickens's portrayal of degenerate East End Jewish life.[12]

> About the middle of the yard, a temporary room had been erected, of dimensions sufficiently spacious for the accommodation of a very large party. It was perfect in every respect, except the ceiling, being built totally without a roof; this deficiency was partially supplied by laths, which were place[d] crosswise in the style of lattice work; these were covered outside, by a variety of green foliage, disposed in such a manner, as to render the sky distinctly visible through its branches: but more perfect light was admitted through handsome sash windows, each side of the room having two. These were decorated with silk curtains, of Pomona green, tastefully festooned up with large bouquets of real flowers. The floor was covered with India matting; cane sophas supplied the place of chairs; excepting in the corners of the room, which were filled with garden pots of an immense size, in which were the finest full grown myrtles. In the windows, were placed, orange and lemon trees, which shed an odoriferous fragrance round the room. At the top of the room, against the wall,

> was placed a small marble slab, on which stood a superb china jar, nearly filled with water; in this, was placed a branch of the palm-tree, the bottom of which was surrounded by sprigs of myrtle and pure willows; near the jar, was placed a small fillagree box, *shut*.[13]

Polack's version of the East End aestheticizes Jewish cultural performances as expressions of light and refinement, in keeping with the tradition of sukkah-building practices all over the world. In this case, elaborate fineries, such as silk curtains, India matting, and cane sofas, present an unusual level of luxury and elegance. The sukkah commemorates the structure in which biblical Jews lived during the period in the wilderness following the exodus from Egypt. Its construction, as Polack notes, must follow certain guidelines, including an unfinished roof created from vegetation and the four species of plants woven together on each day of Sukkot: a citron tree, a palm tree, a myrtle tree, and a willow tree. The above passage expresses what the coeditors of a book titled *Jewish Topographies* describe as "a deep-seated internal and external translocality and transculturality, entangled and interconnected with their respective environments as well as with other Jewish spaces throughout the world."[14] While we may be more familiar with narratives of East End danger, as darkened in contrast with light shining from bullseye lanterns, or of reptilian Jews skulking through dark streets, *Fiction without Romance* constructs the East End as not so dangerous after all, as a cosmopolitan space with ties to historic and global Jewish culture.

Dickens and Polack imagine spatial and temporal dimensions of the East End from vastly different frames of reference. For Dickens, Fagin proves the existence of a primitive racial figure, in the tradition of scientific writing in this period that, as Patrick Brantlinger summarizes, "hierarchized the races, with the white, European, Germanic, or Anglo-Saxon race at the pinnacle of progress and civilization, and the 'dark races' ranged beneath it in various degrees of inferiority."[15] Imagined as reptilian and Jewish, Fagin appears to be a primitive life form, or a form of residue from the past that will inevitably be displaced by more advanced races that have continued to develop. In sharp contrast, Polack's passage creates a version of the past as evidence of Jewish advancement. Her construction begins with the ritual of memory and the writing of Jewish history and homeland as an occasion worthy of the elaborate display of expensive cloth and foliage. Polack suggests that diasporic Jews living in urban spaces remain connected to an ancestral wilderness that ties them to their God and to one another. Both passages root Jewish people in the past; however, Dickens's East End is dead, whereas Polack's is alive with memory and story, and draws from a historiography that weaves Jewish communities together across spatial boundaries while rooting them in place through communal performances of sacred rituals.

Maria Polack may have been the first Anglo-Jewish novelist, but she was not the first Anglo-Jewish writer. By the eighteenth century, Anglo-Jewish men had already begun writing religious manuals for Jewish audiences. David B. Ruderman notes that "the authors of the new manuals were cognizant of the alarming need to inform Jews about basic concepts and ritual acts necessary for the preservation of Jewish life in the home and synagogue." He adds, "They were also painfully aware that these potential readers could only be addressed in the English language," as opposed to Yiddish or Hebrew.[16] By the early decades of the nineteenth century, Anglo-Jewish women began publishing their work for this audience.[17] Sisters Sophia and Charlotte King, the daughters of the infamous money-lender John King, are thought to be the first Jewish women to publish a book of poetry.[18] However, the King sisters seem to have had few, if any, connections with the Jewish community in which their father had been raised.[19] Polack is the first known English Jew to publish a novel as an individual who identified outwardly as Jewish. We don't know what that identity meant to her at the point when she published the novel, but we can see evidence of her interest in promoting Jewish culture in the novel's pages. Michael Galchinsky recalls the extraordinary nature of the emergence of writers like Polack, explaining, "Between 1830 and 1880, Jewish women in England became the first Jewish women anywhere to publish novels, histories, periodicals, theological tracts, and conduct manuals. In their own time, [writers such as] Grace Aguilar, Marion Hartog, Judith and Charlotte Montefiore, and Anna Maria Goldsmid were acknowledged by Christians and Jews alike as the most significant theorists of English Jews' entrance into the modern world."[20]

I've argued elsewhere that in *Fiction without Romance* Polack weaves together an argument against Jewish assimilation and a vision of the English novel as a site of realist aesthetics.[21] Historical contexts likely influenced this blending of cultural concerns. David Feldman notes that in 1830—the publication year of *Fiction without Romance*—"all public offices were closed to professing Jews. They were debarred from Parliament and from civic office and were disqualified from any employment connected to the administration of justice. In the civil sphere, Jews were obstructed from entering professions which demanded a Christian oath: most branches of schoolteaching, medicine and the Bar were closed to them and, for the same reason, Jews were ineligible to take degrees or hold any office at Oxford and Cambridge Universities. Between the years 1830–1871 these political and civil disadvantages were erased," one law and amendment at a time.[22]

Polack's work is therefore situated between a previous era's Jewish Naturalization Act, or "Jew Bill" (1753)—which in a single year extended and subsequently repealed naturalization rights to Jews—and the Victorian era's gradual extension of equal rights to Jewish citizens. James Shapiro accounts for the sluggishness of change, noting, "The buried threat occasioned by the naturalization of Jews had to do with the surprising vulnerability of English social and religious identity at this time: if even a Jew could be English, what could one point to that defined essential Englishness?"[23] Critical debates in *Fiction without Romance* about estrangement between Jewish and English communities not only respond to Polack's cultural moment, but as chapter 2 of this study demonstrates, reflect her choice to put her novel into the service of political reform rooted in respect for religious differences.

Polack and the other individuals in this study wrote from the borders of Victorian culture. They came from marginalized religious groups and were also frequently members of the working classes or working poor. While wealthy or middle-class writers made a habit of meandering through the streets of London before returning to their wealthier homes to write and publish accounts of their travels, East Enders struggling to survive with limited job opportunities or shunned as ethnic outsiders did not always have access to publishers, let alone schools and libraries. Not surprisingly, not many East End residents published their work before the 1880s. The following chapters focus on archival evidence of a thriving intellectual community in the East End in the early and middle decades of the nineteenth century. The archives I've consulted preserve stories, fictions, and subjects shaped as much by the perspectives they preserve as the archival structures in which they are housed. I suggest that these narratives create opportunities for considering the formation of a diversity of spatial identities and the importance of recovering artistic and cultural expressions from racial and ethnic minorities living in the East End that resist or complicate familiar constructions of this region.

The Archive's Visuality

Reading *Fiction without Romance* against the litany of popular constructions of East End depravity fueled my archival quest for evidence of Polack's life and writing. I reasoned that anyone engaged with literary activities must have left a paper trail, especially given the wealth of evidence of learning and attention to local culture on the pages of Polack's novel. I learned very quickly, however, that archival traces of her life and work were scant. With each failed search, I retraced my steps, propelled by my sense of amazement about the absence of materials. Was it really possible that all evidence of the first English Jew to publish a novel had been lost? The fact that the first Anglo-Jewish novel was written by a woman intensified my determination to find paper evidence of her life. Polack and many of her East End neighbors, as I began to understand, were among the first generation to invent Jewish secular literature. Despite the gravity of this revelation, my searches yielded tiny slivers of detail about Polack's life, most of which proved what I already knew to be true—that Polack lived and died, that she was a daughter, a wife, a mother, a teacher, a writer, and a person who took an interest in literary, musical, and theatre activities. Evidence of her life has been preserved in several cultural institutions—a synagogue, a cemetery, and a school. I believed these details to be worthless because the narrative they constituted seemed so slight, and because they failed to address my questions about Polack and her East End community.

In time I came to understand my problem. The quest for information about Polack and her novel came from the outside. My visuality was working against me. The questions for which I sought answers were coming from my bullseye lantern and not from the extant papers or the archival structures that shaped them. My challenge was to find a way to register the stories the archive was inherently capable of narrating rather than insist that the archive address questions I brought from the outside. I had to develop a reading practice attentive to the archive's form, paying close attention to torn or missing pages or its structuring of records linked by folders or book bindings that reflected or forged meaning through their ordering of paper fragments. I had to analyze what was saved for evidence of its provenance. And I had to find ways to read evidence of the archive's processing by curators or other readers. Gradually I came to understand the archive's infrastructure as suggestive of cultural practices, beliefs, and structures of meaning that, in turn, situated evidence of Polack and her novel within a dynamic cultural milieu. To find evidence of Polack's existence required that I stop looking for records of her life and instead approach each archive as a complex cultural matrix that documented, preserved, and shaped records of East End cultural life.

The chapters in this study detail my process of finding or creating such matrices. An early encounter in an archive containing records of the Jews' Free School helped me to see the subtle work of the archive's framing and organizational rituals. Polack's community was concerned about how to educate Anglo-Jewish children as English and Jewish. By reading record books kept by the school administration, I learned that the public recitation of poems had been used to raise funds for the school and to engage students in a form of public humanities that united English and Jewish sites of learning. I stumbled upon Polack's name in these records, on a page dated February 23, 1812: "One of the Boys belonging to the School delivered a suitable Hebrew discourse + another of the School Boys made a Speech in English prepared by Miss Maria Polack for the occasions both of whom conducted themselves to the satisfaction of the Meeting and a Silver medal given to each."[24] Initially, I read this rare and exciting mention as a breakthrough. It didn't reveal much about Polack's teaching or writing life, but the passage anchored her to an East End school. The occasion for the meeting was the anniversary dinner, an event held at the City of London Tavern that raised £139: 2. 6, or US $13,167 in 2020.[25] A subsequent entry in the record book, dated a few months later on May 25, 1812, states, "The President reported that the lines spoken in English by one of the Boys at the last Anniversary were written by Miss Maria Polack. Resolved that a letter be written by new Secretary to Miss Polack thanking her for the same."[26] Polack's name was never mentioned again in the school record book, leading me to conclude that this was simply a fleeting event in her life, a one-time charitable contribution to a local school that, in the end, told me little about her work and reception within her community.

The entries containing Polack's name didn't include the passage she wrote or the name of the student who delivered the recitation. It was only when I began reading across yearly records, cherry-picking references to the annual fundraising dinners, that I began to understand the significance of the brief 1812 mention of Polack's writing and teaching. Subsequent mention of recitations at the anniversary dinner began in 1822, the year when girls were admitted to the school. From that point forward, boys delivered a Hebrew recitation at the dinner while girls presented a poem in English. At the anniversary dinner in 1822, a female student presented an English ode written by Mrs. Henry, better known as Emma Lyon.[27] In 1828 another unnamed female student presented an English ode written by Mrs. Cornwall Baron Wilson. And in 1829 a female student presented an English ode "written by a Young Lady."[28] The secretaries of the all-male board persisted in omitting from the record book the identities of the teachers and students, but what they *did* record, curiously, was an important piece of evidence—all of the poems recited at the charity events by female students were written by women. Libraries might organize records by titles or authors, but charity school record books catalogue information by rituals tied to budgets, philanthropic work, and pedagogical practices. In order to find evidence of Polack, I had to read the record book through its organizational logic, looking for repetitions and rituals. Once I detected the pattern, I could see that Polack had initiated a literary tradition of recitations of women writers—beginning with her own writing—and a pedagogical practice in an East End charity school that used literature written by women to educate Jewish girls.

Similar archival records attested to the fact that Polack's East End community was actively engaged in performative and publishing ventures, in creative, individualized, educational, intellectual work leveraged to combat social and economic inequality and religious and ethnic persecution. The challenge was to find ways of reading seemingly random, unspecific fragments of information, such as the brief appearance of Polack's name in the school record book, and to develop a practice of listening to the voices that, in many cases, didn't appear noteworthy at first because they were silent on questions I wanted them to answer. The Maria Polack I sought in the beginning of this project is not the subject I've come to understand by *not* finding evidence of her life in the archives. Over the course of my research, I've had to learn to accept what I would never find, while reading the archive's framing rituals and structural patterns for evidence of what I didn't know to look for.

Ann Laura Stoler explains that the approach of "mining for treasures" in the archive has been the dominant mode of archival knowledge making.[29] She defines the "archival turn" in archival theory as a "move away from treating the archives as an extractive exercise to an ethnographic one" with the goal of recovering reading strategies that focus on "how history's exclusions are secured and made."[30] With this work in mind, the following chapters focus on the archive's visuality, which, I argue, can distract us from noticing what lies beyond the archive's boundaries or what has been submerged within its contours. I build from Hal Foster's turn to visuality to consider "how we see, how we are able, allowed, or made to see, and how we see this seeing and the unseeing therein."[31] His distinction between that which enables us to see and the process by which we are made aware of our vision's limits recalls the way archives often fail to point to their own exclusions. W. J. T. Mitchell argues that "images are not everything [but] they manage to convince us that they are."[32] I suggest that archives play the same game, creating the illusion of primacy and fulfillment. Indeed, the mythical power of archives, as Derrida and others have so adeptly demonstrated, rests upon our feverish desire for closure and the hope that complete recovery of a subject might be possible if we could only just find the right filing cabinet where the evidence we desire will have been saved and will set the record straight.

Dominant cultural narratives of East End poverty and crime, because of their loud and sensational effects, have diminished our ability to acknowledge literary culture from underrepresented minorities or working classes. Lives of ordinary citizens, or what Hilda Kean describes as lives "conducted off-center-stage in the margins of what has been seen," constitute significant and overlooked sources of cultural production. Such examples of *writing from below* are often the very places where dominant visualities are most explicitly challenged or complicated.[33] Polack's novel, read within the context of East End cultural activities, should prompt us to consider both the conditions and community within which she worked, and the important related question I return to in the chapters that follow: How might we examine what remains for evidence of what was lost or never saved? And what might those examinations illuminate about the very subjects on which the archive remains silent?[34]

Like other scholarly work on archives, I've made my quest for information visible, including descriptions of missteps, challenges, uncertainties, and breakthroughs. My goal is both to chart the process of working with archival materials and to underscore the limits of my vision brought about by my place in time, the archive's losses and silences, and the idiosyncratic uncertainties of my subject of study. I draw from a rich tradition of scholarship that foregrounds the experience of the archival search amid the ubiquity of loss.[35] Richard Altick, Antoinette Burton, Nancy K. Miller, Arlette Farge, Saidiya Hartman, Carolyn Steedman, Seth Koven, and numerous others have demonstrated the value of this mode of scholarly writing that affirms our desire not just to consult archives, but to touch, experience, and witness them.[36] Indeed, the study and creation of archives require a reckoning with both the archival objects under examination and the specific experience of working in archival spaces. They also demand attention to the archive's form and infrastructure, or the way the folders and filing cabinets, the record books, and collected pages shape meaning through the conditions of production as much as the archivist's priority to narrate order out of chaos by making choices about what to save or how to organize extant fragments.

The chapters in the study address the archive's power to create and preserve narratives that emerge partly from collectors and archivists who've selected, processed, and stored historical records, and partly from scholars who have left evidence of their use. On a visit to an archive, for example, I found a note I'd accidentally left on a previous research trip. A scrap of paper covered with notes in my own handwriting marked a place where I'd attempted to interpret a passage from a cemetery accounting book. At the time I wondered, Have other readers seen my note? Did they think it was part of the original archive? And how many fragments have I read as source material that were in fact left by previous readers? Eric Ketelaar reminds us that "every activation [in archives] also changes the significance of earlier activations."[37] *Strangers in the Archive* is thus primarily a study of the version of the East End made possible by the archives I consulted at the moment when I encountered them, and by the existence of fragmentary voices and perspectives read through the archive's structuring forces; its power as a technology of knowledge production; and my own efforts to understand the contexts for Polack's novel writing. The archive is always a moving target, an assemblage of texts that, as Michelle Caswell notes, is "always in a process of becoming."[38]

While they vary, most archives are alike in preserving three stories about themselves: the story narrated by their content and form; the story they preserve about their provenance, or how they came into existence *as* archives; and the story created through their boundaries, or the story *only* they can tell because of the particular collection of records united by their borders and exclusions. Archives produce a visuality that has the effect of privileging what's been saved as more important (because it's been chosen or has survived and is now visible) or more prominent (because it has the final word above lost records), while casting into oblivion anything that's been lost, anything else rendered, by default, less important because of its absence and inaccessibility. Rather than give up on subjects without archives, I show how we might find other points of access, or other ways to think about archives as dynamic and shape-shifting producers of questions capable of animating or exposing knowledge about our chosen subjects. I approach archives as both formal and informal collection systems that live within and beyond institutions—in family trunks, cemeteries, or within book bindings—that frame archival fragments and shape what can be known about their provenance.

The first story of the archive, the story of the archive's content, was unhelpful in my search for evidence of Polack's writing life. When there's no archive, there's no archival content to study. I moved on to the second story, or evidence of what's behind the missing archive, as I began wondering, What kind of narrative can be told when we consider what was saved and omitted from archives of the nineteenth-century East End? It would be too easy and inaccurate to see every archive as an emblem of a particular archivist's values. Certainly, many archivists have stories to tell about their institution's processing of records that reflect—for better or worse—the values of earlier generations. However, missing papers are often the result of other historical forces. For example, one librarian explained that records from Polack's synagogue—London's Great Synagogue—were destroyed during the Blitz. Extant archival records are those that happened to be stored on the side of the building that survived the bombing raids. Records stored on the other side of the building are now lost. Accidents, coincidences, luck, and the unknown are always part of the provenance story—an archival trait that perhaps feeds our feverish desire for recovery. Moreover, while the institution that houses the archive cannot always be held responsible for the archive's content, that institution's identity frames everything it holds and processes. The expert guidance of archivists; the ordering of the records; the context of the repository's other holdings; the institutional funding and cultural or academic status; and the user's experience of handling archival objects are all important factors contributing to the reader's engagement with archival content.

One challenge of this project has been to find ways of reading Victorian archives outside of the colonial violence that made them so compelling to their creators, especially given that, as Judith R. Walkowitz notes, over the course of the nineteenth century "the opposition of East and West increasingly took on imperial and racial dimensions, as the two parts of London imaginatively doubled for England and its Empire."[39] In many cases, fragmentary documents, voices, and perspectives produced by East End residents resist these dominant spatial narratives of the East End or quietly capture evidence of archival absences. This study focuses on the significance of the way archives are bound by borders that separate their content from all other worldly objects, spinning meaning out of the interplay of the particular objects united by systems and forms of containment. The fact that the content in an archive was selected for saving in the first place may lead us to conclusions about how or why it was valued by archivists. And while finding aids may sometimes speak of the archive's provenance or efforts to maintain original order, in many cases such narratives are lost to time. We are therefore confronted by signs of missing narratives from which we speculate, hoping to find traces of the provocations that led archival objects to be bound together in the first place.[40]

My creation of the East End Digital Library (https://eastendarchives.net) was inspired by the question, What if a digital archive were built not just to contain rare historical content or to make fragile objects available to a wider audience, but to facilitate speculative, collaborative scholarship—scholarship that could engage multiple registers and visualities?[41] I've created a digital library of archives at a moment of change when digital technologies grant us power to engage with older narrative forms, such as the multi-chapter monograph and the physical archive. *Strangers in the Archive* is written as a monograph that simultaneously steps beyond its medium through its interactions with digital archives—a dynamic form that responds, in turn, to archival problems raised in the book's content. Central to this work is the question of how repositories recover or create contexts through their content, literary form (letters, journals, epitaphs), infrastructure (loose papers in a file folder, for example, or headstones in a cemetery), and provenance. I argue that in each of these realms—content, form, infrastructure, and provenance—archives have the power to intercede in or shape knowledge of the cultural objects they hold. Thus, reading archives of the East End involves not only acts of tracking down evidence saved, but of finding a way—if possible—to hear and juxtapose the voices governed or produced by the archive's material forms, space, history, and contexts. I've responded to extant physical and print objects in archives of the East End by creating digital archives and editions, dynamic digital maps, sound interviews, digital surrogates of official records, and interpretive exhibits and arguments by students and descendants of the writers discussed in this book. My work has been influenced by the authors of the multigraph *Interacting with Print,* who suggest that "print still has a valuable role to play as a central medium of humanistic communication," and their encouragement to imagine new kinds of scholarship in digital work that foregrounds "process, community, and collaboration over scholarly hermeticism, hierarchy, and charismatic insight."[42] From their prompting, I've created joint projects—a monograph and a digital archive—that expand the boundaries of nineteenth-century London literature to include a range of media records that reflect the power of archives to shape and produce meaning or to preserve or submerge subjectivities.

The *Archive*'s East End

Visualizing East End people and places gave Victorian reading audiences opportunities to wrestle with the rise of the modern metropolis at a moment when social issues—in particular, crime, poverty, sanitation, and sexual violence—became subjects of national debate.[43] In fact, many travelers recording their experiences in the East End sought to improve the lives of the poor or redress systemic social problems.[44] The study of sensational depictions of the East End told from outsiders looking in is, therefore, fundamental to our understanding of nineteenth-century culture and writing about Victorian London. In recent years, scholars have sought a fuller picture of the diversity of London life and literary activities, including Gretchen Holbrook Gerzina's *Black London: Life before Emancipation,* which addresses both the history of Black Londoners as well as the legacy of representations of African and Afro-Caribbean culture from theatre to the written record.[45] Coll Thrush's *Indigenous London: Native Travelers at the Heart of Empire* offers a history of nineteenth-century "Indigenous people who traveled there, willingly or otherwise, from places that became Canada, the United States, New Zealand, and Australia."[46] Both texts offer models for including perspectives from groups frequently underrepresented in studies of London in this period. Their work has been foundational in rendering legible the normalization of dominant subject positions.

Joseph McLaughlin and Tanya Agathocleous have explored the effects of empire fictions on emergent discourses of Victorian London life.[47] Agathocleous's *Urban Realism and the Cosmopolitan Imagination in the Nineteenth Century* carefully delineates how nineteenth-century writers used depictions of the city to shape "a new global consciousness."[48] This work has influenced my own thinking about archival evidence of East End ties to global communities, particularly regarding intersecting diasporic concerns. Paul Fyfe's *By Accident or Design* extends the discussion of Victorian London's global networks by considering its major upheavals in infrastructure.[49] And Pamela K. Gilbert's *Imagined Londons* and *Mapping the Victorian Social Body* lay essential groundwork for the study of Victorian spatial narratives and the rising discourse of disease and mapping in shaping London literature.[50]

Building on this work, each of the following chapters delineates voices from the archive engaged with either a seemingly uncontrollable or accidental urban life or its massive expansion of global networks. Several studies have explored these changes in light of Victorian London's Jewish writers and populations (Susan David Bernstein, William Fishman, Michael Galchinsky, Meri-Jane Rochelson, Nadia Valman and Emma Francis, and Sharon Aronofsky Weltman to name a few).[51] This important work has exposed aesthetic exchanges among Jewish and Christian writers, while underscoring the significance of East End culture in the formation of Anglo-Jewish literary history. Lynda Nead's *Victorian Babylon*, moreover, directly traces London neighborhoods and regions represented in visual culture, including those with large Jewish populations. This body of work locates gaps in readers' vision or their competing visions that complicated debates about the city's transformation into a major metropolitan center in this period. Literary and visual culture were centrally concerned with such challenges, as new forms of art addressed both urban cultural production and the aesthetics of modern representations of the city. As Nead explains, such cultural forms depict London social problems not as a background, but "as an active constituent of historical consciousness."[52]

This study extends previous work by focusing on archival traces of nineteenth-century East End writing and by foregrounding reading strategies informed by archival theory. Chapter 1, "Before the Archive: East End Discourse out of Context," explores patterns that emerge in constructions of the East End as a fallen site, a place once respectable but viewed in the nineteenth century as desperately lost. I argue that archival writing, with its focus on future audiences, stands at odds with nostalgic and retrospective narratives of the East End. This chapter argues that archival records are not just different in content and form from novels and newspapers; I show that archives offer a distinct visuality, born from their unique infrastructure and provenance that reaches forward in time. While fictional narratives frame the East End in an imagined past, as struggling to keep up with the pace of modern London life, archival constructions look forward, preserving evidence for a future audience interested in learning about the past.

Chapter 2, "Archive Models: Maria Polack's *Fiction without Romance* Transformed," begins with a discussion of a unique copy of Maria Polack's novel, *Fiction without Romance*, housed in the British Library and containing an unusual set of paratexts—including the only copy of the novel's subscription list, a common form of nineteenth-century marketing and fundraising. In preserving these rare pages, this single copy of the novel functions as a kind of archive whose provenance and infrastructure shape interpretive possibilities.[53] In this chapter I consider the subscription list as the basis for the creation of a more expansive database that includes subscription data produced by several of Polack's East End Jewish contemporaries. Drawing from the British Library's copy of the book, my database and digital models locate actors in Polack's global intellectual and social networks. Whereas published narratives in this period tend to construct the East End as an outcast ghetto besieged by criminal foreigners, this chapter demonstrates how a single book's history and a database made from evidence of that history are capable of capturing signs of the East End's cosmopolitan global networks. Chapter 2 moves on to consider silences made apparent by the creation of a database that exposes slavery's muted but significant role in Polack's novel and her publishing world.

Chapter 3, "The Noisy Archive: A. S. Lyon's East End Diaries," grows out of two manuscript diaries written from 1823 to 1839 by East Ender A. S. Lyon, a member of Polack's social circle. The diaries chart an ordinary London citizen's attempts to become educated, start a business, and navigate illness and "dullness," or what contemporary readers might consider to be a form of depression. The diaries were stored in Jamaican archives before they were relocated to a family archive in Sacramento, California. This chapter is inspired by Bethanie Nowviskie's advocacy for the creation of speculative digital archives as performance spaces and Shalini Puri's example of "improvised fieldwork" granting access to "localized or vernacular rather than globalized knowledge and memory."[54] I focus on three archives in this chapter: A. S. Lyon's diaries stored in a private family archive; a digital archive I created, the Lyon Archive; and a Jamaican Jewish cemetery archive, the burial place of A. S. Lyon and members of his family. In addition to digitizing published and manuscript materials by members of the Lyon family, the Lyon Archive creates what I call a "talking archive"—that is, an archive containing sound objects, such as podcast interviews and movies, that reflect upon the significant power of voice and silence in our understanding of the East End's cultural life and archival afterlife.

Chapter 4, "An Archive of Lies: Evidence and the Jews' Orphan Asylum Investigations," examines allegations of child abuse at a Victorian charity school and orphanage located in the heart of the East End. The Education Committee issued a report on April 15, 1856, naming the guilty parties. When it became clear that evidence in the report was tainted by coercion, the Education Committee began a new investigation one year later. Interviews and accounts from teachers, students, and community members from both investigations have been preserved in an archive at the University of Southampton. One of the defining features of the Jews' Orphan Asylum archive is its incomplete nature. At some point in the nineteenth century, testimony vanished from the archive. To complicate matters, most of the records include passages where individuals accuse others of lying. Finding the truth about who was responsible for child abuse is impossible in a deceptive, incomplete archive. I therefore approach records and statements as expressions of will and attempts for justice (as these community members understood justice) regardless of whether their statements are verifiable. I build from Natalie Zemon Davis's approach of focusing on the "'fictional' qualities" of archival materials or "the extent to which their authors shape the events of a crime into a story."[55] Records of the investigation at the Jews' Orphan Asylum have a lot to say about how this East End community understood the contours of truth and fiction; how they defined and sought justice; and how they articulated the importance of education for the poor.

Strangers in the Archive makes two significant interventions. First, I offer counternarratives of the East End produced by physical archival materials and their digital remediations. Second, in creating a digital archive to accompany this book, I've produced linked scholarly projects that practice and extend discussions of archival tensions raised in the pages of this study in an effort to challenge dominant historiographies of the nineteenth-century East End. The digital archive contains structural limits in the technology as well as my own limits, both financial and conceptual. My hope is that these projects will nevertheless inspire new approaches to studies of London's ethnic and racial minorities and writing from below. I hope as well to forge archival reading strategies informed by literary-studies methodologies, including literary-studies fieldwork, public humanities, archival creation and theory, and digital humanities. The pages that follow detail a range of approaches to the study of physical and digital archives and the manner in which a single archive can be read or reorganized to register evidence of understudied literary texts and the subjectivities sometimes submerged by those very texts.

Archives of the nineteenth-century East End have remained mostly silent on the subject of Polack—except for a few surprises discussed in the pages that follow. Yet archives containing East End records are brimming with evidence of Polack's social and intellectual world. As a stranger in the archive, I've sought a nearness and knowledge rather than mastery or belonging. Such nearness comes from my handling of crumbling objects, my opening of old books with tight spines, and my acts of rubbing flour into incisions on tilted grave stones. While I can speak to what I've learned through these experiences, my perspective as a stranger will always be shaped by my vision from my own time and place. Thus, the challenge I've faced in writing this book was not just a dearth of archives, but the difficulty of finding analytical methods with which to read extant records as metanarratives about their silencing rituals and patterns of preservation. The following chapters focus on methods of archival study as a practice of reading relations among material and digital objects shaped by conditions known and unknown. How the physical and digital records came to speak, to make meaning and influence interpretive work, is just as significant, I suggest, as the content in any given document. Put differently, reading the archive isn't just about finding evidence of an undiscovered literary work or author, but about knowing what questions and contexts the records speak to in their physical form or through strategic digital transformations.

What follows is a study of the East End that only archives could tell. Individually and collectively, archival boundaries unify and put into play dynamic interactions that showcase identifiable perspectives, voices, and assertions of power. Physical and digital archives structure meaning differently from one another but can sometimes be made to speak to archival silences. The version of the East End discussed in the pages that follow becomes accessible through the very structures that precluded information about Maria Polack, but were suggestive of her intellectual and social networks. I have come to understand that such foreclosures are not, in fact, signs of my failure to find Polack. Abandoning the project at the prospect of an absent archive of Polack's work would have constituted a failure. What I have pursued instead is a way to read absence against and through the pieces that remain. Finding ways to connect the visualities of the physical and digital has changed my thinking about both, while demonstrating the power of archives to animate narratives in startling, sometimes invisible ways.

1

Before the Archive

EAST END DISCOURSE OUT OF CONTEXT

MANY YEARS ago, I found myself eavesdropping on a conversation at a dinner party. An American guest asked an English couple their thoughts about the decision to hold the 2012 Olympics in London. The English woman's eyes enlarged when she responded, "It's horrible. The games aren't just in London. They're in the East End." In an effort to grasp the gravity of her outrage, the American man responded sympathetically, "You must be worried about traffic." "Traffic?" she snapped back. "That's not the problem. The camera crews will descend upon the East End. People will get the wrong impression. They'll think that's who we are." An awkward silence coupled with befuddled expressions followed, prompting the English man to clarify his wife's outrage: "The East End is a place of foreigners. People will mistake us for them."

From my invisible place on the far end of the table, I surmised that the English guests were not concerned that they'd be mistaken for the foreign athletes competing in the games. Rather, they were concerned that Londoners would be confused with so-imagined foreign residents living in the East End. I was struck by their horror, which recalled similar sentiments I'd encountered in nineteenth-century writing. Spatial identities shift over time to accommodate changes in demographics, the built environment, and historical or cultural associations among many other shaping forces. The English woman's outburst suggested that such shifts do not always overwrite earlier constructions of place. For some people, the East End remains a site of universal abjection, populated by those considered to be *not truly English*. In fact, the 2012 Olympic games became a flashpoint for such narratives. A *New York Times* reporter covering the Games characterized the East End as "a sprawling area known for its artists, anarchists and immigrants" and as a place that now feels "light years away from central London, and totally self-sufficient, thanks to a host of [new] enticing restaurants, shops, markets and hotels."[1] The association in this passage with anarchists and immigrants, or with an identity "light years away from central London," replays nineteenth-century constructions of the East

End as a spatial Other—materially, culturally, and spiritually linked to the other side of the earth. The writer suggests, moreover, that the East End continues to be constructed as a place whose value lies in the enticing activities it offers hungry visitors.

The English couple touched upon one of the trademark features of outsiders' constructions of the region. They didn't speak of directions objectively by mentioning specific locations or directional words, such as "east of the Tower" or "north of the River." They used pronouns to stand in place of group identifiers. As one put it, "They'll think that's who we are," while the other clarified, "People will mistake us for them." I wondered, What people? And to whom were they referring as "us" and "them"? The conversation that followed suggested that for some, London's East End is more than just a section of town or a geographic territory situated at the borders of London proper; for this group, as Paul Newland notes, it's a socially constructed site defined by and central to the construction of identities of all Londoners.[2]

It was in the turn to the nineteenth century when this social construction of the East End began to propagate. The discourse of regional Otherness spread wildly throughout print outlets. Decade by decade, the East End was imagined to be a space defined by its exploratory opportunities for wanderers and by its potential to facilitate spiritual uplift among social reformers. Significantly, these constructions of the East End grew from the writing of wandering visitors rather than residents. Gareth Stedman Jones notes that "in the second half of the nineteenth century, Victorian civilization felt itself increasingly threatened by 'Outcast London,'" or by those who lived within the urban sphere but represented a foreign or outsider class because of their economic and/or social position.[3] The expression "outcast London," used in many post-1850s print materials, Jones explains, "symbolized the problem of the existence and persistence of certain endemic forms of poverty, associated together under the generic term, casual labour," or those without permanent work.[4] Deborah Epstein Nord adds that the term "outcast London" was a common feature of nineteenth-century writing that adopted the viewing lens of the male onlooker or "the rambler, the stroller, the spectator, the flâneur—[who] is a man. [. . .] He begins as a visible character in the urban sketch, a signature . . . who is both authorial persona and fictional actor on the city streets, and ends as the invisible but all-seeing novelist, effacing all of himself but his voice in the evocation of an urban panorama."[5] Travelers or flâneurs sometimes recorded their interactions with East End residents in an attempt to bring about economic or spiritual improvements to the lives of the poor. Others focused on the gritty filth and greasy abundance of too many bodies crowding narrow streets. Seth Koven observes that "for the better part of the century preceding World War II, Britons went slumming to see for themselves how the poor lived. They insisted that firsthand experience among the metropolitan poor was essential for all who claimed to speak authoritatively about social problems."[6] It's curious that their attraction to "firsthand" knowledge of the East End didn't inspire interest in stories produced by local residents of the spaces they visited. Instead they focused on constructions of East Enders produced by those who imagined the East End as a cultural step behind modern London. East End culture and people were depicted in many publications as having fallen from a better way of life or as having failed to progress. This body of work, discussed in the pages that follow, offers telling evidence about how the East End was understood and imagined in nineteenth-century published writing and visual culture.

Henri Lefebvre notes that space is never final or fixed, but is born through an interplay of many voices, perspectives, and events. He encourages us to consider the "dialectical character" of spatial formation, and to acknowledge the ways that the social production of space emerges from "a practical relationship, as part of an interaction between 'subjects' and their space and surroundings."[7] With Lefebvre's point in mind, the following discussion integrates published narratives of the East End created by insiders and outsiders alike. I show how these published accounts offer not simply a different genre or type of narrative from those found in archives; they offer a fundamentally different kind of evidence. Writers of travel narratives depicting their own exploits or those of a character typically recount a past event. Their narratives explicitly situate the East End as a place the character or writer travels through and advances beyond. In contrast, archival records of East End writing look forward. Archives, as Derrida reminds us, are created with an eye toward the future's interest in the past. As he explains, "the question of the archive" is always "the question of the future."[8] The archive's version of the East End therefore stands out against a legacy of cultural constructions it disrupts and complicates. The following discussion of that legacy offers a helpful starting point for the chapters that follow.

To speak of a place called the "East End" gives the false impression that the region had fixed boundaries. Pamela Gilbert wisely notes that "there are no Londons other than those of the imagination."[9] I would suggest that the same is true of the East End. According to Alan Palmer, "Confusion over the precise borders of the East End is as great as ever:

newspapers have [. . .] annexed to it Barkingside, Romford and Upminster, which is like extending the West End to Heathrow or to Ruislip."[10] The "traditional limits" of the nineteenth-century East End, Palmer adds, included only "the old Inner London Boroughs of Hackney and Tower Hamlets, together with the western fringe areas of Hoxton and Shoreditch and the dockland overflow into West Ham and East Ham."[11] While narrative and visual cultures shaped understanding of the East End, equally powerful is the fact of geography; for the East End is situated not only outside of the original boundaries of Roman Londinium, but downriver where the trash, smells, and, according to Dickens's depictions in *Our Mutual Friend* (1864–65), dead bodies flowed away from central London and through the East End before heading out to sea. According to some accounts, the Tower of London marks the eastern border of the East End, while the space to the immediate north and west of the Tower of London designates the area known as the "City."

But there's no line marking the eastern boundary of the East End. Thus, where the East End *ends* geographically has been the subject of debate. The area known as the Tower Hamlets, located to the east of the Tower of London, includes a number of "hamlets" or boroughs including Bethnal Green, Spitalfields, Stepney, Whitechapel, Wapping, Mile End, and beyond. The geographical boundaries of the area termed "the East End" shifted over the course of the eighteenth and nineteenth centuries. As the city grew modern in this period, as increasing numbers of people migrated to the East End, and as transportation expanded, boundaries and spatial identities shifted in response. Paul Newland explains that confusion about this area "demonstrate[s] how far it remains a profoundly amorphous, ambiguous space—a space that has never been clearly or adequately defined, delineated or drawn. It is not, and has never been, a village, town or borough. But if it is not a mappable material space, it certainly functions as an enigmatic imaginative space."[12] Throughout the nineteenth century, writers commonly turned to the East End as a powerful emblem of modern urban life and as a space capable of arousing a sense of fear, fascination, and repudiation among readers.

The "East End" as a proper noun with capital E's emerged sometime after 1860 and evoked a sense of deviance, danger, and the sadness of urban poverty. Judith R. Walkowitz notes that the East End in the late nineteenth century was imagined to be "dark, powerful, and seductive" and that popular narratives "held a powerful sway over the social imagination of educated readers."[13] The legacy of associations with the "East" played a powerful role in imagining and shaping knowledge of this area's culture and its immigrant communities. Alex Goody adds that this rhetoric had the effect of "symbolically colliding metropolitan and international connotations of the word 'East' and potentially marking the East End as a racially othered space."[14] The origin of these stereotypes stems partly from late-century East End events, such as an influx of Russian Jewish immigrants fleeing European pogroms in the early 1880s and the terrifying Whitechapel murders. Peter Ackroyd observes that it was in "the middle of the nineteenth century that this salacious and somewhat inaccurate image of the East End first began to be disseminated."[15]

Our challenge is to find a way to understand the shifting nature of the East End in the first five decades of the century outside of the historical frames that emerged in later decades. What can we know about the East End by studying other cultural configurations or narratives? And how do we approach those narratives, including Maria Polack's *Fiction without Romance,* outside of the overdetermining lenses of poverty, imagined racial deviance, and danger? Must Polack's work be read as a deviation from "what we know" about the East End, or might it instead enable us to question what we've come to understand from published accounts of the region? Polack lived in Whitechapel, a place shaped by different diasporas, migration patterns, and communal concerns that shifted over time. Polack's Ashkenazi community included people who may have defined themselves as having intersecting identities—English, Jewish, Russian, Polish, Dutch, Portuguese, or Spanish—whose social standing changed dramatically from person to family to decade. To be an "insider" in the nineteenth-century East End often came with the stigma of being a foreigner, an outsider in London's cultural sphere. Reading this space, then, as one created by insider East Enders such as Polack or outsider West Enders such as Mayhew or Dickens is not always a helpful approach for the study of how the East End's identity emerged through or against multiple subjectivities and identity categories.

This chapter begins with a review of common assumptions by well-known writers and illustrators, such as Dickens, the Cruikshank brothers, and others who held what Nils Roemer describes as "a privileged viewing position."[16] I move on to consider a trajectory of counternarratives that push against popular constructions of the East End. I suggest in these discussions that we can better address the complexities of East End spatial narratives in this period by foregrounding an array of contexts, texts, and perspectives.[17] This requires us to consider not just sensational stories by well-known authors, but narratives produced by East End writers, ethnic and racial minorities, children, and the burgeoning East End periodical press and printing industries in this period. The East End was a site of confluence among various geographical places across and beyond London and, as chapters 2 and 3 of this study suggest, throughout the Atlantic world. A study of place, of course, is not the same subject as a study of the construction of place, and it is here where the challenge of approaching East End archives and writing about the East End meet in this chapter.

The Visitor's Gaze

A great number of factors led to the construction of the East End's amorphous identity, including its name. Is it really an end, we might wonder? Might it be read more productively as a beginning, or as a space that opens on the eastern side of the Tower of London? Printed records indicate that as early as 1756 a place known as "the East End" had already been identified as separable from the rest of London. *A New and Accurate Description of the Present Great Roads and the Principal Cross Roads of England and Wales, Commencing at London,* which includes a chapter titled "The Eastern Roads or Those Going from the East End of London," makes this distinction clear.[18] Another text published in 1782 titled *The London Guide, Describing the Public and Private Buildings of London, Westminster, & Southwark* includes a reference to the white tower in the Tower of London: "[T]his erection stands on the north of the Thames, at the east end of London."[19] In this instance, the first letters of "east" and "end" are lowercase e's. Prior to the 1860s the place name "East End" appeared variously with capital and lowercase letters. Dickens referred to Whitechapel in his 1837 novel *Oliver Twist* as "the eastern suburbs." Variations in the spelling suggest that even if the East End's exact location was understood to have a distinct character early in the nineteenth century, its formal name or status as a proper noun remained in flux.[20]

Yet the name of this space was not the only reference point in flux. In 1797 Johann Wilhelm von Archenholz, a Prussian writer and historian, described features of the East End that persisted in later formulations. In *A Picture of England: Containing a Description of the Laws, Customs, and Manners of England,* Archenholz explains, "There has been, within the space of twenty years, truly a migration from the east end of London to the west."[21] He continues, "The east end, especially along the shores of the Thames, consists of old houses, the streets there are narrow, dark, and ill paved; inhabited by sailors and other workman who are employed in the construction of ships, and by a great part of the Jews. The contrast between this and the west is astonishing; the houses here [in the west] are mostly new and elegant; the squares are superb, the streets straight and open, nor is any city in Europe so well paved."[22]

Noteworthy in this passage is the elision of people, architecture, and aesthetics. According to Archenholz, the "east end" is populated by "old houses" and rickety streets. Elegance appears in the West End with its open streets that supersede those found in Europe. A short time later Pierce Egan picked up on this conceptual framework in his novel *Life in London* (1823), illustrated by brothers Isaac Robert and George Cruikshank.[23] The novel tells the story of three friends and their raucous adventures throughout London, including visit to sites east of the Tower. It is in the East End where they drink wine, become loose-tongued, and make comparisons between the high-class gentlemen's club "Almack's at the West End" and the eastern social space of "All-Max in the East."[24] In the image by the Cruikshank brothers, the rowdy adventures arrive at a pub where they flirt and dance with East End locals (fig. 2). According to Egan's narrative and the Cruikshanks' corresponding visual image, by 1821 the East End had become a destination for entertainment, drinking, and consummate partying. While Egan's narrative keeps its focus on the perspectives of men who travel around London, the Cruikshanks' illustrations showcase the "lowbrow" people they meet in the East End. The

FIG. 2. "Lowest Life in London," by Isaac Robert and George Cruikshank, from Pierce Egan's *Life in London* (1823)

image title, "Lowest Life in London," draws upon the invisible position of authority against which the construction of "lowest" peoples and places have been imagined.[25]

The caption, "Tom, Jerry, and Logic among the unsophisticated Sons and Daughters of Nature at All Max in the East," situates East End foreignness against the presumably refined world of West End sophistication. Almack's refers to exclusive upper-class social and dance clubs in London. The slippage from real place to imaginary site construed as its uncultivated opposite, All-Max in the East, underscores how geographical places—real and fictional—are constituted through their relations with one another. The illustration seems to mock the East End as a destination for trifling West End adventures. At the same time, it recalls the role of book illustration in defining the East End's baseness through its use of a racist and xenophobic lens.

Joseph McLaughlin wisely observes that "empire, the increasing 'globalization' of culture, and contact with others [stood out] as *the* social facts most important to the specificity of the urban fantasies that circulated around London at the turn of the [twentieth] century."[26] Yet texts produced by Egan and the Cruikshanks indicate that similar fantasies took root much earlier. John Marriott recalls that "Black seamen had landed in East London ever since it emerged as a major maritime centre [in the 1790s]. Along with Asian lascars, they were vital to the crews of British shipping but since they possessed few rights, and shop owners felt under no obligation to provide for them once they reached London, many were simply abandoned and had to fend for themselves until a return passage could be found."[27] Egan's and the Cruikshanks' depictions are troubling on a number of fronts, including their characterization of East Enders as low, wild, and uncivilized. This version of the East End's identity is constituted through the perspective of West Enders who go "slumming" for entertainment. And the disturbing depiction of dancing Black East Enders recalls contemporary images of enslaved people forced to dance for their captors. According to Rodreguez King-Dorset, "The slave traders used the word 'dance' to describe the way they made the slaves move about in the hope that exercise would keep them healthy. They did this by whipping them so that they moved about, even when they were in irons. . . . In no sense was the traders' enforced exercise 'dance' as it was understood in African culture."[28] The picture and corresponding descriptions are remarkable for their endorsement of these stereotypes and their portrayal of "lowest life" people springing into action to entertain West End visitors.

Efraim Sicher notes that both Egan's writing and the Cruikshanks' illustrations were classic examples of "new technologies of representation of London, such as the magic lantern, the diorama, and photography, which radically altered the versatility of the optical image and the visibility of the observer."[29] Like so many popular texts from this period, Egan's narrative privileges the imagined objectivity of the visitors. Sicher adds, "London was, in Egan's words in *Life in London,* a 'complete cyclopaedia,' captured by a *camera obscura* that represented the nation's wealth and health, without the viewer being seen."[30] While the three adventurers appear in the image of the East End pub (wearing tan, blue, and green jackets), the artists drawing the image are invisible. The illustration thus effectively buries other perspectives of East End identities through its endorsement of racist stereotyping and its critique of regional culture constructed by an invisible and authoritative lens.

Dickens deployed a similar kind of invisibility in *Oliver Twist,* where characters float easily across geographical borders. The young Oliver is locked in Fagin's Whitechapel apartment but later escapes; while Fagin moves from his East End home to the Maylies' middle-class neighborhood, the very space that becomes Oliver's home later in the novel. Dickens's depictions of the eastern suburbs lead us to wonder about both their porous edges and the impulse to imagine the East End through a racializing lens, as a space defined by the presence of social deviants and racial others who can be seen from a place of hiding. London is both a background and a driver of action in the novel, propelling Oliver forward in his progress from poor parish boy to wealthy Christian hero. Indeed, long before he visits, Oliver imagines London as a place suitable for anyone either willing to work or desirous of hiding. The narrator explains,

> London!—that great large place!—nobody—not even Mr. Bumble—could ever find him there! He had often heard the old men in the workhouse, too, say that no lad of spirit need want in London; and that there were ways of living in that vast city, which those who had been bred up in country parts had no idea of. It was the very place for a homeless boy, who must die in the streets, unless some one helped him. As these things passed through his thoughts, he jumped upon his feet, and again walked forward.[31]

Despite his misguided impression that he might camouflage himself, it is in the bustling modern metropolis where Oliver is continually sought out and discovered—first by the Artful Dodger and later by Mr. Brownlow and Nancy. With each encounter, Oliver either moves into or is rescued from identifiable areas within the city of London.

The reader's first encounter with "the neighborhood of Whitechapel" occurs just after Oliver is kidnapped from his errand for Mr. Brownlow.[32] Nancy and Bill Sikes, acting under Fagin's command, drag Oliver through Clerkenwell, Smithfield, and finally to Whitechapel to a house "in a ruinous condition" where Oliver is ultimately locked up in his cell.[33] The narrator continues, "The rooms up stairs, had great high wooden chimney-pieces and large doors, with paneled walls and cornices to the ceilings: which, although they were black with neglect and dust, were ornamented in various ways; from all of which tokens Oliver concluded that a long time ago, before the old Jew was born, it had belonged to better people, and had perhaps been quite gay and handsome: dismal and dreary as it looked now."[34] The apartment's architecture, its paneled walls and cornices, stand as evidence of the better people who once lived in the Whitechapel apartment. The "great" and "high" chimney and doors suggest wealth and grandeur, while the architectural flourishes provide evidence of a people attuned to the aesthetics of finery. All that's left of these "better" residents who abandoned the apartment long ago are the decaying features of the space covered in black dust.

Oliver entered London expecting a bustling city of possibility. Instead, he finds himself imprisoned in a dark world strikingly out of step with other London regions. From a place of hiding in Fagin's Whitechapel apartment, Oliver gazes at life beyond his prison window:

> There was a back-garret window, with rusty bars outside, which had no shutter; and out of this, Oliver often gazed with a melancholy face for hours together; but nothing was to be descried from it but a confused and crowded mass of house-tops, blackened chimneys, and gable-ends. Sometimes, indeed, a ragged grizzly head might be seen, peering over the parapet-wall of a distant house: but it was quickly withdrawn again; and as the window of Oliver's observatory was nailed down, and dimmed with the rain and smoke of years, it was as much as he could do to make out the forms of the different objects beyond, without making any attempt to be seen or heard,—which he had as much chance of being, as if he had lived inside the ball of St Paul's Cathedral.[35]

Here Dickens teases readers expecting a continuous progress narrative with evidence of gradual improvement in the struggling protagonist. Instead, we encounter a period of faltering as Fagin progresses toward his goal of poisoning his victim. Oliver does finally grow beyond his spiritual and economic impoverishment by becoming an upper-class hero who lives far away from East End squalor. But it's in Whitechapel, in the barren, grizzly, and lifeless place of imprisonment, a place once alive with elegance, where the novel's competing trajectories of progress and stagnation intersect.

In later scenes when Oliver and Bill Sikes travel through Spitalfields, the narrator recalls the muted signs of East End life. They begin their journey in a "cheerless morning" where they witness "the somber light only serving to pale that which the street lamps afforded: without shedding any warmer or brighter tints upon the wet house-tops, and dreary streets. There appeared to be nobody stirring in that quarter of the town; for the windows of the houses were all closely shut: and the streets through which they passed, were noiseless and empty."[36] As they move further west, people emerge and activity resumes. Oliver notices "[t]he public–houses, with gas-lights burning inside, were already open,"[37] and shops "[b]y degrees [. . .] began to be unclosed."[38] By the time they reach Shoreditch and Smithfield, the street has "swelled into a roar of sound and bustle."[39] Whether we view this space through Oliver's prison windows or with a larger view to the street, Dickens consistently describes the eastern suburbs as "still as death."[40] The resulting version of the East End contrasts with the modern metropolis not only because of its location downriver but also because it has failed to advance in the march toward modernity and new life. This kind of characterization can be read, as Clive Bloom notes, as a version of the East End "at once truncated . . . and that in turn is truncated into a cobbled street, a blind alley, a gaslit corner. The real and the tangible of history become the fractured scenario of nostalgia for history, a ruined memory of a landscape now reduced to its significant effects, glimpses of a lost place that never quite existed."[41] Such an image reveals nothing of the East End's artists, schoolteachers, or musicians. We see instead broken-down homes and bodies caught in a flash of insight by a trapped child.

The choice to present the East End as having fallen from a more perfect past was a common feature of nineteenth-century novels. George Eliot mocked this trend in *Daniel Deronda.* In one noteworthy passage, Deronda conjures an image of himself "[l]ying dreamily in a boat, imagining one's self in quest of a beautiful maiden's relatives in Cordova elbowed by Jews in the time of Ibn-Gebirol . . . Or if the scenery of St Mary Axe and Whitechapel were imaginatively transported to the borders of the Rhine at the end of the eleventh century, when in the ears listening for the signals of the Messiah, the Hep! Hep! Hep! of the Crusaders came like the bay of bloodhounds."[42] Although written in different decades, Deronda and Oliver are alike in their use of a nostalgic lens from which they construct East End Jewish culture. Deronda sees East End crowds as descendants of the once-refined medieval culture thriving in the years before the rise of bloodthirsty Inquisitors. Elsewhere I've suggested that Eliot makes fun of Deronda in this passage for the absurdity of his nostalgic vision.[43] Dickens, in contrast, seems less critical of Oliver's construction of East End cultural decay. In Fagin's Whitechapel apartment, Oliver feels a sense of longing and companionship with the better people who once lived there. Dickens's depiction of Whitechapel's demise, marked by criminal types, renders Fagin's downfall inevitable.

What Oliver sees of Whitechapel in the once-loved but degraded ornate interior space has some historical grounding. Gareth Stedman Jones explains that "in the first quarter of the nineteenth century, the two most distinctive industries of East London were silk-weaving and shipbuilding. In the forty years after 1830, both industries collapsed. Neither industry was able to surmount the technological threats posed by industrialization."[44] He adds,

> It is estimated that the East London silk weaving industry employed 50,000 persons in 1824. The long decline of the industry reached crisis proportions in the 1830's when in some years 30,000 were said to have been unemployed. Although there was some migration to other silk centres, a substantial number remained. Many took to casual work in spells of unemployment. According to a Poor Law Report in 1837, "a considerable number of the weavers are fellowship porters and are employed in unloading vessels at London docks during seasons of distress." By the end of the 1840s the resort to casual labour by unemployed handloom weavers had become well established.[45]

The "extreme distress" brought about by Industrial development and economic turn was recognized, according to Alan Palmer, as "'peculiar to the poor of Spitalfields' as early as the winter of 1806–7, had spread the length of Brick Lane to envelope much of Bethnal Green, especially along Hackney Road."[46] Signs of the declining silk industry are evident everywhere in *Oliver Twist*, particularly in the relationship between Saffron Hill, where Fagin teaches young boys to steal silk handkerchiefs, and the abandoned East End with its closed-up shops, dark streets, and grizzly-headed inhabitants. Not all forms of poverty are created equal in *Oliver*

Twist. Saffron Hill's despair stems from its failure to rise to a level of self-sufficiency and productivity, whereas the eastern suburbs—the location of Fagin's apartment—appear to be beyond redemption.

Dickens did not invent a discourse on East End degradation; such images flourished in the years before the publication of *Oliver Twist.* Social conditions led to a poorer quality of life for many East Enders. Expressions of fear or anxiety about foreigners emerged from multiple, sometimes overlapping, contexts. Writing just a few years after the publication of *Oliver Twist,* John Fisher Murray declared, "The Jewish Quarter . . . is literally the New Jerusalem: here we Christians are foreigners."[47] He continued by noting bodily distinctions among Jews living in the Jewish quarter: "Here, every face is of the shape and somewhat of the complexion of a turkey egg; every brow penciled in an arch of exact ellipse; every nose modelled after the proboscis of a Toucan. Locks as bushy and black as those of Absalom about, and beards of the patriarchal ages."[48] Murray underscores physical differences as proof of the essential un-English qualities of East Enders. Later chapters in this study will address the rise of crime in this period that may have played a role in propagating such disturbing constructions. But the depiction of "lowlife" people in these passages with distinctly racialized physical features stems from rising forms of racism, xenophobia, and anti-Semitism that fed dangerous and disrespectful spatial narratives. The urge to collapse social problems with racial, ethnic, or religious deviancy raises the stakes of the invisible viewing position from which they were drawn. Contrasting accounts by writers with different access points or levels of familiarity certainly exist but have not always received the same kind of attention. As the next section demonstrates, East End writers were quick to note these flattening narratives that reduced East End spaces into images of loss and degeneracy.

Counternarratives

Well-known, sensational narratives of East End danger have long shaped thinking about Victorian London. Travelers' accounts of the region commonly collapsed constructions of racialized deviancy with the fact of poverty. Given the dominance of these narratives, we're faced with the challenge of finding ways to hear local, quieter constructions of the same streets and regions. Archival interventions create opportunities to recenter perspectives coming from other places, as we'll see in the following chapters. But we can also approach such depictions with an awareness of the writers' relationship to the specific places they depict. John Hollingshead, for example, straddled two aesthetic and political worlds as an East Ender who grew up poor but later became a successful journalist. Hollingshead published a series of articles in 1861 during one of the coldest winters on record. His accounts of people struggling to survive appeared in the *Morning Post* with the title "Horrible London." These accounts were later revised and republished as *Ragged London in 1861*. According to Hollingshead, poverty was not an East End problem, but a London problem. As he explains, "The evils of overcrowding in courts and alleys are, unhappily, not confined to the eastern end of the metropolis. There are almost as many dark holes and corners within a few yards of [the wealthier section of London] Regent street or Charing Cross, which shelter almost as much sickness, crime, and poverty, as any back hiding-places in [the East End's] Whitechapel or Bethnal Green."[49] It's unclear why he felt such an intervention was necessary. The passage nevertheless stands as a reminder to us and his contemporaries that Whitechapel's back hiding-places were comparable with those in other regions in London.

Born in Hoxton, Hollingshead knew well the despair he described in his essays. In his words, "I have lived in it and amongst it ever since I could walk and talk, and I speak with some authority when I say that I know what it is."[50] His writing is unusual in its focus on the lives of ordinary citizens. Unlike Mayhew's more famous portraits of street people, Hollingshead's examples slide variously between an alignment with and detachment from his subject. The dominant narrative of East End life depicts poverty so abject that no one seems capable of escape. Hollingshead's history offers a corresponding narrative of possibility. Not only did he leave the East End where he was raised, but Hollingshead also emerged a successful writer who later achieved even more success in the London theatre. Thus, his text works from multiple geographical directions by calling attention to poverty while doing so from the position of one who managed to escape such a fate as an adult.

Charles Booth adopted a different tactic in his 1885 study of London poverty. Unlike Hollingshead who flaunted his East End subjectivity, Booth created as much distance as possible from his subject through the creation of poverty maps. The prompting for this work was a survey of working-class London neighborhoods published in the *Pall Mall Gazette* in which the author claimed that "one out of four Londoners lived in abject poverty."[51] Booth was suspicious of these findings. As Albert Fried and Richard M. Elman explain, "He thought they were inspired by religious or political ideology, or by the desire for sensationalism, rather than by a concern for the truth."[52] In response, Booth conducted a follow-up survey to investigate. He gathered reports, statistics, and other official records in an effort to discern the truth about the plight of London's poor. The result was *Life and Labour of the People in London* (1889). His now-famous color-coded maps allow viewers to study class differences and crime by gazing at his street-by-street guide.[53]

Booth's goal was to provide statistical accuracy to prove the foregone conclusion that London's East End was dominated by abject poverty and despair. His results upended his assumptions.[54] William Fishman explains that while Booth's maps depict a large population of people struggling to survive, they simultaneously show that "65 per cent [of the population of the East End] lived above the poverty line."[55] John Marriott adds,

> We must [. . .] exercise a degree of caution in viewing nineteenth-century East London as a place of unmitigated poverty and desolation[. . . .] Booth found that approximately half of the adult males were in regularly paid occupations described as skilled, professional or merchant, while less than ten per cent were in irregular, casual employment, the remainder being semi-skilled. East London in the late nineteenth century was therefore dominated for the most part by skilled and semi-skilled workers and their families, who tended to determine the course of industrial struggle; they also inhabited and largely controlled the area's cultural landscape. There were members of the labour force who possessed genuine levels of skill, and could command regular employment providing them with relatively comfortable means[. . . .] Historical accounts of East London have neglected this stratum of skilled labour, and yet it is one which needs to be considered in order to provide a more complete—and complicated—picture of the social composition of the area.[56]

Neither Booth nor Fishman overlooks the fact that much of the East End struggled with poverty. Their point, rather, is that "the levels of poverty in Whitechapel compared favourably with districts such as Southwark, Greenwich and Bermondsey."[57] We might wonder why these areas haven't been sensationalized in the same manner as the nineteenth-century East End.

One answer to this question has to do with the style of reporting used to cover the Whitechapel murderer in 1888–89. This singular event lent credence to decades of writing about East End social and economic deviancy. Later accounts, in turn, read earlier nineteenth-century culture anachronistically through the lens of the murders. This is not to suggest, of course, that the East End suddenly became unexpectedly dangerous in

1888 when the first Ripper murder victim was discovered. Rather, writing about this event drew from and extended a tradition of constructing the East End in ways that entrenched assumptions about the relationship between immigrants, poverty, and crime. Today we are left with a seldom-questioned narrative reinforcing the idea that the story of the East End is one of universal and absolute danger and poverty. Recent book titles such as *London's Shadows: The Dark Side of the Victorian City* build on this trajectory by reducing the East End to a dark and shadowy nether world.[58] What gets lost in this construction are stories of the East End's intellectual and cultural life, such as East End theatre history, the rise of East End literary culture, the popularity of music and art led by locals like Simeon and Abraham Solomon, or the creation of the Spitalfields branch of the School of Design, where their sister Rebecca Solomon enrolled in art classes. The school was created in 1837 for the study of Ornamental Art. Female students attended in the morning hours and studied drawing, painting, working with casts, designing, and wood engraving. By 1850 the school enrolled two hundred students.[59]

The image published in the *Illustrated London News* in 1843 (fig. 3) depicts a bustling space of artistic creativity where locals would learn art as

FIG. 3. "School of Design," from the *Illustrated London News* (1843)

a trade, an opportunity for economic mobility, or to expand their knowledge of art and aesthetics. We may wonder, what if the story of the East End focused on the artists who attended the classes at the Spitalfields branch of the School of Design in place of Fagin and turkey-headed bargainers? Or better yet, what if a construction of the East End juxtaposed images by Dickens, the Cruikshanks, Polack, and Rebecca Solomon in an attempt to capture the contested nature and dynamism of London spatial narratives in this period? A more helpful path forward would find ways to register multiple views of the East End emerging from different subject positions, experiences, and perspectives, and would find ways to read them as expressions from their sources rather than statements of fact about their objects of study. Privileging one set of views or narratives not only leads to overdetermined characterizations but has the potential to inflict harm. Sander Gilman's study of the Whitechapel murderer investigation points to the effects of persistent racism and anti-Semitism, which led to biased detective work and the continuation of murders.[60] Centering writers like Polack and the East End diarist A. S. Lyon can lead us toward a productive unsettling of grand narratives of the East End's universal abjection, while recalling the importance of the heterogeneity of its resident voices. Indeed, such an approach is more in keeping with the nineteenth-century's actual demographics. As Heidi J. Holder points out in a discussion of theatre in this period,

> Minority characters in the West-End theatres were overwhelmingly low and comic (and marginalized), beginning with those seen in the various adaptations of Pierce Egan's *Tom and Jerry* in the 1820s and continuing through Paul Meritt and George F. Rowe's *New Babylon* (Duke's Theatre, 1879) and Joseph Derrick's *Twins* (Olympic, 1884). But as early as Edward Fitzball's *The Negro of Wapping* [1838], London's minority populations were given central roles. And, as in *The Street Arab*, what could be a negative class- or race-based stereotype is given a twist in the end.[61]

Holder's analysis recalls both the division—indeed competition—between East and West London theatre and the way in which the selection of plays performed in the East End accommodated participation from local minority ethnic and racial groups living in the East End.

East Enders were well aware of the way their lives and communities were misrepresented by outsiders. Like Hollingshead, Arthur Morrison was born in poverty in the East End and later became a successful writer. The following passage, published as "A Street" in *Macmillan's Magazine* in 1891, not only resists the popular and reductive historiography of East End abjection, but also offers a striking rebuke of the casual dismissiveness of popular depictions of the region:

> It is in the East-end. There is no need to say in the East-end of what. The East-end is a vast city, as famous in its way as any city men have built. But who knows the East-end? It is down through Cornhill and out beyond Leadenhall Street and Aldgate pump, one will say; a shocking place, where he went once with a curate. An evil growth of slums which hide human creeping things; where foul men and women live on penn'orths of gin, where collars and clean shirts are not yet invented, where every citizen wears a black eye, and no man combs his hair. Our street is not in a place like this. The East-end is a place, says another, populated by the unemployed. The unemployed are a race whose token is a clay pipe, and whose enemy is soap. Now and again they migrate bodily to Hyde Park with banners, and furnish surrounding police courts with disorderly drunkards. Still another knows the East-end only as the place whence come begging letters; where coal and blanket funds are in a state of permanent insolvency, and somebody is always wanting a day in the country. Everybody has his own notion of the East-end,—usually nothing but a distorted conception of some incidental feature of the place. There are foul slums in the East-end of course, just as there are in the West-end; there is want and misery in the East-end, just as there is wherever men and women gather together to fight for food and a roof; but it is not always of a spectacular sort.[62]

Morrison's interest here is to detail the unquestioned vision of those who presume to understand the East End as a place where "human creeping things" live. Through their "distorted conception of some incidental features," their assumptions fall short. Indeed, in the hundred years preceding Morrison's observations, narrators of popular accounts of London commonly equivocated in their descriptions of the East End, landing somewhere between curiosity, confusion, and distrust of their subjects. In many cases, such accounts present a kind of relative or relational tension that worked to create a divide between East and West End cultures. They expose, on the one hand, the existence of *both* dismissive and respectful views of East End life, and, on the other, the prominence of complicated heavy-handed assumptions that the East and West were essentially separate spheres—one defined by universal culture, collars, and soap, and the other by poverty, filth, and crime.

Evidence of similar relational tension appear in W. T. Stead's infamous exposé of child prostitution in *The Maiden Tribute of Modern Babylon*, published in June of 1885 in the *Pall Mall Gazette*. Stead's goal was not just to expose the immorality of child prostitution, but to generate interest among readers in passing the Criminal Law Amendment Act of 1885, which proposed raising the age of consent for sexual acts from thirteen to sixteen. In his five articles, Stead inventoried the intimate details of young girls—ages four to fourteen—who were abducted, drugged, raped, and/or sold into a life of prostitution, sometimes even by members of their own family desperate for money or one less mouth to feed. In trying to criminalize the vices of the rich, Stead argued that the criminal figure is not exclusively a product of the dark seedy streets of Whitechapel. The worst criminal figures in Stead's narrative live in middle-class or well-to-do homes in West London. Rather than reading the social and moral problems in London as the result of East End criminal behavior, in *The Maiden Tribute of Modern Babylon*, Stead suggested that the horrible social deviants are West End men encroaching on innocent girls living in regions throughout the metropolis.

The first installment of *The Maiden Tribute*, published in July of 1885, included an interview with an unnamed East End man under the subheading "Confessions of a Brothel Keeper." Readers learn that this man "formerly kept a noted house on Mile-End road [in the East End], but who is now endeavouring to start life afresh as an honest man."[63] He adds, "The East is the great market for the children who are imported into West-end houses, or taken abroad wholesale when trade is brisk. I know of no West-end houses, having always lived at Dalston or thereabouts, but agents pass to and fro in the course of business. They receive the goods, depart, and no questions are asked."[64] This same man proceeds to offer details about his former East End brothel, and about the movement of girls—"Maids, as you call them—fresh girls as we know them"—who are lured from East London and then moved to brothels in West London. In a subsequent section titled "A Dreadful Profession," included in the same day's article, Stead describes his conversation with a "highly respectable midwife" to whose house "children were taken by procurers to be certified as virgins before violation, and where, after violation, they were taken to be 'patched up,' and where, if necessary, abortion could be procured."[65] Stead adds, "[T]he existence of the house was no secret."[66] Such stories are disturbing enough, yet what lends strangeness to these accounts is Stead's choice to frame the problem of child prostitution as one with East and West counterparts. Why mention London geography at all? If the goal is to change British law, and to show that child prostitution is a problem everywhere in the city of London, why delineate East from West—especially when both play an active role in the procurement and abuse of young girls? We might put the question a different way: What does Stead's attentiveness to London geography enable him to say about London vice?

Robert L. Patten claims that "a hermeneutics of literary geography helps to recover the aesthetics [. . .] which embody ways a culture organizes itself [and] allows us to ask why a place is made, why it is a place to start from or come to, and why, because of those starting and ending points, the spaces and journeys signify in particular ways."[67] According to Patton, literary geography is not a meager reference to the location of plot action; rather, both setting and place function centrally as part of a work's aesthetics and its political engagements, and in the significance of what texts say and mean by alluding to place. This point becomes all too clear in Stead's subtle challenge to simplified constructions of a refined West End and a socially deviant East End. In the subsequent subsection of his article titled "Juvenile Prostitution in the East and West," Stead makes the following pronouncement: "In the East-end of London vice is much more natural than in the West."[68] Echoing Egan's and the Cruikshanks' depiction of natural lowlife, Stead expresses his view of the inevitable or irrecoverable nature of East End crime. The passage continues by elaborating on the essential differences in the way East Enders and West Enders engage in the culture of prostitution. He explains,

> [T]he taste for extreme youth does not seem to have developed in the crowded East. Here and there are cases, and there are vast strata where the children cohabit from preposterously early years, but that is quite distinct from prostitution. In the most fashionable houses of ill fame [located in the East End], such as Mrs. Jeffries's, Mrs. B———'s, J———'s, and others, any stranger ordering young children of very tender age would be looked at askance. These things are only done for old customers.[69]

Stead's East End has a decided disadvantage in its natural proclivity for vice; the upside is that those who hire prostitutes at least still prefer adults over children. He neglects to elaborate on why he believes "vice is more natural" in the East, but earlier discussions concerning the procurement of young girls suggest that economic forces are at work in this characterization. He implies that it's more natural that someone struggling to feed their children might sell one of them into prostitution. Seemingly offhand references to the places where girls are procured or where they go to be "patched up" helped the campaign to pass the Criminal Law Amendment Act in 1885. In the end, *The Maiden Tribute* created a version of London out of a number of competing discourses. The reductive East and West moral or economic division may be at work, but is complicated further by other resistant narratives that contradict one another in the coverage of child prostitution. Ultimately, they express not a separation, but an undercurrent of relations linking East and West ends of London. Stead's point is that London vice traversed borders. However, his use of East and West recalls an entrenched and uneven relationship, even as he attempts to overturn it with a narrative of widespread metropolitan sexual deviance.

Past, Present, and Future

The range of perspectives we encounter from Egan and Cruikshank, Dickens, Hollingshead, Morrison, and Stead raise important interpretive problems about the way spatial identities are formed through available written records. As Victorian Britain became wealthier economically, more powerful globally, and more progressive technologically, images of a degraded or stunted East End proliferated, deepening the divide between West and East London, while suggesting that rising poverty and danger were primarily East End problems. The resulting construction of the East End emerged not just through the visions of privileged affluent observers, but from the experience of border crossings, or from those traveling from West to East London or across the river to record what they perceived to be a problem coming from elsewhere, and involving people peripherally connected to London.

Myths of archival truth toy with our thirst for new or hidden knowledge, and frequently echo the discourses of light and darkness used in constructions of the East End. Saidiya Hartman considers this metaphor's implications in her quest to recover absent archives of the Atlantic slave trade, noting,

> In Western Philosophy, knowledge has been conceived of primarily as an ocular function. To know is to see and to see is the inception of thought. The mind has been described as an inner eye and knowledge as a series of visual perceptions or pictures. Sight is the sense elevated above all others in apprehending the world. Not being able to see clearly is tantamount to ignorance, and since early modernity the ignorance of the West had

> been projected onto Africa—the heart of darkness, the dark continent, the blighted territory.[70]

Indeed, the early nineteenth century drew from these very images of darkness to signal East End depravity and its symbolic alignment with depictions of Africa. William Booth's *In Darkest England and The Way Out* (1890) and Margaret Harkness's *In Darkest London* (1891) framed East End poverty in light of Henry Morton Stanley's earlier *In Darkest Africa* (1890).[71] None of these works can be read outside of Conrad's depictions of Marlow in *Heart of Darkness* reflecting upon "the monstrous town" while gazing upon London, as he states, "And this also . . . has been one of the dark places of the earth."[72]

The English couple I discussed at the start of this chapter may be responding to a version of the East End that emerged in the nineteenth century, but their insistence on a sustained separation of spheres and a unified control of narratives of nation reflect contemporary concerns about definitions of place and belonging. As I write these words, recent newspapers debate President Trump's proposal for a wall between the United States and Mexico, dividing families at the border and placing children in cages as punishment for stepping over the line. I suggest that to see the construction of the nineteenth-century East End outside of recent debates in the United States about cages and wall building would be a mistake. Texts written about nineteenth-century East Enders as deviant foreigners point to the very tensions that continue to inform racist definitions of nation and exclusionary borders. This body of work is not about the past. It's about a vision still dividing communities around the globe. My hope is that a reading of the East End through the lens of archives and critical archive studies will expose some of the damaging effects of flattening places into depictions of universal abjection, or of linking crime and social deviance to marginalized ethnic and racial communities. Violence recorded, preserved, and repeated by each generation of writers must be part of our own reckoning not just with the past and present, but with the thread that unites them.

The following chapters examine archival texts produced by East Enders that disrupt and advance narratives and images I've discussed in this chapter. In some cases, archival records explicitly challenge popular stereotypes of the East End. Others are silent on their intentions, offering instead a vision that reflects an intimacy with East End people and culture. Read alongside one another, the East End becomes a contested space difficult to pin down or prop up as a dangerous underworld of dark shadows. As I trace my search for archival evidence of Maria Polack's writing life in the following chapters, I consider the varied work of that evidence as it creates conflicting constructions of the East End that often push against familiar narratives. The nature of the archive is to prompt hope and desire, to give rise to the impulse to continue searching against apparent absences. Such an approach inevitably stirs up questions about what might have been saved or hasn't yet been found. In archival romances calm is restored only once questions are answered, and the scholar can enjoy the illusion of making the story whole.[73] In real life, the story always remains incomplete, not just because of missing objects, but because the past and origins of archival content are always implicitly fragmentary and biased. While archives may not provide closure to our questions, they do still find ways to narrate or reflect evidence of pasts from which they were born and perspectives of the witnesses who gathered records in anticipation of our arrival.

2

Archive Models

MARIA POLACK'S *FICTION WITHOUT ROMANCE* TRANSFORMED

IN HER 2012 *New York Times* article titled "New Novel of the Harlem Renaissance Is Found," Felicia R. Lee recounts a story almost too good to be true. An unknown manuscript of a novel by Claude McKay "was discovered," Lee explains, "in a previously untouched university archive and offers an unusual window on the ideas and events . . . that animated Harlem on the cusp of World War II."[1] Lee continues exaltingly:

> This literary detective story began in the summer of 2009, when Jean-Christophe Cloutier, a doctoral candidate in English and comparative literature, was working as an intern in the Rare Book and Manuscript Library at Columbia. He was going through more than 50 boxes of materials belonging to Samuel Roth, a kind of literary pariah who died in 1974. . . . No one knew of a connection between Mr. Roth and McKay, Mr. Cloutier said, as he came upon the roughly 300-page double-spaced manuscript, bound between cardboardlike covers bearing the novel's title and McKay's name.[2]

Like a scene from *Raiders of the Lost Ark*, audiences learn about the unearthing of a lost treasure, a prized cultural object found against all odds. Lee's fashioning of this event as a "literary detective story" dramatizes the sense of mystery, while mention of "untouched . . . archives" smacks of what readers love about archival romance narratives. To make the story even better, not only did the cave *not* collapse on the treasure seeker, but that seeker is the very person we would hope to make such a discovery—an earnest graduate student interning at the library.

The revelation of a lost novel by McKay is certainly worthy of attention. Yet the tone of triumphalism in Lee's account conjures troubling mythologies of discovery that taunt us into believing archives are a place of recovery work, where original truths can be rescued from obscurity by eager, well-intentioned scholars. In my first encounter with the article, I bristled at Lee's framing of the event. After all, Cloutier hadn't *only* discovered a new primary source; he'd exposed a host of unrecognized questions about the archive's creation and provenance. The article raised unanswered questions about Roth's relationship with McKay. For example, what led to the failure of the finding aid and cataloguing process? Was the loss of these materials the result of an archivist's oversight? Or did Roth intentionally bury the manuscript? Or perhaps McKay had no interest in publishing the novel? Lee was silent on such questions. Her job was to report the story of romance and discovery. And our job was to moon over the unexpected joy of unearthing a lost source and to wonder—as I did, I admit—why does this never happen to me? Readers everywhere were charged by the affective power of the archive, its withholding tendencies upended by the seduction of recovery.[3]

I knew this affective power well from my efforts to find archival traces of Maria Polack's life. My interest grew out of a single sentence in Michael Galchinsky's groundbreaking study *The Origin of the Modern Jewish Woman Writer:* "When Maria Polack's novel *Fiction without Romance; or, the Locket-Watch* appeared in 1830—the first novel to be published by an English Jew, in the year of the Jews' first efforts at parliamentary emancipation—the Jewish public sphere was nonexistent."[4] I was hooked instantly by the parts of the story omitted from Galchinsky's sentence. Was Polack really the first Jewish novelist in England? What prompted her to write a novel—a literary form foreign to early nineteenth-century Jewish culture? Why had we lost track of such a monumental feat? And was Galchinsky's claim right that the Jewish sphere was *completely* nonexistent? Maybe it was just difficult to find. Polack was clearly educated, as *Fiction without Romance* attests with its numerous references to books, plays, poems, and important cultural figures and events. How did that come to be? Where did Polack find books to read? Where did she find the money to subscribe to lending libraries? Records of Polack's life are limited. To date, a lost source by Polack, like the one Cloutier found by McKay, has never surfaced. The challenge I faced—that we all face with archival quests—was how to read extant archival traces and fragments as metanarratives about those who created, collected, or preserved them. And what could those fragments tell us about lost pieces of the story?

Baffled by the challenge of locating evidence of Polack's career, I made my way to the British Library. Although I had in my possession a photocopy of *Fiction without Romance,* I wanted to place my hands on an original copy of the book.[5] As I waited expectantly in the muffled quiet of the British Library's reading room for my book to arrive, I recalled what I'd learned about this strange novel. *Fiction without Romance* was published on May 30, 1830, and sold for 16 shillings. Converted into modern value by the National Archive's Currency Converter, the 2017 equivalent value (the most recent year available) is £54.24.[6] According to the National Archives, in 1830 this amount would be the equivalent of four days' wages for a skilled tradesman. Clearly, this was not a cheap paperback. When I planned my visit, I had assumed the novel would show signs of its costliness. Yet my first view of the book was a disappointment. I was struck by its plastic cover. The librarians were unable to determine if it had been published originally without a cover or if the old cover was replaced from overuse. I resigned myself to make the most of the disappointing object. I tried to reassure myself that holding one of the few extant copies of the book was still powerful despite its plastic mask.

I proceeded to open the stiff boards, feeling the tugging of a tight binding that unfairly represented the book's stature. Another betrayal, I thought. Surely this old novel must have been handled by many before me. By now the binding should have stretched from use, from nearly two hundred years of hands forcing the spine open for hours at a time. Next I turned over the cover to focus on the book's first pages. At precisely the moment when I might have caught a whiff of dusty old-book smells, I noticed a problem. The title page was wrong. I hastily compared my photocopy of the novel with the British Library's copy. My inspection of ink smudges on the pages of both copies indicated they'd been printed either at the same time or by the same printing press. But the title pages didn't match. In the weeks that followed, I contacted librarians at the four libraries that owned hard copies of *Fiction without Romance* requesting reviews of the paratexts in their copies.[7] Their helpful replies confirmed that the British Library's *Fiction without Romance* included not only a different title page, but an entirely different set of paratexts from those included in every other extant copy of the book.

While trying to interpret the existence of two versions of a book published just once, I mulled over Galchinsky's claims that there was no Jewish public sphere in 1830. Since the beginning of my work on this novel, I suspected that Polack would have had difficulty publishing without support from her community. I returned to archival sources with hopes that they would show signs of a public or communal sphere cognizant of Polack's literary activities. My efforts always ended in failure. The reviews announced the publication of the novel but offered little else. My archival quests were similarly unproductive. Without evidence, it seemed likely that Galchinsky was right. Or even if he wasn't, I had no way to support my theory that Polack's East End community must have endorsed or supported her literary venture. Without evidence of this context, I had to find other ways to fill in gaps of the story. As it turned out, the strange title page in the British Library's copy of the novel widened the scope of my search. Other clues surfaced as I made my way through the unique copy of the book. Turning one crisp page after another, I discovered two additional paratexts absent in other copies of the novel: a subscription list and a page titled "To Subscribers." These seemingly insignificant pages would ultimately open the door to a larger story about both Polack's path to publication and her Jewish public sphere. The existence of the British Library's copy of *Fiction without Romance* made it clear that my job was not to recover the lost story of Polack's writing life; it was to learn how to read unofficial and unexpected archives, to account for textual silences, and to make meaning out of an odd set of paratexts.

In search of clues about the British Library's strange copy of the book, I corresponded with another library's online help desk. I asked if their holdings included published or unpublished materials by nineteenth-century East Enders. The reply clarified some of the challenges I faced in my search to find contexts for Polack's novel. The person at the help desk explained, "Whilst true working class 'east enders' have often recorded their memories etc in the 20th century through published and unpublished writings and visual and oral material I am not aware of any doing so earlier partly because they would not have had the literacy skills and also because they would not have understood the relevance in recording their lives."[8] Offered with the best of intentions, this response reminded me I was not only pushing against a legacy of assumptions about the East End's putative cultural depravity; I was also confronting the effects of a silent archive, for missing evidence bolstered assumptions that the East End cultural record had *only* one kind of story to tell. The respondent assumed that because they were unaware of East End writing, it must not exist. They reasoned, moreover, that the absence of writing by East Enders proved a universal deficiency in literacy skills among residents of the region. The respondent made one final assumption I knew I had to challenge: East Enders would not have understood the value of recording their lives. Polack wrote a novel, not an autobiography, but her footnotes indicate that she drew from personal experience in her work of fiction. The existence of *Fiction without Romance,* with its signs of Polack's learning and her ability to navigate the publishing market, hinted at the misleading nature of East End stereotypes. I was frustrated by my inability to challenge these narratives. Without records verifying East End intellectual and cultural production, Polack's novel seemed like an exception to the presumed rule of universal East End cultural degradation.

When I stumbled upon the British Library's paratexts, however, I knew they furnished proof of the existence of East End intellectual life. Gérard Genette explains that a "paratext is what enables a text to become a book and to be offered as such to its readers, and, more generally, to the public."[9] Title pages, notes, acknowledgments, and the like function as "more than a boundary or a sealed border, the paratext is, rather, a threshold, or . . . 'vestibule' that offers the world at large the possibility of either stepping inside or turning back."[10] A title page doesn't simply announce the novel's title; it mediates, preparing and shaping readers' impressions and experiences with the text. In this vein, the paratexts in the British Library's copy of *Fiction without Romance* pointed to contexts previously unknown to me, contexts I wouldn't have thought to consider as a significant feature of the novel's content, the author's intellectual reach, or the book's provenance. The subscription list in particular—a collection of names and addresses of those who publicly endorsed Polack's literary accomplishment—pointed to the existence of a community willing and able to support the first Anglo-Jewish novelist. Remarkably, this single copy of the book had preserved the identities of 147 subscribers from throughout England and the Atlantic world. Although 147 names constituted a small list by 1830s standards, it was formidable enough to suggest a rich and diverse field of social actors. I knew nothing of the reasons people bought subscriptions or their relations with the author. I was struck, however, by the inclusion of addresses alongside many of the subscribers' names indicating that one of the highest geographical areas of concentration on the list came from Polack's Whitechapel neighborhood. Apparently, a sizable number of East Enders had the ability to purchase a book valued today at about US $100. The inclusion of names of prominent people in Polack's community offered additional clues about her contacts with scholars, educational reformers, painters, musicians, playwrights, and philanthropists. Indeed, the range of identities of Polack's subscribers not only situated the author within a broad community, but also preserved traces of the methods she used to reach her global audience. I came to understand that the British Library's ugly plastic cover protected an unofficial archive, curated by Polack, containing evidence of a Jewish public sphere in 1830.

The book archive, as I'll refer to it in this chapter, is composed of a collection of unique paratexts stored in the British Library's copy of Polack's novel. My characterization of a book as an unofficial archive, or as a repository that preserves and orders documents that speak to the author's publishing venture, draws from Giorgio Agamben's claim that "the archive is situated between *langue*, as the system of construction of possible sentences—that is, of possibilities of speaking—and the corpus that unites the set of what has been said, the things actually uttered *or* written."[11] The "or" in Agamben's phrasing accounts for the possibilities of absence, or the unwritten uttered thoughts substantiated through extant records. Put differently, Agamben suggests that the archive is full not only by the existence of saved writing, but by its affirmation of utterances and speech possibilities that may be absent from paper records.

With this point in mind, the following discussions trace the coordinated appearance of existence and loss in Polack's book archive. In addition to researching the identities of individual subscribers, I've transformed the list's content into a one-dimensional flat database. My subsequent analysis of the list benefits from the database's ability to reorganize content and to find patterns in gender distribution, subscriber locations, and social actors whose support may have influenced the rise of Jewish literary culture in this period. Despite the benefits of the database archive, I make clear in the following discussion that transformations of the list have the power to expose submerged contexts and subjectivities or to raise new questions about East End literary culture. The challenge was to find a way to create and read visual models made from my database with an awareness of the information they suppress and reveal. My work builds from Michel-Rolph Trouillot's description of the four moments when silences creep into the archive: "the moment of fact creation (the making of *sources*); the moment of fact assembly (the making of *archives*); the moment of fact retrieval (the making of *narratives*); and the moment of retrospective significance (the making of *history* in the final instance)."[12] While records of Polack's life and publishing ventures are scant, evidence of her professional practices can be gleaned from both the book archive's static paratexts and the dynamic power of the database, which produced models that point to the players in her community. Trouillot's categories are neither conditional nor mutually exclusive. Thus, while Polack's subscription list might fall into Trouillot's category of "the making of *sources*," the collection of paratexts included in a single copy of Polack's novel constitutes her own work of fact assembly, or "the making of *archives*." My database archive, drawn from Polack's list and transformed by the database's dynamic structuring capabilities, exposes or creates new or little-known narratives of East End intellectual culture.

Maria Polack's "To Subscribers" notice bound with the British Library's copy of the novel offers a palpable example of unwritten utterances stored in the book archive. She writes, "The laying this little work before the Public, having been attended with considerable expense, and the number of Subscribers not being as large as might have been expected, it is earnestly requested, that those Ladies and Gentleman who have obligingly honored the author with their patronage, will extend their kindness still farther, by not lending their books, as they may be had at most Circulating Libraries."[13] Her note makes a request—that readers refrain from loaning their copies of the book—while simultaneously admitting her failure to meet the costs of production. Like contemporary novels containing collections of paper fragments, such as J. J. Abrams and Doug Dorst's *S.* and Zachary Thomas Dodson's *Bats of the Republic,* evidence preserved in the British Library's copy of the book frames the novel's content and our engagement with that content. Andrew Stauffer's Book Traces project similarly records evidence of unique inscriptions and marginalia preserved within book covers that account for their use, circulation, and reception over time. While Polack's letter to her subscribers may not provide an account of a reader's interaction with her novel, its existence in a single copy of the book captures rare evidence of Polack's connection with subscribers. Like other objects in the book archive, the note illuminates features of Polack's community relations, her funding model, and her understanding of the way her contemporary readers accessed books in circulating libraries.

Of all the British Library paratexts, the subscription list was the most difficult to decipher. I wondered why addresses appeared alongside some but not all names on the list. And I struggled to understand the rhetorical effect of this particular cluster of names on Polack's audience. Initially I approached these questions by creating a map with dots marking the locations of her subscribers' residences. In time I realized such a map would create the same kind of argument used against East Enders by making reductive spatial claims about East End stasis. I sought instead a method of representing the dynamism of East End cultural forms and expressions. I reorganized the content of the list using an Excel spreadsheet and Gephi visualizations. Gephi is a tool that creates visual models showing the relations among names and addresses on the list. Rather than accept the list on its own terms, I intentionally transformed its content to broaden my analytical scope.

Johanna Drucker and Lisa Gitelman among others have helpfully cautioned against viewing data or data structures as records of truth or neutral repositories of objectively rendered information.[14] As Gitelman explains, "Data are familiarly 'collected,' 'entered,' 'compiled,' 'stored,' 'processed,' 'mined,' and 'interpreted.' Less obvious are the ways in which the final term in this sequence—interpretation—haunts its predecessors."[15] Similarly, in restructuring Polack's data, I've engaged in an interpretive process. My goal was not to use data to advance absolute declarations about the East End. With an awareness of the ways all data has been shaped by bias and interpretation, I use the data from the list to propose helpful provocations that elucidate features of the novel's content and hidden social networks. The following discussion builds from Lauren F. Klein's caution against reading data as a source of neutral information. I focus instead on the data's ability to point to "the limits of our knowledge."[16] It was the effects of my reordering that exposed such limits, demonstrating in the process crucially important evidence of subjectivities suppressed by the static lists and only hinted at in the database transformations.

Author, Novel, and Book

Polack's preface to *Fiction without Romance* indicates that this was her first publication. Additional works, if they were written, remain undiscovered.[17] A few other sources touch upon fragmentary details of Polack's circle. Polack's father, Ephraim Polack, was buried on May 3, 1812, in the Jews' Burial Ground on Brady Street. At the time of his death, Ephraim Polack lived on Mansell Street in Goodman's Fields in the East End. According to a Chancery record for the Goodmans [*sic*] Fields Estate, Ephraim Polack leased his home at 23 Mansell Street on October 4, 1804, and he or his heirs held the lease for 17 ½ years.[18] Anglo-Jewish historian James Picciotto claims that Ephraim Polack is the father of Maria Polack and the grandfather of another writer named Elizabeth Polack.[19]

According to the *Great Synagogue Marriage Records,* Maria Polack married Lipman Pollak—the spelling is noteworthy—on August 11, 1813, a little over a year after Ephraim Polack's death. According to Angela Shire, Lipman is described in these records as "Desc. from a Priv[d] Member: Lipman s. of Isaac Pollak." The entry for Maria reads, "Desc. from a Priv[d] Member: Miriam d. of Ephraim Polack."[20] On marrying, Lipman, the son of Isaac Pollak, evidently took the spelling of his wife's name. Maria Polack died on January 9, 1849, and was buried the following day in the Brady Street Cemetery.[21] At the time of her death, Polack lived at

84 Leman Street, Goodman's Fields.[22] Her husband died the following year on August 24, 1850, and was buried the next day. Lipman was interred in Brady Street Cemetery with his family.[23]

Maria Polack's birth records have not been found. However, she and her family make an appearance in the 1841 English census.[24] At the time, Maria and Lipman Polack were living on Mansell Street in Whitechapel. The record states that Maria Polack was 55 and her husband was 50 in 1841.[25] In this particular census year, ages of adults were cited to within the nearest five years of their actual ages (Lipman appears as 50, Maria as 55, Elizabeth as 25, Martha as 15).[26] The actual age of Maria is difficult to determine from this record, but it suggests that the span of her age would fall between 55 and 59 on June 6, 1841, the day on which the census taker arrived at her home. Similarly, Lipman's age on this date would fall between 50 and 54 years old.

The record describes Lipman's occupation as tailor and Maria's as "teacher of M." Two additional people were in their home during the census taker's visit: Elizabeth, age 25, with the occupation of author, and Martha Polack, age 15, with no occupation. Lipman is the only one in the family born abroad. When I first read the 1841 census record, I was confused about how Elizabeth and Martha were connected with Lipman and Maria. In chapter 4 I address details that emerged in later stages of my research. In these early stages, I struggled to understand how these people came to live together or their relationships to one another. My confusion was further muddled by contradictory historical accounts. Picciotto's claim that Ephraim was Elizabeth's grandfather suggests that she was likely Maria and Lipman's daughter.[27] However, since Maria Polack's husband was also named Polack, it's also possible that Elizabeth was Lipman's sister and Maria Polack's sister-in-law—mentioned in other records discussed below. Martha died two years following the date of the census in 1843.[28] Another death record notes that Maria Polack gave birth to a son, Ephraim Polack, whose burial took place on January 8, 1816.[29] I had earlier relied on available database resources. As time passed, new resources became available to augment the scope of this family's story while also raising new questions about their ties to the East End and other sites in England and the West Indies.

According to the UK Register of Duties Paid for Apprentices' Indentures, Lipman worked as an apprentice to Ephraim Polack, a tailor.[30] Lipman's name also shows up in the *Proceedings of the Old Bailey*, when he testified as the victim of larceny.[31] His own words were recorded on the day of the trial, May 26, 1819:

> I am a tailor, and live in Mansell-street, Goodman's-fields. On the 25th of May the prisoner came to my house and asked for some clothes for Mr. Jacobs; my sister called me down—I told him to send Mr. Jacobs himself for them. About three-quarters of an hour after he was gone I received information, and then missed the table-spoon off the beaufet [*sic*]. I went to a coffee-shop in Church-street with an officer, took him into custody, and asked him for the spoon; he said he gave it to Jacobs—he then pulled it out of his breeches-pocket.[32]

This man—the prisoner—was found guilty and transported to Australia for seven years. It's difficult to know if the unnamed sister was the Elizabeth Polack listed on the census record. While justice seems to have been carried out for spoon stealing, at least by nineteenth-century standards, this tiny anecdote supports the criminal construction of the East End. Much of what we can know about any place rests upon the kinds of institutional records that have been saved and/or digitized. In this case, it was the Old Bailey records—official accounts of criminal activities—that support a vision of the East End as violent or criminal. As I scrolled through its holdings, I was left wondering what kind of narrative of East End life would be possible if evidence had been saved of literary societies, charity work, or musical performances. The fact that criminal records were not only saved but also selected for digitization frames and limits questions we can ask of the available resources while also casting shadows upon other potential sources we may not know to look for in our searches for understudied writers like Polack. In sum, the existence of an admittedly helpful digital resource, such as the Old Bailey records, emerges through a host of questions and promptings invisible to us. In this case, the decision to preserve crime narratives works like a bullseye lantern, entrenching stereotypes of London spaces while pushing other potential narratives into darkness.

Polack's *Fiction without Romance* takes place far from the crowded streets of her home in the East End. The plot of the novel focuses on two contemporary problems. First, Polack emphasizes the importance of educating—or enlightening, as she puts it—English readers about Jewish culture and religious practices. In an effort to quell English prejudice and Christian efforts to convert Jews in this period, Polack argues for greater cross-cultural exchange between Jews and Christians in literary culture and in day-to-day life.[33] Second, *Fiction without Romance* critiques the demise of traditional Jewish religious values and rituals. In her anti-romance novel, Polack argues for the preservation of Jewish religious and cultural traditions at a moment when many Anglo-Jews were abandoning or reforming such practices to assimilate into English culture. Young children of any religion, the novel argues, must learn the value of rational, enlightened thinking in order to become morally responsible adults; but reason, the novel argues, is best taught alongside—not in place of—religion.

In her two-volume novel, Polack narrates the stories of two families and two worlds that converge when the daughters of each become friends. In the English plot, the narrator tells the story of the infant Eliza whose mother dies shortly after learning that her husband, Charles Courtney, was married to another woman at the point when she married him. In defense of his sister's honor and in a fit of rage, Edward Frederick Desbro stabs Courtney and, believing him dead, flees with the illegitimate Eliza to a village in Devonshire. Eliza is raised by Reverend George Howard and his wife, Jane Howard. The Reverend's widowed sister, Mary Wallace, assumes the role of Eliza's preceptress. Together, the Howard/Wallace family and Desbro provide a model education for Eliza that helps her to develop a rational mind through the study of academic subjects, including literature (in particular the moral tales of Jean-François Marmontel and Maria Edgeworth), geography (with the help of globes), and music. Eliza meets a diverse range of people and cultures in Devonshire and London under the supervision of her wise teacher, Mrs. Wallace. By novel's end Eliza has learned to navigate courtship rituals, has founded a Sunday School for the poor, and lives happily among friends in London.

The second part of the novel, the Jewish plot, recounts the story of a London Jewish stockbroker named Mr. Zachariah. In his first visit to Zachariah's home, Desbro is pleased to meet such an educated and refined Jewish man and to meet his well-mannered children and grandchildren. Desbro befriends the eldest child, Jacob Zachariah, and many years later sets up a meeting between his niece, Eliza, and Jacob's daughter, Rebecca. The teenage girls become good friends. Rebecca teaches Eliza about the observance of Jewish rituals and the sad misfortunes of her sister, Sarah, who eloped with a non-Jewish man. Living in isolation from her family, Sarah gives birth to a child who later dies while she awaits her husband's return from a trip to France. Sick, alone, and grieving, Sarah finds her way back to her family just before dying herself. This is not the only interfaith marriage in the novel. A subplot details the misfortunes of the Anglican Mrs. St. Clair, whose marriage to a Catholic man leads to similarly devastating consequences.

Fiction without Romance addresses interrelated concerns about enlightenment values, the importance of female education, and religious pluralism in England. These subjects, though timely and important, were hardly original in 1830, the publication year of *Fiction without Romance.* Dozens of novels from the previous four decades emphasized the importance of educating daughters or cautioned female readers to resist the allure of seductive rakes. In her depictions of happy and sad marriages, philandering seducers, fallen women, and runaway brides, Polack revives earlier debates over the educational and social role of romance and realist fictions.[34] If we pay exclusive attention to the story of Eliza—her education, her mother's history, and her negotiation of her culture's courtship rituals—Polack's novel would seem to be fairly unremarkable. Yet, two details make this otherwise standard tale extraordinary. First, Polack is one of the first to publish a novel depicting the struggles around Anglo-Jewish integration. And second, unlike other novels in this period, in *Fiction without Romance* Polack uses the friendship between Jewish and Anglican families as a platform on which to argue for respect for religious difference. Polack's readers would likely have been familiar with other contemporary novels that explored similar subjects, such as Maria Edgeworth's *Harrington* (1817) and Sir Walter Scott's *Ivanhoe* (1819).

One of the most curious features of Polack's novel is the choice to situate the action in two distinct geographical locations—Devon and London. The former is the location where Desbro takes the infant Eliza to be raised by her guardians, the Reverend Mr. Howard; his wife, Jane Howard; and his sister, Mrs. Wallace. The novel opens with an idealization of this rural environment: "Amongst the many picturesque and romantic scenes, with which Devonshire so profusely abounds, there is not a spot more beautiful than that on which stood the residence of Mr. Desbro. It was built in the cottage style,—small, yet elegant, and replete with every convenience that could render it the abode of domestic comfort, without any of those superfluities, which, in the present age of fashionable refinement, are too often erroneously considered as necessary."[35]

The "fashionable" world makes a striking appearance in descriptions of Eliza's visit to the Selby family—neighbors living in a nearby estate. The Selbys' daughters are shallow snobs who've been ruined by the vacuous glitter of London society. Eliza's innocent comment that "I should think the healthy air of Devonshire much more likely to prolong existence than that of London" is made fun of by her neighbors for its naïve provincialism. The exchange, however, draws out the novel's tensions over the refinements of rural culture compared to the potentially damaging effects of fashionable life in London.[36] It's in Devon where Eliza meets Henry Cooper, the young man who turns out to be her half brother. He arrives in the country for the improvement of his health.[37] Despite the benefits of Devon, however, the action of the second volume of the novel shifts to London for the completion of Eliza's education. Desbro laments features of Eliza's seclusion in the country, wondering to Mrs. Wallace, "Is it not a pity, that so fine and accomplished a creature, should remain buried in obscurity?"[38] Following subsequent discussions, the sixteen-year-old Eliza moves to London, where she meets the Zachariah family. Repeated travels between settings raise questions about how an East End Jewish writer would have learned about rural Christian communities in Devon. It's possible that Polack visited the region prior to writing the novel. Jewish communities in Devon and Cornwall were well established by the eighteenth century, and several names on her subscription list had contacts in both Devon and London.[39] While the subscription list hinted at her ties in these regions, it was only once I'd decoded the identities of specific names on the list that I began to sense the gravity of the novel's dual settings.

According to the title page in the British Library's copy of *Fiction without Romance,* Polack was a resident of London at the point when her neighbor, J. Wertheimer of Mansell Street, printed *Fiction without Romance.* Despite her father's death many years earlier, on the title page Polack places herself under his authority—as the daughter of the late Ephraim Polack. Mention of her title of "Mrs." assures her readers that she writes under the approval of a husband. Gary Kelly notes that in this period "by publishing, a woman put herself in a 'double bind'. As a woman she was supposed to be domestic; once published she became public, risking loss of femininity."[40] As the century unfolded, these social pressures would ease. Linda H. Peterson explains that Victorians witnessed a gradual "flowering of literary professionalism" for women made possible by "the burgeoning of print culture and the opening of new genres for women writers."[41] Like many of her contemporaries, Polack took advantage of these emerging opportunities. Yet she remained tied to the practice of aligning herself with men in positions of authority—not just her father and husband, but also the printer J. Wertheimer. It is likely that Wertheimer printed enough copies for subscribers and one additional copy for Polack to submit to the publisher Effingham Wilson for consideration to publish. Once they agreed to publish the novel, new copies would have been printed along with a new title page listing the publisher's

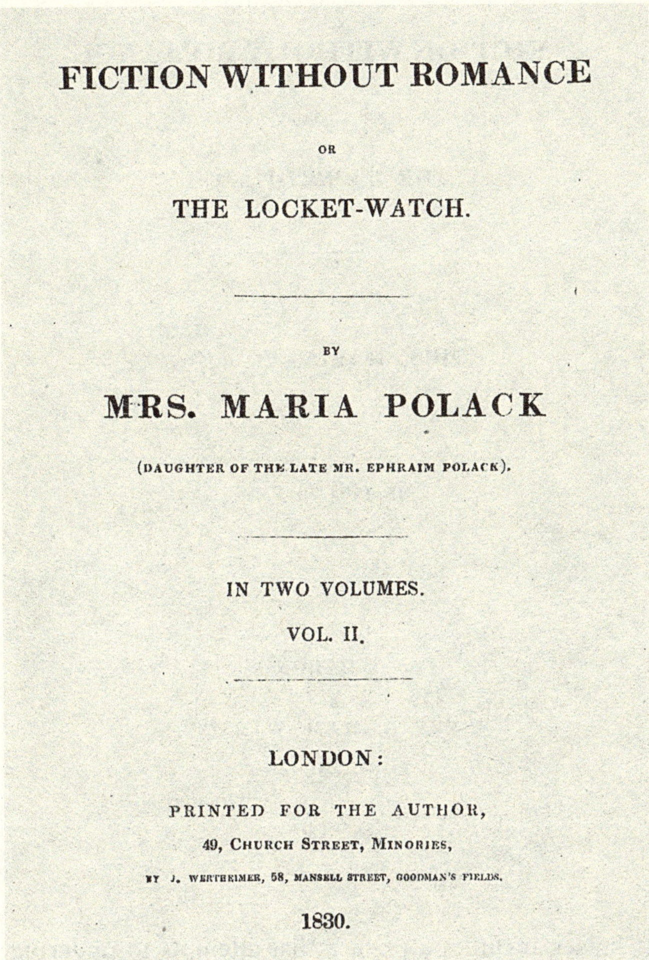

FICTION WITHOUT ROMANCE

OR

THE LOCKET-WATCH.

BY

MRS. MARIA POLACK

(DAUGHTER OF THE LATE MR. EPHRAIM POLACK).

IN TWO VOLUMES.

VOL. II.

LONDON:

PRINTED FOR THE AUTHOR,

49, CHURCH STREET, MINORIES,

BY J. WERTHEIMER, 58, MANSELL STREET, GOODMAN'S FIELDS.

1830.

FIG. 4. Title page of the British Library's *Fiction without Romance* (printer's copy). (© British Library Board, 1153.l.1, n.p.)

name. At that point, the subscription list, created to make an appeal to the publisher, would no longer be necessary. The published copy, containing the second title page displaying Effingham Wilson's name, is the version saved by all of the libraries except the British Library. The printer's copy (the British Library copy), submitted to the publisher for consideration, aligns Polack with her East End supporters. Polack needed to make a strong appeal to this group in order to raise funds to cover printing costs.[42] In contrast, the published copy not only aligns the East End author with a West End publisher, but also removes evidence of her local East End support network.

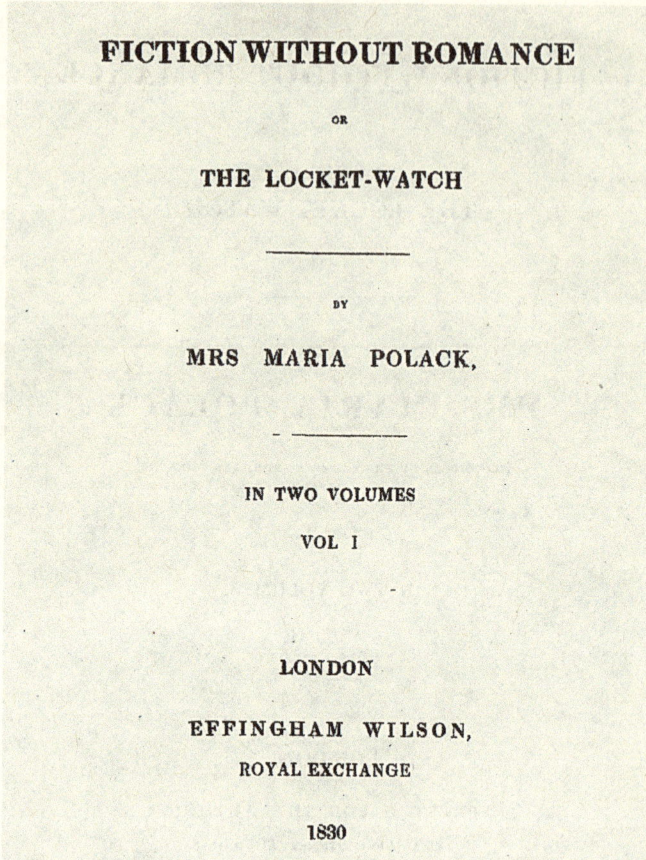

FICTION WITHOUT ROMANCE

OR

THE LOCKET-WATCH

BY

MRS MARIA POLACK,

IN TWO VOLUMES

VOL I

LONDON

EFFINGHAM WILSON,

ROYAL EXCHANGE

1830

FIG. 5. Title page of *Fiction without Romance* (1830) (publisher's copy)

In both copies Polack includes a preface that attempts to underplay the boldness of her desire to publish. Michael Scrivener recalls that the preface to Emma Lyon's *Miscellaneous Poems* (1812) includes "a strenuous framing process" similar to the one used in *Fiction without Romance.* According to Scrivener, "Women were not supposed to write poetry, but large numbers of women wrote anyway—and even larger numbers of women wrote in other genres as well, especially the romance and the novel. . . . Separate-spheres ideology was powerful enough to force from almost every woman writer some gesture of visible obedience to its authority."[43] Polack expressed her obedience on the novel's title page and the preface, where she includes statements that seem to diminish her boldness. She writes, "[T]he author's most delicate feelings are put to the test."[44] Yet her next statement offers a subtle reversal of her role as submissive first-time author. She claims, "I am not so presumptuous as to say, that I do not fear criticism; nor am I so pusillanimous as to shrink from it. I shall receive it as the wholesome chastisement which a judicious tutor bestows on the pupil whom he wishes to train towards proficiency."[45] Polack places herself in the role of the student awaiting "wholesome chastisement" from her teacher/critic. At the same time, she subtly teaches her audience how to offer an appropriate critique of her work. Criticism, she claims, should be "wholesome" and delivered by "a judicious tutor" to the "pupil" he hopes to "train." The gendered language (teacher = he; student/author = she) is meaningful in light of Polack's professional identity, listed on the census record as "teacher." Despite the performance of feminine submissiveness, in her preface Polack expresses her vision of how book reviews should work. Sadly, she never received the kind of feedback she requests. Several reviews mention her novel without commentary—wholesome or otherwise—on the quality of the writing or her treatment of her subjects.[46] One anonymous reviewer from the *London Literary Gazette and Journal of Belles Lettres, Arts, Sciences, Etc.* noted it was "evidently the production of one anxious to benefit by the inculcation of excellent principles—the leisure hours of many of our young readers may be much worse employed than in the perusal of these well-meaning pages."[47] Although the tone seems placid and withholding, this reviewer's phrasing suggests that Polack was probably writing to an audience of "young readers."

Polack's Social Networks

Numerous once-blank books containing lists of every kind have been preserved in the London Metropolitan Archives. The unnamed record keepers presented details of celebrations, names of construction workers, identities of teachers, records of badly behaved children, donors to charities, and financial records from local cemeteries—all presented through the structuring logic of the list. Earlier register books from the period before 1820 were written in Hebrew or Yiddish. Given that Hebrew moves from right to left, the list books followed suit. Pages filled from the right-hand side of the volume, moving forward in time as they reached toward the left. At some point between 1800 and 1820, record keepers began using English to keep track of institutional affairs. Rather than waste the book's remaining blank pages, they simply turned their books upside down and continued writing in English on the remaining blank pages, beginning anew from the left to the right side of the volume. These archival treasures document a moment of cultural transition by joining two languages with a buffer of a few blank pages. I gazed at these volumes with a mix of curiosity and confusion. For whom did they compose such extensive lists? And why did they continue to save records long after the subjects seemed relevant? What did they want readers to understand from their columns of data preserved in daybooks, diaries, and meeting notes? My training as a literary scholar had never introduced "lists" as a form of nineteenth-century rhetoric or writing. What was implied by the stacking of information? The documents were written by men, and most were written about men or schoolboys. When I later stumbled upon Polack's two-columned subscription list with an alphabetical arrangement of individuals and the inconsistent inclusion of addresses, I recalled the record books I'd studied in the archives and the community's habit of presenting precise data in stately rows. Polack's list reflected an interest in order and clarity. Read against evidence in the archive of this community's interest in excessive attention to organizational details, the missing addresses on Polack's list seemed more like record-keeping flaws than absences.

Subscription was a common form of book publishing in the eighteenth and early nineteenth centuries. William St. Clair explains that throughout "the romantic period, there was often an element of charity, raising money for a widow or giving a start to a local lad or lass without a patron, and the subscribers were often local nobility and gentry."[48] Polack's subscription list was one way of making an appeal to circulating or subscription libraries looking to expand their collections. According to Solveig C. Robinson, "Under the subscription system, authors or booksellers would appeal to potential readers to pledge funds. When enough funds were pledged or collected (for obvious reasons, cash in hand was preferred), the project would proceed. Assuming the author actually completed the promised work—which didn't always happen—the bookseller would arrange to have the text printed, usually in quantities at or just slightly in excess of the numbers spoken for."[49] Using the subscription process to cover the cost of printing was a form of publishing "on commission" which, according to St. Clair, established an arrangement in which it was "the author [not the publisher] who was the investor who accepted all the costs and the risks, and the publisher who took a royalty on sales."[50] Polack's note "To Subscribers" exposes her printing investment and miscalculation. The list itself, with its inclusion of well-known subscribers, would have made a powerful argument in her pitch to publishers. The choice to include an address clearly mattered, for 73 out of 147 subscribers included addresses alongside their names. Addresses may have functioned as a status symbol; an identifier to prevent confusion of common names; or an indication of a geographical competition. It's also possible that subscribers wanted to prove that even those living in the East End were respectable enough to consider a novel worthy of their hard-won earnings. It's likely that the inclusion of addresses held several meanings at once.

Polack's list of prominent leaders included the Rothschilds, who purchased five copies of the novel; the Montefiores, who purchased two copies; and members of the Goldsmid family, who bought an impressive total of seven copies. Other noteworthy figures stand out as well. Hyman Hurwitz, the first Professor of Hebrew Literature at the University of London, purchased one copy. Emma Lyon (Mrs. A. Henry), a well-known Anglo-Jewish poet, purchased a copy, along with several members of her family, including A. S. Lyon, the subject of the next chapter. And Joshua Van Oven, a well-known East End physician and a "Hebrew scholar and promoter of Jewish education" who "supported Hyman Hurwitz's establishment of a Jewish private school" and who later founded and served as president of the Jews' Free School in Whitechapel, also purchased one subscription.[51] Mr. Neumegen, a prominent educator in London's Jewish community, purchased a single subscription. And John Braham, the famous London tenor, purchased two subscriptions. In Polack's time these names would have provided further evidence of her respectability given that revered and accomplished communal leaders were willing to endorse her literary endeavors.

Polack's list complicates what we've come to assume about her East End neighborhood. While popular or sensational writing often claims that this part of London was universally riddled with poverty, crime, and degeneracy, the subscription list suggests alternately that the East End was a region inhabited by people actively engaged with the cultural, philanthropic, and religious concerns of their day—people, that is, involved with the publishing and printing world, synagogue life, education and educational reform, hospitals, and charities. Reading Polack's novel within the scope of her London connections places both book and author within a particular cultural milieu. One of the most interesting features of the subscription list is its resistance to the bifurcation of London geographies. In addition to including addresses from the East and West ends of London, the list includes addresses from the West Indies, Ireland, and throughout England.

From the moment I first gazed at the subscription list in the British Library's reading room, I was baffled by Polack's global reach. I wondered

Subscribers Names.

A

Mr. S. Abrahams, *Sun Square*
Widow of Colonel Andrews,
Mr. Lewis Aarons,
Mr. Assur, *Leman-street*
Mr. Mark Abrahams,
Mr. Alexander, *Cannon-street*
Mr. Lewis Abrahams,
Mr. Ansell, *Savage-gardens*

B

Mr. John Braham, 2 *Copies*
Mr. S. Bonfil,
Mrs. Barlin,
Mr. Joel Benjamin,
Dr. Boret,
Mr. D. Braham,
Mr. Moses Barnett,

C

Mr. Solomon Cohen, *Canonbury*
Mr. Benjamin Cohen, 2 *Copies*
Mr. Isaac Cohen,
A friend,
Mr. I. Cohen, *Mansell-street*
Mr. Canstatt,
Miss Cruse,
Mr. Myer Cohen,
Mr. Castello,
Mr. Calisher,
Mr. John Crabb,
Mr. Woolf Cohen, *Dublin*
Mr. Solomon Cohen, *Birmingham*

D

Mrs. Davidson, *Park-crescent*
Miss Dias,
Mrs. N. Davis,
Mrs. Davis, *Castle-street*
Mr. A. Davis, *Quadrant*
Mrs. Davis, *Strand*

E

Mrs. Joel Emanuel,
Mr. S. H. Ellis,
Mrs. Ebdell,
A friend

F

Mr. Flavel,

G

Mr. Edward Goldsmid,
Mrs. Edward Goldsmid,
Mr. Nathaniel Goldsmid, 2 *Copies*,
Mr. Isaac L. Goldsmid,
Mr. Aaron A. Goldsmid,
Mr. Aaron Goldsmid,
Mrs. Gottheimer,
Miss Granger,
Mr. J. Goldscheider,

H

Mr. Hyman Hurwitz,
Mrs. Lemon Hart,
Mr. Hart, *Barbadoes*,
A Gentleman
Mrs. A. Henry,
Mr. Michael Henry, *Jamaica*, 2 *Cop.*
A Gentleman,
Mrs. Harrington, *Brompton*,
Mrs. Harris, *ditto*,
Mr. Hyams, *Borough*,
Mrs. Harley,
Miss Hernden *Maidstone, Kent*,

I

Mrs. Israel, *Gloucester Place*,
A Lady,
Mrs. Joseph, 29, *Minories*
Mr. M. A. Joseph, *New Square*,

FIG. 6. Subscription list, *Fiction without Romance*, printed for the author (printer's copy). (© British Library Board, 1153.l.1, n.p.)

about this obscure East End writer's relations in Jamaica. Parsing the subscription list data hinted at unexpected familial and social contacts that would gradually take shape over years of tracking down seemingly tangential clues about the Polack family. In addition to connecting East Enders to the West Indies, the list pointed to the significance of the novel's mysterious settings in Devon and London. But the import of those settings was legible only once I'd unpacked the components of each name on the list: name, gender, title, and address. I entered this data into a spreadsheet. Next, I tracked down additional details about individual subscribers to supplement information about their residences. After

SUBSCRIBERS NAMES.

Mr. I. Joseph, *St. James's Place*,
Mrs. Henry Jonas,
Mr. Israel Isaacs,
Mr. Michael Jacobs, *Cottage-lane*,
Mrs. L. Isaacs, *Houndsditch*,
Mrs. J. Joseph, *Brixton*,
Mrs. L. Jacobs, *St. Helen's*,
Mr. J. Jonas, *Little Prescot-street*,
Mr. David James,
Mrs. Z. A. Jessel,
Miss Isabella Johnson, *Exeter*,

K

Mr. R. A. Keyser,
Mr. Joseph Kisch,

L

Mrs. Moss Lyons, *Kent-road*,
Mr. Lewis Lyons, *Holborn*,
A Lady
Mrs. Lousada, *Lower Bedford-place*,
Mrs. M. Levien,
Mr. N. P. Levy,
Mr. Lewis Lazarus,
Mr. Isaac Lyon, *Duke-street*,
Mrs. M. Levy, *Prescot-street*,
Mrs. S. Levy, *Wellclose-square*,
Mr. Harris Lazarus,
Mrs. J. W, Lyon,
Mr. Hart Lyon, *Barbadoes*,
Mr. A. S. Lyon, *ditto*,
Miss Levy, *Leadenhall-street*
Mr. S. I. Lee,
Mr. S. Lazarus, *Wells-st. Spitalfields*,

M

Mrs. Montefiore, *Park-lane*, 2 *Copies*
Mrs. Micholls, *Broad-street*,
Mrs. Myers, *Albany-street*,
Mr. M. Moses, *Dover*,
Mr. Lewis Morris, *Bethnal Green*,
Mrs. Morris, *ditto*,
Mrs. Myers *Peters-alley*,
Mr. Magnus, *Prescot-street*,
Mr. J. Millingen *ditto*,
Mr. R. Myers,

N

Mr. C. L. Newton,
Mrs. A. L. Newton,
Mr. Neumegen, *Highgate*
Mrs. I. Newton, *North-road*,
Miss Nathan, *Kent-road*
Mr. John Nathan,
Mr. Nathan, *Plymouth*

P

Mrs. Alfred Philips,
Mrs. Periente,
Mr. John Pollock,
Mr. Marks Polack, *Jamaica*
Mr. Benjamin Polack, *ditto*
Mr. Jonas Polack, *ditto*

R

Mrs. N. M. Rothschild, 5 *Copies*
Miss Raphael,
Miss E. Reynolds,

S

Mrs. S. M. Samuel, *Park-crescent*,
Miss Selig,
Mr. S. Stiebel,
Mrs. J. Spurling, *Peckham*,
Mr. Solomon, *Pall Mall*,
Mr. Joseph Samuel, *Jews Hospital*,
Mrs. E. I. Symons,
Mrs. S. Solomons, *Charing Cross*,
Mrs. Samuel, *Bury-street*,
Mrs. Sampson, *Clapham-road*,
Mr. P. Solomon, *Bevis- Marks*.
Mrs. Aaron Solomon, *Heneage-lane*.
Mr. Solomon, *Sandy-street*,
Mrs. Stroud,
Mr. H. Solomon, *Strand*,
Mrs. Solomon, *Magdalen-row*,
Mr. George Sammell, *Hatton-garden*
Mrs. Salmon, *Piccadilly*,
Mrs. W. W. Simpson,
Mrs. Sampson, *Oxendon-street*,

T

Mr. S. Tournoff, *Manchester*,

V.

Mr. Joshua Van Oven,

W

Mr. Williams, *London Infirmary*,
Miss Worms,
Mrs. Mark Woolf,
Mr. John Warburg,
Mr. Ellis Williams, *Wellclose-square*,

adding similar subscription list data from four other East End publications from this period, I was able to make more sense of the geographic information. But even in the first stage, having entered just the details from Polack's list, the significance of the geographical connections was illuminating. Arthur Kiron has argued that "a circum-Atlantic network of Jewish publishers, authors and translators living in three port cities, London, Philadelphia, and Kingston, Jamaica became increasingly visible during the 1840s articulating these rhetorical strategies in print. This group can be considered a distant sub-culture. . . . The main actors were printers and preachers, merchants and professionals. They adopted

English [rather than Hebrew] as their primary language of communication."[52] In fact, the network Kiron identifies was already visible by 1830. According to evidence supplied by the subscription list, it was formed not by printers, preachers, merchants, and professionals, but by Anglo-Jewish women who created intellectual communities throughout the Atlantic world with their invention of Jewish secular literature.

Polack's subscription list had many stories to tell. Most of the subscribers had London addresses. Yet several people on the list—including members of her own family—resided in the West Indies. Benjamin Polack didn't include his address on the list, but the Legacies of British Slave-Ownership website recounts that he lived in the parish of Westmoreland in Jamaica in this period and was awarded two claims from the government on November 9, 1835: the first for £104 and 15 shillings and 3d for five slaves; the second a claim of £122 and 15 shillings and 0d for seven slaves.[53] Such claims were made to slave owners as compensation for losses brought about by abolition. Jonas Polack, another subscriber, had two claims, both dated December 21, 1835: in the first he was awarded £19 10 shillings and 10d for a single slave; in the second he received £78 3 shillings and 5d for four slaves. Mark Polack has one claim dated February 15, 1836, for £174 11 shillings and 10d for nine slaves. Another record notes that the subscriber "Mr. Hart Lyon, Barbadoes [*sic*]" was awarded £38 16 shillings and 9d on April 4, 1836, for one slave in "Barbadoes" (*sic*). Hart Lyon was born in 1796 in Cambridge, England, and is the brother of A. S. Lyon and Emma Lyon Henry. All three siblings added their names to the list. "Mr. A. S. Lyon, ditto" was living in Barbados in 1830 when *Fiction without Romance* was published. A third Lyon appears via mention of his wife: "Mrs. J. W. Lyon," whose residence is missing from the list. Records from the period indicate that J. W. Lyon lived on Mansell Street in the East End—the same street where Polack and her father lived at various points in their lives. Lyon's wife, Mrs. J. W. Lyon, was a member of the Hart family whose name also appears on Polack's list.

Tracing these family lines demonstrates a tangled familial and social network among Polack's subscribers, or what Wai Chee Dimock describes as a "crisscrossing set of pathways, open-ended and ever multiplying, weaving in and out of other geographies, other languages and cultures" or "input channels, kinship networks, routes of transit, and forms of attachment—connective tissues."[54] The existence of West Indian subscribers takes on added significance when read through the novel's setup of travels and attachments between Devon and London. Characters in the novel travel frequently. They pass through Exeter on the way to London;

they journey to Clifton for the restoration of health; and they travel back and forth from Exeter to Eliza's rural home, Greenwood Cottage. References to jaunts from one place to another might signal entirely different social worlds. While London is privileged by several characters for its cosmopolitan sophistication, the narrator occasionally challenges such logic. At the same time, mention of Henry Cooper's upbringing in America suggests that behind the twinning of city and country is a plot linking England and Atlantic sites. The subscription list, however, makes this tie even more explicit. Several subscribers, for example, had residences in port towns in Penzance, Falmouth, Plymouth, and Exmouth—all in spatial proximity to the novel's setting in Devon. These port towns had direct ties with Atlantic trade in the late eighteenth and nineteenth centuries. The particular collection of subscribers' names and residences, I came to realize, creates and reflects social and economic ties among the East End, the West Indies, and Devon.[55]

For example, the name "Mrs. Lemon Hart" on the subscription list appears with no location, but she was a well-known figure in this period. Mrs. Lemon Hart (née Mary Solomon, 1758–1852) was a member of the Society of Hebrew Literature and died in Euston Place, London.[56] Her surviving husband, Lemon Hart, was born in Penzance, located in the southwest of England. He made a fortune as an importer of rum from Jamaica and elsewhere in the Caribbean, becoming at one point the official rum supplier to the British navy and a leader of the Jewish community in Penzance, located about a hundred miles west of the novel's setting.[57] Lemon Hart had residences in Penzance and London, and he owned plantations in Jamaica and Barbados. A second name from the list, "Mrs. Lousada, Lower Bedford-place," was married to Emanuel Lousada, a merchant in the firm of Barrow and Lousada based in Sidmouth, Devon, and 11 Lower Bedford Place in London. The Legacies of British Slave-Ownership records note that Lousada was a London West Indian merchant who partnered with Simon Barrow to transform Sidmouth into a resort town. Lousada served as the high sheriff of Devon from 1842 to 1843.[58] Men like Lemon Hart and Emanuel Lousada were more than well-known figures in this period; they were extraordinarily wealthy and well connected. And their money, used to fund Polack's novel, came from their participation in West Indian slave economies.

While direct mention of Atlantic slavery is absent from the novel, its embeddedness in the subscription list is telling.[59] Marisa J. Fuentes has argued compellingly for a "methodology that purposely subverts the overdetermining power of colonial discourses. By changing the perspective of a document's author to that of an enslaved subject, questioning the archives' veracity and filling out miniscule fragmentary mentions or the absence of evidence with spatial and historical context, our historical interpretation shifts to the enslaved viewpoint in important ways."[60] Fuentes's approach prompted me to reconsider the list's power to silence the very enslaved subjectivities it evokes. More than just a paratext operating from the border zone between the novel and the world, the subscription list facilitates the privileging of one set of perspectives (Polack's social circle) while submerging evidence of the enslaved laborers who underwrote their privilege. I am unable to recover information about the identities of the enslaved people whose identities are evoked by the list. In contrast, records of the enslavers can be found quite easily. In this way, the book archive reflects oblique structures of power by preserving records of white plantation owners while excluding evidence of the lives of those they enslaved—the very people whose labor funded the book's production costs.

Priya Joshi has described a kind of transnational study "where the cultural and economic hegemony of the metropolis is no longer dominant, so that other circuits and relations, long-obscured in the centre-dominated model, become evident."[61] Polack's subscription list facilitated such a study, which began with my efforts to decenter West London by foregrounding the existence of Jewish cultural production in the East End. Decoding the identities of the names on the list enabled me to extend this work by registering archival silences about the system of slavery driving the novel's funding and marketing strategies. What came clear through these readings were clues about the novel's key sites of engagement—the Atlantic port regions in Devon and London—that operated as more than just settings of country and city; I came to understand them as spaces that structure the silence of slavery's violence elided from the novel's content. And in pointing to this critical silence, the subscription list helped to subvert what I had previously conceived as the solipsism of the novel's English-Jewish plot.

The Database Archive

Regardless of their form, archives are never stagnant entities. Each user of an archive easily alters its content or form. A misplaced hand can accidentally tear a corner. Turning pages too quickly can generate paper dust. Opening a book without proper care can break its spine. We may be used to thinking of digital archives as dynamic entities that stand in contrast to static paper archives, but in fact the two are entirely unlike one another with regard to their shape-shifting tendencies. Yet their dynamism isn't limited to the reader's handling of pages. I worked in one physical archive that lost a box of materials halfway through my research on this book. Such mistakes are not uncommon in underfunded cultural heritage institutions. The experience of losing materials transformed my memory of what I'd lost and my hope of finding the missing box during future visits. Indeed, most archives are susceptible to these kinds of distortions or disruptions. When we work with databases, this kind of dynamism seems like an advantage or affordance. We may reason that databases can reorganize or regroup names on Polack's list according to gender or street address, thereby clarifying geographical or gendered patterns in the data. In contrast, changes in the form of paper records—breaks, tears, and disappearances—are more often read as a disruption or loss. Yet both examples recall the essential nature of all archives as unstable and dynamic. We might agree with Wolfgang Ernst's vision of digital archives as not so much a "a question of reactivating objects, but [one focused on the] . . . relations" among parts.[62] I'm suggesting that digital tools are not unusual in enabling interactive relations, for paper objects are also implicitly susceptible to alterations brought about by archival activations. The difference between them, rather, is that digital archives expand the range of types of interactions whereas similar shifts in paper archives are more commonly treated as a loss. Such differences have everything to do with the way we use digital and physical archives, and our relationships to the materials we find in them.

Despite their abilities to process data and to register interactions within the data, Excel and Gephi cannot interpret the patterns they reveal. It takes human intervention to explain and make sense of the models formed by these digital tools. Indeed, it takes humans to create the digital tools and to design the models in the first place. Despite these facts, Richard Jean So notes, "literary scholars have long cast a suspicious and critical gaze toward modeling, which strikes them as offensively simpleminded and naïve: models run counter to the deep and intensive reading that literary critics take pride in, the exposing of nuance and singularity in texts, writers and human beings."[63] Scholarly resistance seems to originate in part from our shift from close to distant reading, or when we turn our attention away from words and toward models made from words. Perhaps we fear we'll lose track of essential features of the writing once it's framed by and mediated through the apparatus of digital platforms. In response, So suggests that "rather than see the model as a potential antagonist, an entity that has brought forth intractable empirical truths that one must accept or reject, the reader is encouraged to reason with the model and its maker to better grasp the data."[64]

In what follows, I build on So's proposition by reasoning with my models and the subscription data used to make them. My database archive does not represent empirical facts about the rise of East End literary culture. Rather, it functions as a mechanism for registering otherwise invisible contexts and for raising questions about Polack's readers and literary contexts. Drawn from my own database archive of subscription data, my models build on Andrew Piper's claim that models are "constructions of new kinds of realities."[65] Models, he argues, "do not just represent history, but also *make* it"[66] through their strategic data transformations. The result is not a direct representation of reality, but a vision of what the database archive suggests or questions once it has been reformed in ways that speak to the relations of its parts.

For the sake of analogy, we might consider Dickens's depictions of the East End discussed in earlier parts of this study. What we see of Fagin's East End den is not the actual East End, but a fictional depiction; it's a narrative construction translated, or remodeled, through Dickens's perspective, writing style, and modes of analysis. Dickens's inaccuracies have not prevented readers from interpreting *Oliver Twist* as a legitimate representation of Victorian London. My subscription list database and Gephi models offer a parallel construction of Victorian London.[67] The database, composed of an available sampling of subscription list data, will of course distort the resulting models, just as Dickens skews portraits of London by filtering them through his writing and perspective or through his marketing objectives. But the skewing of narrative—either from novels, databases, or archives—doesn't invalidate their interpretive work. We might instead read them *as interpretations* of a world the author sought to capture. The models I discuss in the following pages don't offer conclusive answers to questions driving my study of Polack and her East End community. They are silent on questions relating to the contours of power or unspoken events that might have inspired Polack and her artistic circle. Despite their deficits, however, the models have the power to identify patterns and contexts that reflect upon the conditions in which Polack wrote her novel—conditions that raise new questions and prompt opportunities for further analysis.

In order to identify these pathways, following my initial entry of details from Polack's list, I scaled up by aggregating data from four additional subscription lists from East End publications in this period. Selecting authors or texts with East End ties who published by subscription meant that I was excluding many other texts; my data set represents only East End authors who published their work and used subscription to do so. The database archive, integrating five subscription lists, might reflect atypical or exceptional authors who had the ability to leverage subscription to their advantage. Or perhaps they were typical, but evidence of similarly published books no longer exists. It's difficult to know for sure how to situate these five publications among the body of work produced in the East End in this period. Still, despite these uncertainties, the aggregation of data from five lists revealed illuminating details about East End readers and writers in the first half of the nineteenth century. Once I'd entered my data, the spreadsheet swelled to absorb over two thousand names and related details about subscribers. The models drawn from the database offer the additional benefit of identifying patterns human eyes cannot possibly register when gazing upon such a large quantity of data.

From there I used Python, a programming language, to cross-reference names and addresses and to fill in missing information. As I added new names and locations, my curiosity about the global dimensions of the database archive grew. The process of parsing and building a dynamic database shifted my thinking in ways I hadn't expected. In my last step, I turned to Gephi to transform my data pulled from five subscription lists into three visual models: a Social Network Model (fig. 7); a Spatial Network Model (fig. 8); and a Female Subscribers Network Model (fig. 9). My methods were informed by Ted Underwood's point that "instead of measuring things, finding patterns, and then finally asking what they mean, we need to start with an interpretive hypothesis (a 'meaning' to investigate) and invent a way to test it."[68] My early exchange with the help desk respondent who wanted me to believe East Enders couldn't write or didn't see the value of their written narratives presented me with a challenge. I began by creating models to investigate such claims. Along the way, I identified specific questions that would help me to address dimensions of the Jewish public sphere that extended through East End literary culture. For example, I sought methods of interpreting the types of people who purchased subscriptions to literary texts or East End publications. Were women or East Enders more likely to support local East End authors? Were male subscribers willing to publicly endorse women's literary activities? The names on the list included titles, such as Mr., Mrs., or Miss, which helped me to determine the stated gender identities of most subscribers. The inclusion of addresses aided my question to situate subscribers in specific regions of London or elsewhere. These two details—location and gender—were not entirely comprehensive or uniform, but their inclusion on most entries enabled me to generate questions that could be addressed by quantifiable data.

A static list printed on paper doesn't allow for transformations; it also doesn't facilitate comparative thinking from one list to the next. Did Polack, for example, have an unusually large number of women subscribers in comparison with the number or ratio of female to male subscribers on lists by her contemporaries? With paper lists I can manually count titles to get a sense of gender distributions. With a database I can work more efficiently by tracking repetitions of titles or by measuring gender and geographical identifications relationally. Ultimately, in the absence of an archive containing evidence of Polack's writing and cultural contexts, the database archive hinted at features of the community's public identity and interest in reading materials. I began by creating columns in my spreadsheet that parsed the following categories of information: a unique record number for each entry (used for reference); the title of each publication; the year of publication; the name of the author/editor of the publication; the gender of the East End author/editor; the name of the subscriber; the gender of the subscriber; an indication of whether the subscriber was a London resident; the city name of the subscriber's residence; the nation of the subscriber's residence; and the region within London of the subscriber's residence (East London, West London, other). Next, I entered subscriber names and filled in the remaining column information. The complete data set includes details pertaining to 2,192 subscribers. My goal was not to track every London author or to study every region of London. Rather, I wanted to create a data set of East End authors who used subscription to market or support their publications. Driving my analysis were questions about how this data could speak to the culture of the East End—its interest in literary activities; its support for Jewish women writers; and its intellectual reach throughout the East End, London, and the Atlantic world.

Evidence of the rise of Jewish literary culture should lead us to wonder about other East End "outcasts" whose literary production has been elided by the emphasis on both a rising commercialization of literary and print culture in this period and the authors made famous and wealthy by that process. The first model, the Social Network Model (fig. 7), registers evidence of East End literary output and community support for such output.[69] The nodes, or circles, displayed in green on the model, represent the five East End publications used in this study: H. V. Bolaffey's *Hebrew Grammar* (1820); Miriam Belisario's *Sabbath Evenings*, a book on

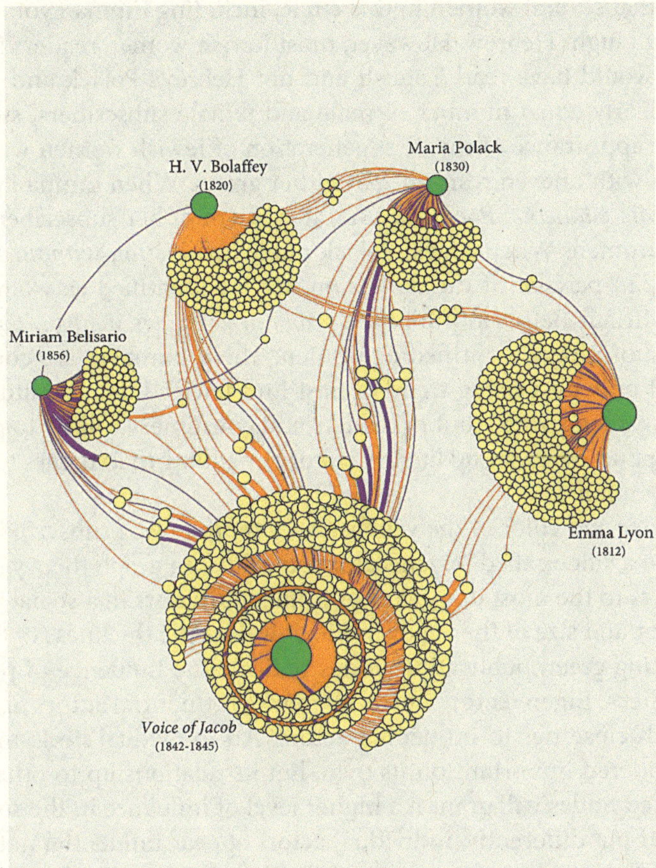

FIG. 7. Social Network Model

the practice of Jewish rituals (1856); the *Voice of Jacob,* the first sustained Anglo-Jewish periodical that used subscription from 1842 to 1845; Emma Lyon's *Miscellaneous Poems* (1812); and Maria Polack's *Fiction without Romance* (1830).[70] The *Voice of Jacob* was produced and printed in the East End, although contributing writers came from all over the world.

The green publication nodes on the model are connected to one another by edges, or the lines running through the model. Yellow nodes (circles) represent the individuals who subscribe to the publications. An orange connecting edge marks the subscriber as male. A purple connecting edge marks the subscriber as female. Not surprisingly, the majority of Bolaffey's edges or subscribers were men, since his text was Hebrew and most women in this period did not read Hebrew—although it's worth noting that several women in this circle, including Emma Lyon, not only read but taught Hebrew. However, most Jewish women readers from this period would have read English and not Hebrew. Polack and Belisario had a nearly equal number of male and female subscribers, suggesting that the appearance of this first generation of Jewish women writers was not met with uneven resistance by either group. When Emma Lyon published *Miscellaneous Poems* in 1812, 18 percent of her subscribers identified as women. When Maria Polack published *Fiction without Romance* in 1830, 44 percent of the names on her list identified as women. And when Miriam Belisario published *Sabbath Evenings* in 1856, 64 percent of her subscribers identified as women. These numbers are contextualized not only by a rising trend of East End Jewish literary culture inclusive of women writers, but of readers and consumers willing to publicize their support for East End literary culture by adding their names to a public subscription list.

The size and color of the yellow nodes representing subscribers correspond to a value called "eigenvector centrality." In graph theory, "centrality" refers to the most dominant or influential actors in a social network. The color and size of the yellow node as well as the thickness of the edges connecting green publication nodes indicate the influence of particular subscribers. Eigenvector centrality marks influential actors and/or actors with close ties to influential actors. An individual node might not be considered important on its own, but its relationship to other highly connected nodes will grant it a higher level of influence in the social network. Or put differently, individual actors appear influential not just because of the number of connections (edges) they have with other nodes, but through their connection with those who have a high number of connections many other nodes. Thus, a node with high eigenvector centrality will be connected to other well-connected nodes. In turn, the most influential nodes can be measured against other well-connected nodes, enabling comparative analysis of the prominent actors in a community.

The five clusters on the graph represent the five authors and their subscribers. The larger the green publication node, the higher that author's eigenvector centrality. The node representing the *Voice of Jacob* is the largest node in the model, suggesting that it's the most influential because it has a great number of subscribers in common with all other authors. Placement on the page is also significant in cases where the number of subscribers was so great it was difficult to see the width of the edge. In these instances, edges that appear spatially closer together represent a greater number of subscriptions. For example, three distinct rings appear around the *Voice of Jacob* green node. Those subscribers represented by the ring of yellow nodes closest to the green node bought three or more subscriptions. The second yellow ring, touching but slightly larger and further from the center green node, marks those who bought two subscriptions. The outermost ring of yellow nodes represents those who purchased a single copy of the periodical. *Voice of Jacob* subscribers represented with large yellow nodes are well connected with the most influential subscribers in the network—that is, those who purchased subscriptions to a greater number of publications in the network.

The *Voice of Jacob* was published every two weeks from September 16, 1841, through August 18, 1848, at which point it merged with the *Jewish Chronicle*—a periodical still published today.[71] It's clear from the model that the *Voice of Jacob* has the largest number of edges or connections to other writers in the model. In comparison, Emma Lyon has more subscribers than Polack, but she's got the least number of subscribers with connections to other influential East End publications, such as the *Voice of Jacob*. The only periodical in the model, the *Voice of Jacob* is important to this story and to Polack not only because it emerged from the East End, but also because it created a global network of readers that mirrors the names and networks on Polack's subscription list. Popular nineteenth-century accounts of East End danger may want us to believe this was a ghetto space cut off from global markets and influence, but subscription list data has a different story to tell. As the model suggests, the lists provide evidence of the East End's global intellectual communities. Publications by these writers reflect outlets and prompters in global literary and print communities that continued to expand in size and geographical spaces throughout the century. Some of this growth may be attributed to British colonial interests. For example, in many cases, the names on the lists reflect family or social ties among Atlantic Jewish communities. Emma Lyon, Maria Polack, and Miriam Belisario all had family living in the West Indies. Subscribers from the combined five lists broken down by nation reveal a sizable number from the Atlantic world: England had 1,615 subscribers; Jamaica had 256; St. Thomas had 80; the United States had 65; Gibraltar had 40; Curaçao had 24; and Barbados had 16.

The next model, the Spatial Network Model (fig. 8), was generated from the database archive of all five lists. The Spatial Network Model presents a subset of 290 subscribers known to have London addresses.[72] Once again, the green nodes mark the publications, while the yellow nodes identify subscribers. Edges or lines connecting nodes represent

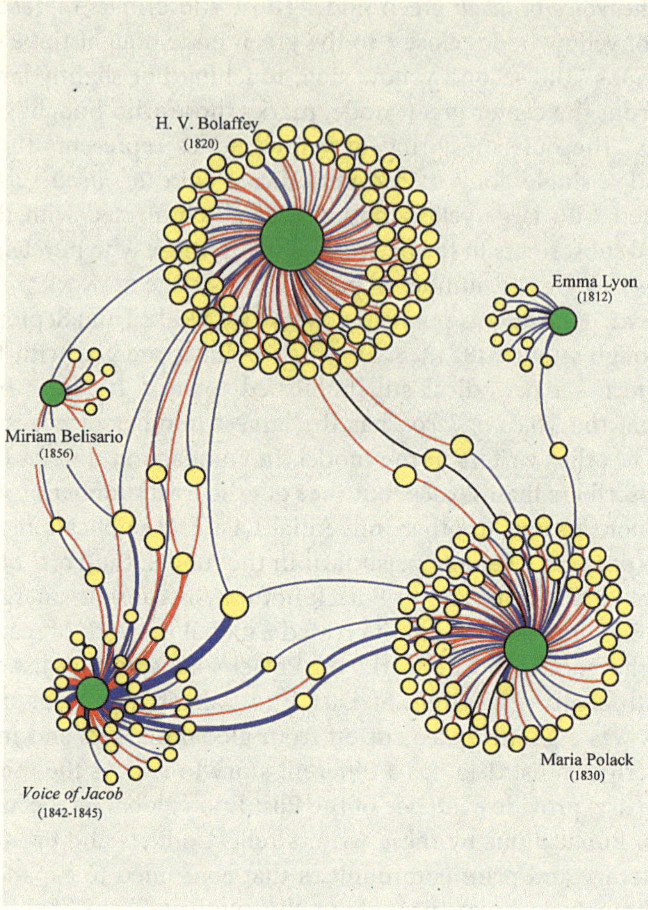

FIG. 8. Spatial Network Model

the locations where subscribers lived. A blue edge indicates that the subscriber had an East End address. And a red edge is used to mark subscribers with known West End addresses. Subscribers from England with unknown addresses have been omitted from this model, as have those with addresses outside London. As chapter 1 suggested, the boundaries of London regions, such as East End and West End, shifted over time. Hence these models cannot provide accurate arguments about geographical boundaries. But they can still hint at patterns of support based on relational spatial configurations. The narrowing of data according to London locations shows the diminished importance of the *Voice of Jacob* in this social network. Polack and Bolaffey have far more subscribers with known London addresses in comparison with other authors in the model.

One of the challenges of reading location data is that people move or have multiple addresses. Edward Goldsmid, for example, moved from East to West London between the period covered in the subscription data I've collected. Therefore the location model can be useful only insofar as it is capable of tracking stable actors. Despite these challenges, even in its less-than-ideal form, the model suggests a general patterns of significance among the relations of its parts. As the Spatial Network Model indicates, among addresses I've been able to trace (67 out of 147), Polack had 40 East End subscribers and 33 West End subscribers. Fourteen of Polack's subscribers appear on the *Voice of Jacob* list and, among those whose 1830 addresses are known, six lived in the East End while another six lived in the West End. According to this model, while East End print networks were linked to cultural spheres in East and West London, many subscribers throughout London were willing to invest in and publicly endorse the publication of a novel by an East Ender. Chapter 1 discussed a nineteenth-century trend of separating East and West End cultural spheres; the data models I've created from subscription data suggest alternately that literary culture emanating from Polack's Jewish community flowed across geospatial boundaries. The larger nodes in the Spatial Network Model suggest, once again, greater influence of subscribers with a higher number of subscriptions. The thickness of the lines indicates the number of subscriptions individuals purchased. Thus, those who purchased five subscriptions are represented by a thicker line than those who purchased a single subscription.

Expecting data models to capture a neutral or complete sphere of influence would be as unreasonable as expecting a passage from a Dickens novel to offer an accurate representation of London. Dickens frequently used a realist lens in depictions of Victorian London. Even though his crafted narratives cannot be read as objective statements of fact, they function as valuable sources for the study of Victorian London. Models can be read similarly. As Piper notes, models allow us to see a "process of surrogate reasoning, an assemblage of externalities that allow mental inferences to be made about meanings in the world that are not readily at hand . . . to arrive at an appropriate approximation of a given territory."[73] The key is to read the data as an "approximation" or suggestion. Models can help us to ask questions we hadn't thought to ask or register contexts hinted at obliquely by subtle or unrecognizable features of the data.

Both archives discussed in the chapter—the book archive and the database archive—remain incomplete, fragmented registers of the cultural objects they model. Their forms and shaping protocols—or the form in which they forge connections—suggest larger patterns that reflect upon features of their content or raise new questions about otherwise undetectable patterns among their cultural contexts. Similarly, the subscription list models provide visual delineations of spatial identities or of overlapping literary interests. They help us visualize how many of Polack's readers were not unique to her, but in fact were active players in the cultivation of a network that supported Jewish women's literary culture. Thus, while the database may not function exactly like physical archives, it displays what Marlene Manoff calls "archive effects" or the "ways in which digital media bring the past into the present."[74] Manoff's point speaks not simply to the accessibility or the creation of digital surrogates but also to the power of transformed content. When content moves from list to database and from database to visual model, or when it's framed by new boundaries and made to interact with content not part of its original container, we have an opportunity to consider the narratives it generates or exposes and the methods by which its archive effects mediate those narratives.

The Female Subscribers Network Model (fig. 9), for example, creates a narrative by a pointed shuffling of information presented in the database archives. This model details information about 322 female subscribers compiled from all five lists.[75] The green nodes represent the female authors. The smaller yellow nodes surrounding them mark their subscribers. And eigenvector centrality is once again marked by the size and darkness of the nodes. The edges are uniformly drawn in black since gender does not need to be represented (all subscribers are self-defined females). However, the thicker edges represent a larger number of subscriptions, whereas a thinner line marks a smaller number of subscriptions. In the Female Subscribers Network Model, the *Voice of Jacob* remains the most influential actor in the publication network, evidence of which appears in the great number of larger yellow nodes around the *Voice of Jacob*. Not surprisingly, Bolaffey's importance is diminished, for women wouldn't have subscribed to a Hebrew grammar this early in the century. Emma Lyon's position is also reduced in this model, although that may be the result of the fact that her book was published much earlier—in 1812—than were the rest of the texts in the model. Belisario appears to be the second most important figure because of the multiple large yellow nodes on the edges connecting her to the *Voice of Jacob*—the most influential actor in the network. Once again, thicker edges in this model demarcate a greater

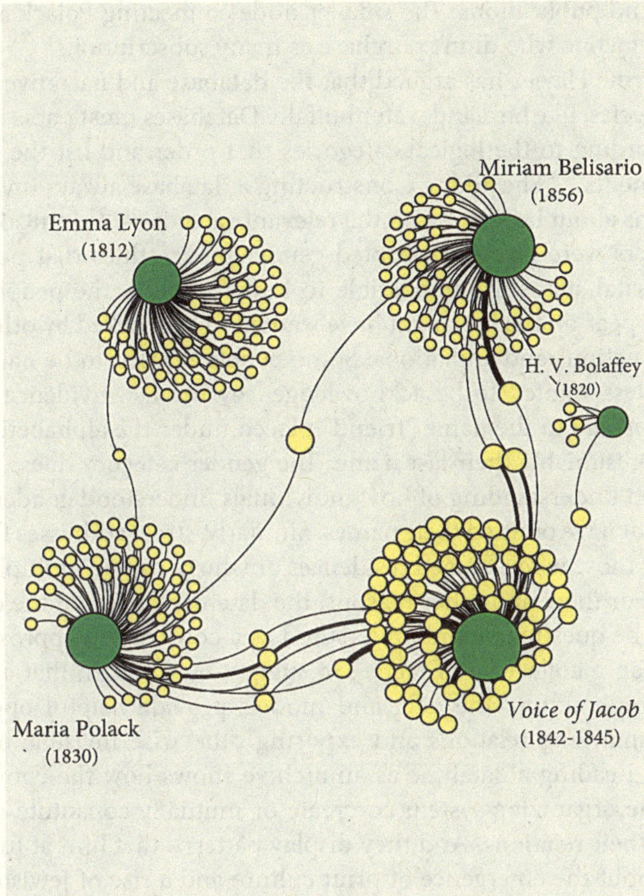

FIG. 9. Female Subscribers Network Model

number of subscriptions. Polack's connection to the *Voice of Jacob* appears to be significant in a different way than Belisario's. Polack had more subscribers in common with the *Voice of Jacob,* but the smaller node size suggests that the subscribers were less influential. In contrast, Belisario had fewer subscribers in common with the periodical, but those who subscribed bought multiple subscriptions to other works in this network. Miriam Belisario and Maria Polack are linked by a single subscriber, but it's one with a large yellow node, indicating that this person had significant influence because she subscribed to a greater number of publications in this social network. Put differently, the connecting thread with the large node marks someone who made a habit of purchasing subscriptions to East End publications. The smaller node connecting Polack and Lyon marks someone who didn't purchase as many subscriptions.

Katherine Hayles has argued that the database and narrative are "different species, like bird and water buffalo. Databases must parse information according to the logical categories that order and list the different data elements."[76] She adds, "Constructing a database always involves assumptions about how to set up the relevant categories."[77] In 1830 Polack's subscribers were given or adopted gender binary titles that pointed to their marital status. It's impossible to know whether the people whose names appear on the list might have wanted to be marked by other kinds of constructions and affiliations. Some people refused to be named, but nevertheless wanted to be acknowledged by the list. Evidence of their wishes appears in the name "friend" placed under the alphabetical category of presumably their last name. The gender category doesn't give us a nuanced understanding of how individuals understood gender or why they might have omitted their names. Similarly, street addresses fail to account for those who changed residences or who occupied multiple homes at once. For these and other reasons, the data used to build the database ought to be questioned and understood as a constructed approximation rather than a collection of facts. I'm suggesting, though, that even as a partial construction, the data and models provide helpful opportunities for analyzing relations and exposing otherwise invisible or subtle contexts. Reading a database as an archive shows how the components within the organizing system co-create or mutually constitute meaning through their relations. And they display patterns that hint at fuller narratives about the emergence of print culture and a rise of Jewish secular literary culture that challenge better-known stories emphasizing the East End's cultural isolation and social depravity. At the very least, the database archive and models give us sound reasons for questioning claims made by louder, more sensational narratives about the East End.

From Book to Database to Novel

My journey to understand Polack's book and contexts began with a lesson about the value of not judging books by ugly plastic covers and expanded to consider how interpretive challenges and revelations emerge through an archive's flexible forms. Despite their limits, the spreadsheet and models made from its data have the potential to capture important dimensions of the East End's intellectual networks, and to construct models that document how East Enders forged literary cultures and print practices in London and throughout the Atlantic world. The degree of dynamism of archival content emerges through an understanding of silences, the parsing of content, and the reconstruction of provenance, which together create archives that can be read not for their hidden treasures, but through the relations of their parts. In what I have found or created, evidence of a Jewish cultural matrix rendered invisible by the selection of names on the list, emerges from Polack's intellectual networks in the East End and throughout the globe. While my digital transformations and corresponding models retain many gaps in the narrative of Polack's life and work, they nevertheless clarify or expose the existence of a large public sphere Polack and her novel entered and expanded. At the same time, I've argued that the preservation of little-known details from one community have the power to overwrite subjectivities in related communities. It was through the list and the novel's emphasis on London and port cities in the southwest of England that I was able to decode a submerged legacy of slavery that financed the novel and the labor of enslaved people overwritten by a narrative, no less important, emphasizing the value of female education and respect for religious and ethnic diversity in England.

While we might be used to thinking of archival structures as holding tanks capable of preserving evidence of a seamless past, in this chapter I've explored reading strategies aimed at accounting for the consequences of the archive's simultaneous acts of hiding and preserving evidence of the past. My thinking has been helpfully shaped by Anjali Arondekar's point about registering the archive's ability to confound. In Arondekar's words, "The intellectual challenge here is to juxtapose productively the archive's fiction-effects (the archive as a system of representation) alongside its truth-effects (the archive as material with 'real' consequences), as both agonistic and con-constitutive. . . . The imperative here is not about founding presence but more about *confounding* our understanding of how and why we do archival work."[78] In a later chapter I'll turn questions about the archive's fictional powers in a new direction. Here, however, I wish to recognize that the presence of Polack's list in a single copy of the book does not speak to the promptings for that artifact—the operations of power that led to her book's funding model. The single copy of the list has the effect of exposing not just two narratives—one related to East End literary culture and another to British slavery in the West Indies—but of the way these narratives are mutually constituted by a single artifact in the archive. In preserving one narrative, the archive encodes the other as a submerged story. The archive's dual operations might be rendered legible, I suggest, through reading acts that highlight the interactions among multiple archives—lists, books, and databases—capable of transforming archival structures from static list to dynamic database, and in the process recontextualize archival evidence.

The paratexts and related archives of Maria Polack's novel narrate a story about what was saved and lost, and the values that have shaped our assumptions about women's writing, the history of the novel, Jewish literary history, the East End of London, and slavery in the West Indies. Locations named and found in the book archive expose the import of spatial formations in East End literary culture quietly suggested in the pages of Polack's novel. Subscription lists transformed by digital archival structures and modeling tools point to the existence of actors, musicians, writers, teachers, and painters as contributors to the dynamism of East End culture in this period. Such methods push against arguments that flatten conventional stereotypes while opening up conceptions of place produced by a diversity of social actors. Ultimately, the book archive and database archive prompt us to question both what we think we might already know about the East End and what else we might ask about those who left, prepared, or abandoned records of its dynamism.

3

The Noisy Archive

A. S. LYON'S EAST END DIARIES

In 1812, at the age of twenty-three, Emma Lyon published *Miscellaneous Poems.* Maria Polack's *Fiction without Romance* wouldn't emerge for another eighteen years. When it was published in 1830, Emma Lyon's name appeared on the subscription list. They were both Anglo-Jewish literary firsts; Emma Lyon is believed to be the first self-identified Jewish person to publish a book of poetry and Maria Polack the first to publish a novel.[1] And both used subscription as a method of funding their publications by drawing support from a broad range of people, including those in their religious community. Scholarly interest in Emma Lyon's poetry has grown in recent years, along with interest in her father, Solomon Lyon, a well-known Hebrew scholar born in Bohemia in 1755.[2] His great-great-great-granddaughter Naomi Cream, also a scholar, explains that eighteenth-century Bohemia was an unwelcoming place for Jews.

> In the wider community, anti-Semitic rules prevailed as Lyon grew up: laws regulated settlement, trade and occupation. The Jewish population was restricted by a system which allowed marriage only after the age of twenty-four and on receipt of a "Familiant" number, which passed to an eldest son on the death of his father. A junior son had to wait for his elder brother to die before he, in his turn, could inherit the number and get his own marriage permit. Furthermore, had these young men lived in Prague [not far from Bohemia], they would have had to wear the Jewish badge, described variously as a yellow collar over the coat or a yellow strip on the left shoulder.[3]

Not surprisingly, Solomon Lyon made the decision to leave Bohemia for England. He settled in Portsmouth in 1781 before finding his way to Cambridge University to work as a Hebrew instructor. While he could teach at Cambridge, Solomon Lyon could neither enroll as a student nor hold a faculty appointment. Cream adds that Cambridge University "functioned as an institution of the Church of England; Catholics, Dissenters and Jews were barred because they could not declare themselves to be members of the Church on graduation."[4] Unable to support his large family through teaching and publications, Solomon moved again, eventually finding his way to London and Fleet Prison, where he served time for debt.[5] In 1812, eight years before her father's death, Emma Lyon attempted to ease her family's financial troubles by publishing her book of poetry.[6] One of the poems in the collection, "The Soldier's Farewell," was set to music by Solomon's former student Isaac Nathan (1792–1864) and was performed by the well-known tenor John Braham (1774–1856).[7]

As far as we know, Polack emerged on the public stage with less fanfare than Lyon and has remained in the shadows of scholarly studies of Anglo-Jewish literature or London literature.[8] Despite their status as minor writers, Lyon and Polack made remarkable literary contributions. Galchinsky has traced the development of Jewish writers *after* the 1830s. Books by Lyon and Polack, as well as the unknown "Daughter of Israel" who wrote a school textbook in 1818, *The Jewish Preceptress; or, Elementary Lessons: Written Chiefly for the Use of the Female Children, Educated at the Jews Hospital,* point to an earlier emergence of Jewish women's secular literature. Galchinsky omits Lyon and Polack from this trajectory presumably because he's interested in the genre of romance as a key platform for Jewish women's literary concerns in this period.[9] As Polack's title suggests, she was more interested in fiction *without* romance.[10] Yet the omission of these writers has had the effect of occluding their significance in Anglo-Jewish literary history as well as that of the East End Jewish community who supported their publications.[11] If we proceed instead by recognizing works by Lyon and Polack at the start of Galchinsky's trajectory, relevant questions about the timing of their publications and their regional contexts become legible. In particular, the eighteen-year gap between Lyon's and Polack's publications, a period during which no known literary works by Anglo-Jewish women appeared in print, becomes both visible and curious.[12]

Michael Scrivener and others believe Emma Lyon continued to write poetry after her marriage to Abraham Henry in 1816, even though none of her work has survived.[13] A violent assault by William Simmons in June of 1812 shortly after the publication of *Miscellaneous Poems* may have triggered her choice not to publish again. The attack could also have intimidated other Jewish women writers.[14] According to Scrivener, when Lyon's friends, a Mr. and Mrs. French, visited her home in Marylebone the day after the assault, they found her "confined to her room, by the very severe indisposition occasioned." They encountered Simmons during their visit. Angry words between Daniel French and Simmons ensued. Simmons called French "a damned Jew" just before attacking him physically.[15] Although French was initially held in jail, Simmons served time for his "violent conduct" toward Emma Lyon.[16] Scrivener's analysis of court records leads him to wonder about Emma's behavior the day after the attack:

> Was his [Simmons's] violent conduct only verbal? If it were just verbal, would she have taken to her bed and confided first to Mrs. French? She was assaulted—at least verbally, perhaps physically—by a drunken anti-Semitic Simmons. After confiding to Mrs. French, Emma Lyon then witnesses her friend Daniel French beaten up, arrested, and tried for assaulting her attacker. Although French is acquitted and Simmons and his accomplice are convicted and sentenced to six months in the house of Correction, she now associates her literary ambition with violent anti-Semitism and public notoriety, if not shame, possibly rape. She had to testify in court on behalf of Daniel French, and we know she was accompanied by two of her brothers.[17]

Although Lyon never published again, her name appears on the list of subscribers in books by Anglo-Jewish women and East End charities.[18] Her public abandonment of literary activities coupled with the absence of books by women in her community could be explained by her attack. We might wonder, then, What prompted Polack to break the silence eighteen years later?

In search of an answer, I turned to archives for evidence of contact between Lyon and Polack. From 1816, the year of her marriage to Abraham Henry, until 1829, the year before Polack published *Fiction without Romance*, Emma Lyon Henry lived in Hayden Square in the City, the region abutting the East End. Emma Lyon obviously knew about Polack's novel, since she purchased a subscription. They likely attended the same synagogue, the Great Synagogue, located in the heart of the Jewish East End. Indeed, their books attest to their knowledge of Jewish history and weekly rituals of religious observance. During Saturday synagogue services they might have sat together in the women's balcony, towering above the men's section on the first level of the sanctuary. It's possible that they never spoke before, during, or after services lasting the better part of the day—although such behavior seems unlikely given that most religious gatherings aim to facilitate some kind of communal connectedness. Even if they remained exclusively focused on prayer on synagogue days, they likely crossed paths in the streets or in the schools where they taught. Might Lyon have advised Polack on subscription publishing? Perhaps Polack used her synagogue affiliations to spread the news about her book, which would explain why four members of the Lyon family bought subscriptions. The archive remains silent on these subjects. If Polack and Emma Lyon, or other East End women for that matter, engaged in literary camaraderie, the evidence is missing from extant sources in the public archives I consulted.

In the following pages I recount my unexpected encounter with a descendant of the Lyon family, Diane Lyon Wead, who generously shared copies of a diary written by Emma Lyon's brother during his residence in the East End. Abraham Septimus Lyon (1804–1872), better known as A. S. Lyon, kept a diary in 1823 at the age of nineteen, a year in which he sought to educate himself by studying French, dancing, horse riding, and reading. He kept a second, intermittent diary from 1826 to 1839 charting his gradual fall into financial loss and emotional despair.[19] The final pages of the second diary describe his travels to Barbados and ultimately to Jamaica where he settled for the remainder of his life.[20] At the point when I met Diane, I'd more or less given up on finding a connection between the Lyon and Polack families. My hope returned when I learned about the East End diarist who lived just a few blocks away from Polack and her family.

Unlike large public institutional archives situated in bulging buildings with websites, online catalogues, archivists, and posted business hours, the Lyon family archive lives in a cedar trunk in the bedroom of Diane's cousin, Annabel Foster-Davis. Family members are the only ones who know about its existence. The diaries' hand-scrawled faded words inscribed on brittle ivory pages were originally bound within silk covers. Annabel's mother had the pages and cover of one diary professionally restored. More recently Annabel has had the remaining diaries repaired. During my visit to her home in Sacramento, California, to photograph the diaries, I noticed Annabel's tender handling of the archival objects in her cedar chest. She inherited from previous generations both the artifacts and the manner of caring for them. When Annabel and her family made the decision to immigrate to the United States from Jamaica, the diaries and related family papers were among the small number of objects she was able to bring with her. They remain essential lifelines to family stories and people in Jamaica.

My early experiences working with the diaries presented several interpretive challenges, including my inability to see how they fit in with the other materials in the archive. The transcriptions I used had been typed by another cousin, the scholar Naomi Cream, who worked from photocopies of the original diaries stored in Annabel's trunk. Throughout my experiences studying the diaries, I struggled to fill in Lyon's references to places he visited or people he met. And I was baffled by his use of the diary form as a record of his struggles to make something of himself. What purpose did the diary serve? And why did he hold on to this early record for the remainder of his life and for future generations? How do we understand his choice to write the word "Private" on the first page of the diary?

How to read is, of course, the first and most difficult order of business in archival encounters: how to construct meaning from the pieces left behind, from their arrangement in the box or folder, and from our spotty knowledge of their history. Arlette Farge suggests helpfully that "archives bring forward details that disabuse, derail, and straightforwardly break any hope of linearity or positivism. This eruption of words and actions shatters established models, broadens the norm, displaces conventional wisdom once and for all, and often adds a certain confusion to things that had been previously considered simple."[21] I would add that such challenges are relevant not just for the content housed in the archive, but also for the archive's history. Indeed, one of the abiding principles and professional practices of archivists is an attentiveness to *provenance*—or the "individual, family or organization that created or received [archival] items." The Society of American Archivists explains that the "principle of provenance . . . dictates that records of different origins (provenance) be kept separate to preserve their context."[22] Archivists thus process archival materials with an eye toward preserving evidence of the history and origins of these collections. Steven L. Henson notes that the principle of provenance "holds that the significance of archival materials is heavily dependent on the context of their creation, and that the arrangement and description of these materials should be directly related to their original purpose and function."[23]

While arrangements and descriptions of archival origins make sense from the perspective of archival management and development, Bethanie Nowviskie notes that it has ineffectually transferred to the creation of digital archives. In "Speculative Collections" Nowviskie emboldens us to deviate from this model of archival development when turning to digital tools and platforms. She explains, "Digital humanities collections—archival and otherwise—are more likely to be taken by their users as memorializing, conservative, limited, and suggestive of a linear view of history than as problem-solving, branching, generative, non-teleological. *This is a design problem.* We're building our digital libraries to be received by audiences as lenses for retrospect, rather than as stages to be leapt upon by performers, by co-creators."[24] Digital archives, she adds, are "not the improv platforms they should be: spaces for projection, planning, performance, speculation. Whether we're talking about born-digital records or those historical documents and artifacts that have undergone the phase-change of digitization—once they're online, I don't want *special* collections, anymore; I want speculative ones."[25]

From my frustrated desire to connect Polack to the Lyon family and my inability to read the significance of the diaries' archival contexts, I created the Lyon Archive—a digital archive launched with Nowviskie's vision in mind. I began building with a question: What if the study of Lyon's diaries involved a form of interpretation rooted in speculative performances? What if they were situated in a space for co-creators? I set out to design a digital space for repositioning the diaries within a digital public archive open to contributors and interpreters. I believed this stage would foreground the importance of the process of making and building—a scholarly praxis Galey and Ruecker characterize as "making as a form of knowing."[26] Ultimately my goal was to build an archive focused on more than just the creation of digital surrogates of print materials or the preservation of relics from the past; I sought methods of putting scholarly actors and agents into dialogue with one another. I would use digital platforms to move us away from the static or backward-looking archive toward a conceptual stage capable of prompting interpretive exchanges. Instead of separating items from different origins and pasts, in keeping with the long tradition of provenance, the Lyon Archive reaches forward in time through its reliance on movies, metadata, sound, and image to imagine or register the records that *might* have been saved of A. S. Lyon's East End intellectual world.

Jarrett M. Drake, a former archivist, has been outspoken in his suspicion of archival work and archival reform, arguing that the imposed silences in the [physical archive's] reading room echo or replicate forces of power that shaped what has been saved or lost. Drake explains, "Silence is an important exercise of control and power. By preventing or discouraging verbal communication between people, the enforcers of said silence . . . remove our human instincts to connect with other human beings *as* human beings. How oppressive it is of archivists to expect users to consult documentary records that chronicle the peaks and valleys of humanity—love, hate, war, abuse, joy, humor—and display no auditory or affective response."[27] As a noisy archive shaped by its dissonance and multiple perspectives, the Lyon Archive emphasizes individual perspectives as well as intersecting, disagreeing voices through its inclusion of podcast interviews with members of the Lyon family; student exhibit essays; and a soundscapes map that imagines what A. S. Lyon might have heard on his daily journey from the East End to the West End of London. Digital objects—voices, images, and sounds—respond to the digital diary's place on a stage unhinged from the silence of the reading room. They strive to reverse the chronological sequencing found in physical archival records that reach back toward the illusion of origins. At the same time, I use the digital archive space to explore the interpretive potential of speculation and wonder. My prompting for such a model comes from Ann Laura Stoler's provocative question, What if "imagining what *might be* was as important as knowing what was"?[28]

The Lyon Archive includes recordings of talking, listening, and responding, hauntings of voices we cannot hear—those that were never saved or in their own time might never have been heard. The noisy Lyon Archive is designed to facilitate a reevaluation of the nineteenth-century East End, which, as this study argues, has been constructed with generalizations and one-directional stereotypes that fail to register evidence of its dynamic cultural activities. I begin with the understanding that reading is a form of listening, and listening is always an interpretive act. As a multimedia archive, the Lyon Archive preserves and clarifies as much as it occludes. I have charted methods of reading what we *can* hear while developing an attentiveness to silences imposed and revealed by the archive's framing powers and curation of select evidence.

My questions about Emma Lyon's relationship to Maria Polack will likely never be resolved conclusively because records of their lives have not survived. Rather than see that fact as a limit or end to questioning, the Lyon Archive seeks methods of registering these and other related archival silences and gaps. To that end, the following pages focus on several archive stories. In the next section I describe my accidental discovery of A. S. Lyon's diaries, an event that happened on a ride to a historic Jamaican Jewish cemetery. The first archive story in this chapter details the challenge of reading the diaries as part of a family archive rather than a public institutional archive. My knowledge of the archive's location in Annabel's home places the diary in a longer trajectory as a family diaspora story from Bohemia to the East End, to Jamaica, and finally to Sacramento, California. My reading of the diaries locates evidence of A. S. Lyon's literary interests, which surface both in references to what he reads and from his constructions of self modeled after popular writing from this period. The second archive story focuses on the digital Lyon Archive, created using Omeka.org, to study the Lyon family's literary legacy. Sound and multimedia objects in the digital archive evoke a sense of wonder and inspire new interpretive possibilities regarding Lyon's diaries. Finally, the third archive story focuses on evidence in the Jamaican cemetery, the site of A. S. Lyon's grave, of Jewish literary culture developed through emerging traditions of epitaph writing. I conclude the chapter by reading this memorial space, containing epitaphs engraved in the East End and subsequently shipped to Jamaica, as an archive of Atlantic literary and print culture. In their own way, each of the archive stories provides evidence of the discursive practices, emotional bonds, and cultural registers of East End literary history during the very period when it supposedly didn't exist.

Finding What Wasn't Missing

Locating evidence of the East End in Jamaica was a lucky accident that happened not in a library or archive, but in a car driving to a Jewish cemetery. As a volunteer on a public humanities project, I was working with a group to create a cemetery inventory, or a catalogue of writings, architectural details, and descriptions of the physical conditions of the graves. The fractured gravestones were, in most cases, the only surviving accounts of individual lives, as earthquakes, hurricanes, and fires have destroyed most other Jewish community records in Jamaica. In their shaggy rows and oblong shadows, the stones preserve records of a community's remembrance acts. Families of the dead, literary scholars, architectural preservationists, historians, and other curious volunteers met once a year to study and record earlier generations' attempts to create a space of memory making and memory keeping. While the dates on the headstones organize the archival content chronologically, patterns in shape, texture, stone type, and writing style link the graves to global cemetery movements. We may be used to thinking of archives as containers of objects organized by folders and filing cabinets. The cemetery archive houses an equivalent in rows of graves, layers of dirt, Hebrew and English inscriptions, and the surrounding boundary walls. Each of these structuring objects and borders creates order out of the chaos of loss.

I returned to Jamaica for several years holding out hope that someday I would find evidence of Polack's Jamaican subscribers in libraries and archives I visited during my trips. I was unsure of how such an association would recast my impressions of the East End, but I assumed that hard evidence would provide clues and clarity. My faith in archival recovery faded over time. But the cemetery called me back. I was drawn to its poetry and languages, its use of incised imagery and story to honor the dead and to process the trauma of loss. It was in my fourth year of volunteering in Jamaica that I experienced a little luck. Just after finishing breakfast, we realized the transportation company had sent the wrong size van. Our leader approached one of the new volunteers, who had just arrived with her husband. "Diane, could your husband drive a few of us to the cemetery? It's not far. The van they sent is too small for all the volunteers." I observed the conversation passively with jet-lagged eyes, warming my hands on a mug of coffee. Moments later we were nudged out of the dining area to the vehicles that would take us to the cemetery. Three of us squeezed into the back of the car driven by Mike, Diane's husband, while Diane navigated. We were instructed to follow the van through Kingston rush-hour traffic to the historic Orange Street Cemetery, Jamaica's only Jewish cemetery still in use. I made small talk with the strangers in the front of the car as we pulled out of the hotel driveway.

"So, what's your interest in cemetery work?" I asked Diane.[29]

"I grew up in Jamaica. I live in Florida now," Diane explained, "and I'm researching my family history. My great-great-grandfather and his family came here from England. They're buried in the cemeteries we'll visit this week. I've never been to the cemeteries—in fact didn't know they existed until recently."

"From England? What's your family name?"

"Lyon," she replied.

"Are you related to Emma Lyon?"

As the car shifted suddenly, I fell on top of Lauren, sitting to my right. Mike mumbled in frustration, "How am I supposed to follow this guy? He's swerving everywhere." The car jolted again, as I plunged to my left on top of Toni, who clung to the door handle.

"Yes. She was a writer," Diane continued, turning around to look at me. "She published a book in 1812. You've heard of her?"

"Of course. She was one of Polack's subscribers." I couldn't believe my ears. Lyon was not well known. Meeting a relative was ridiculously implausible.

"Who's Polack?" Diane asked, turning toward me while keeping one eye on the van. I told her about my interest in the East End's relationship with the Caribbean. Within minutes we discovered we'd been studying the same circle of people from different sides of the ocean. The car came to a screeching halt to avoid mowing down a stray dog and her pups. Mike spotted the van at the end of an alley, and, in an effort to catch up, turned into a crowded neighborhood with loud horns and chuckling goats. We caught up to the van, but our hopes were dashed when it turned the wrong way down a one-way street. Mike shook his head in frustration. As the car jolted forward, a line of chickens jumped in the road, which gave me a moment of anxious stillness to collect my thoughts. I'd been so completely focused on dusty archives and spaces of the dead that I'd lost track of their connections with the living. Diane turned to look at me pointedly with questioning eyes before asking, "Do you want to read the diaries?"

"What diaries?" My mind searched for a possibility I had never thought to consider.

"I have transcriptions of two diaries written by my ancestor A. S. Lyon, Emma's brother. He was living in the East End when he wrote the diaries. I've got two more at home. One was kept by his wife, Sarah Lindo, during her trip to Paris. And another is written by someone we don't know. But we know he's a Lyon."

The car swerved again. From his tense-looking shoulders, I sensed Mike's growing frustration. Toni continued to clutch the door handle, while I perched awkwardly in the middle seat trying to keep my balance as we turned sharply through overcrowded streets. I struggled to make sense of this strange luck. Here I sat in a crowded car, with a driver attempting to deliver us alive to a cemetery, listening to a stranger offer to share diaries from the nineteenth-century East End—the very artifacts for which I'd spent years searching. *Do I want to read the diaries?*

"Yes. Please," I blurted emphatically. "I have to read them. When can I get them?"

"They're in my suitcase. I'll get them for you as soon as we get back to the hotel. Oh, but there's one condition."

"A condition?" As the car swerved again, I lost my balance. In dismay Mike confessed, "I've lost him. Can someone call for directions?" Horns blasted as street dust floated upward. Commuters passed our car on their way through the thick morning heat. While we waited to get directions, Diane and I continued talking, pushing away the noise and smog, giddy that we'd found a shared interest in her family.

"Diane," I demanded, "what's the condition?"

Diane turned around again to look at me. "You're welcome to read them, but you can't use the diaries in your work. They don't actually belong to me. They belong to my cousin Annabel who lives in Sacramento.

My other cousin, Naomi, transcribed them. I'm sure you'll enjoy reading them, but Naomi and Annabel might not like it if you used them in your research."

This seemed suspicious. What were they hiding? And how could I read personal diaries written by someone in the circle I'd been studying for years—years!—and *not* quote from them? What if I found juicy information? How could I write my book and ignore that amazing detail, knowing full well it existed but I wasn't allowed to mention it? Would it be better to read the diaries and forget their content? Or should I forgo the pleasure of reading them altogether? Hours later I found myself surrounded by fragments of historic debris, rows of tall stones, and piles of dirt. While I wilted from the midday Jamaican sun, I came to the conclusion that I would always regret not having read the diaries. What kind of scholar passes up an opportunity like this? So, I might have to ignore what I'd learned. There was still pleasure in knowing and in choosing to know. And after all, years of archival research had taught me that I probably wouldn't find anything relevant in the diaries. Sensational dramas unearthed in private family archives are the stuff of romance.

We returned to the hotel with a fine coating of dust stuck to our bodies by insect repellant and sunblock. Diane brought copies of the diaries to the lobby. I grabbed them as politely as possible and raced back to my own room to begin reading under the hotel's dim lamp. I scrutinized references to the East End, everything A. S. Lyon mentioned reading, every play he saw, and every person he met. I learned about Lyon's health problems, his descent into poverty, and his reluctant decision to leave England for the West Indies. While preoccupied with what I was going to do with all the material I wasn't allowed to mention in my book, the name found me—Polack. It jumped off the page in full glory. My eyes recognized the letters before my brain could interpret their meaning. I couldn't be sure if this was my Polack, but I remember feeling both a rising hope and despair in that moment of recognition.

I cornered Diane at breakfast the next morning. "Can you clarify what you mean by, 'You can't use the diaries in your work'?"

Diane offered helpfully, "Maybe if we ask my cousins? I don't really know Annabel. We've emailed, but I've never met her in person. I don't know why, but I know she wants to protect the diaries. We need to respect her wishes."

This conversation was the first of many I would have with Diane, Naomi, and Annabel about the significance of the diaries for the historiography of London's East End, nineteenth-century Atlantic literary culture, Anglo-Jewish cultural formation, and Jamaican print and literary activities. In the months to come, all three cousins granted permission to let me use the diaries in my research—which culminated with this chapter—and in a class I would later teach. The diaries are remarkable for their descriptions of the daily occurrences of an ordinary citizen moving through the streets of London, Scotland, France, Barbados, and Jamaica. A. S. Lyon narrated a world in which he struggled to carve a place for himself as a young Jewish man who had no access to a university education or the support of family money.

Like all other archival records, the diaries alternately expose and submerge details of A. S. Lyon's life. While I had full access to the diaries, the rest of the content in Annabel's cedar chest remained off-limits. Eventually I made my way to her house to photograph the diaries. During my visit I was never invited into the bedroom to rummage through the contents of the archive. Why would they invite me? Their archive was not created for the public. It was a personal archive created lovingly by family members who wanted to preserve a record of their history and memories. They were willing to share some materials, but others recorded private family affairs. It wasn't until I worked with this limited-access archive that I realized how the presumption of full access had guided my previous work in open public archives. But in fact, their holdings are just as incomplete. It was the family archive at Annabel's house that helped me see how full access fed the illusion of wholeness. Moreover, unless they leave evidence of their framing protocols, the work of collectors and archivists can be made invisible to users of the archive. On occasion I've asked archivists about when the library acquired their materials or the names of those who donated or processed collections. Some libraries were able to answer my questions. In some cases, the archivists just don't know because the records were missing. Others responded with guarded or incomplete answers. While working at Annabel's dining room table, listening to her open and close doors at the far end of a long hallway, I felt a similar boundary. Only in this case, I faced a limit brought about by the distinct features of discrete family archives that actively curate and hide because they are, understandably, private by choice.

Lyon's descendants have generously granted permission to let me photograph, digitize, teach, map, and visualize data from the diaries in ways that have not only illuminated the importance of Lyon's cultural contexts but also reminded me of the fear families experience when their personal family papers cross the threshold from private trunk to public archive. The diaries were connected with other objects, enjoined by the walls that keep them hidden from the world. While I've never seen the cedar chest, frequently when I ask Annabel a question about her family she'll reply, "I have something else you might want to see." These conversations remind me that while I know the trunk isn't bottomless, I can't determine its contours or the limits of its holdings; nor can I conceive of the intricate ways each item's significance speaks through its relations with other items beyond my reach.

The Diaries: From London to Kingston

On August 3, 1823, Lyon wrote, "Played another game of chess with George. Lost it, not very well. Played a few games of crib with Polack. Lost a shilling. Retired to rest at half past 11 o'clock without supper or anything else."[30] Upon reading this passage for the first time, I was surprised to learn that Maria's husband, Lipman Polack, was a gambler. Numerous references to gambling throughout the diaries convinced me that this was a common activity among members of this crowd. In another passage written on November 3, 1823, Lyon wrote, "Rose a little before 7 o'clock. Busy in the counting house. Went to riding school with Mr Polack. Busy in the counting house. Read."[31] Had they been raised with money, both men would have learned to ride as children. Learning these skills as adults suggested a desire for upward mobility or for lessons that had to be learned later in life for those without the benefit of wealthy parents to foot the bill.

It was Lyon's final mention of the name Polack that brought me back into confusion about these families. On December 10, 1823, Lyon wrote,

> Rose at a little before 8 o'clock. Wrote a little French. Busy in the counting house. Wrote a very long letter to Zip. Went over to Polack's. Spent an hour there to console Mrs P for the loss of her father, a very good old man who died at the advanced age of 79, without a struggle, at the moment he was saying his prayers. Such an end must be wished for by everyone who has a fear for him in whose power it is so to call us at his divine pleasure. Retired to rest at 12 o'clock.[32]

I stopped in my tracks. Maria Polack's father, Ephraim Polack, died in 1812. The diary entry was written in 1823. Could this be her father-in-law? Or maybe this was a different Polack family? I was unable to derive clues from the surrounding passage.

I was flummoxed. And I was angry. How hard would it have been to mention the first name or an address? Just when I thought I'd had a breakthrough, the archive receded, yanked out of my conceptual powers by the rude fact that diarists tend not to document their sources. After years of searching for clarity, I can say with absolute certainty as I type these words that I have no idea if Lyon refers to Maria Polack and her family in this diary entry. My only option was to make the painful decision to ignore the diary's inclusion of the name "Polack" and read the diaries instead as a key to the social circle Maria Polack shared with Lyon. I tried to cheer myself by recalling that it wasn't all bad news. I'd been granted access to two diaries from a private family archive that recounted the activities of someone known to Polack and who subscribed to her novel. I read A. S. Lyon's descriptions of visits to multiple synagogues, his efforts to become educated, and his enjoyment of theatre and reading as a key to Polack's world. The diary offered a window into East End cultural activities in this period. It also functioned as a reminder of what I might have learned about Polack had one of her diaries been saved.

The earlier 1823 diary details Lyon's intention of accounting for his time. In one typical entry dated Sunday, May 4, 1823, he wrote, "Rose at quarter past 7. Wrote. Took writing lesson. Wrote a French exercise. Took a French lesson. Busy in the counting house. Read. Went to Mr Wiffens for Kate. Read. Retired to rest at 12 o'clock."[33] The second diary was kept from 1826 to 1839 and deviates considerably in content and style from this early representative passage in the first diary. In the later diary, Lyon moves away from the list-like accounts and toward more detailed descriptions of social interactions, business troubles, family feuds, unrequited love, and rising feelings of despair. Not only does the writing become more meditative in the second diary, but it creates a pattern of imaginative time travel as Lyon names future points in time or events he anticipates. For example, in an entry dated 24 Tuesday [January 1826] during his visit to Scotland, Lyon wrote,

> Rose at 9. Read. Out. Went to the court. Had a sight of the great unknown Sir Walter Scott, but whose countenance [shown?] not the least sunshine of intellect. Went from thence to the Infirmary and had a lesson for all my life, both as regards content and pride. It will teach me the former in as much as I cannot say I am more worthy to leave in perfect health, any more than the poor sufferers who laid [ ] on the bed of sickness, pain, sorrow and, I may add, certain death, from the then present state of the ward [ ] . . . in approaching the [ ] the poor sufferers lingering in the stairs and casting [a] gloomy eye towards the door of operation, no doubt with the painful reflection of perhaps I am the next. The countenance [of]

> these poor fellows was certainly distressing. Wrote home. Mems. Retired to rest past 1.[34]

Lyon's mention of a "lesson for all my life" signals his processing of Infirmary horrors as a learning opportunity to consider his own inevitable future death.[35] Implied by this logic is a construction of his current moment of learning as separate from his future moment of death. In the years following the Scotland trip, Lyon, along with his brother and business partner James Lyon, fell into gradual financial ruin. Later diary entries comment on financial struggles and failing health. More than just a mechanism for a daily retrospective, Lyon's second diary, as the above passage suggests, situates daily events in light of futures he envisions and from which he imagines looking back. This is one of the many ways the author of the second diary emerges as a character situated within a progressive continuum of past, present, and future.

One of the noteworthy features of the second diary is Lyon's mention of books he reads or seeks. While he's mostly silent on his interpretations of those texts, inclusion of his intellectual curiosity helps to explain the shift in his writing style from choppy list in the early diary to narrative fluidity in the later. Andrew Piper notes of readers in this period, "It was through romantic literature where individuals came to understand their books, and it was through their books where they came to understand themselves."[36] In her study of Joseph Woolley, another nineteenth-century working-class diarist, Carolyn Steedman explains that her subject's "response to literature can be read out of his own prose style, and out of the allusions he made to the books he named" as he "made meaning out of literature."[37] Lyon's second diary, with its better-developed prose style combined with allusions to books he read, plays he attended, and lectures he heard, contains numerous instances of the diary's power for emotional or intellectual processing in a manner that echoes many of the texts he mentions reading. With increasing frequency and complexity, Lyon's diary entries evolve into clear expressions of interiority and a growing self-reflective awareness of his emotional development. In such passages, he frequently hints at his own process of becoming and his rising awareness of future and past versions of himself.

Worries about money are one of the dominant topics in the diary. Indeed, the diary's concentration on despair about his business failures and disagreements with his brother James leave readers wondering what outlets Lyon might have had for processing his emotions. Shifts in the style of writing over the thirteen years of diary-keeping suggest that writing provided some help with anxiety. It's difficult to know if A. S. Lyon's diary entries recount a worsening situation or if his writing becomes less guarded over time. When a family member falls into debt, Lyon notes, "9 Tuesday Rose at half past 7. Out with Henry. Certificate. W. End. Home 4. To Harts. Chess etc. Retired to rest past 11."[38] Michael Lobban recalls the significance of certificates and their role in bankruptcies in this period:

> In contrast to ordinary debtors, insolvent traders had long been able to use the bankruptcy courts, where they could be freed of all their past debts and avoid the threat of imprisonment, provided they obtained a "certificate of conformity." The legislature drew a distinction between trading and non-trading insolvents, since it was felt that the failure of traders was generally the result of their blameless reliance on other traders who did not pay their debts, whereas non-traders had only their own folly and extravagance to blame for their insolvency.[39]

Lyon's entry is brief, unspecific, but pointed. He not only witnesses the fall of friends into bankruptcy while engaging in a personal struggle to avoid the same fate, but he likely also reads the dangers of his precarious state through memories of his father's imprisonment for debt.

Lyon's return to the subject of bankruptcy in the very next entry, written on May 10, 1826, expresses a more pressing sense of despair signaled by mention of the "blue devils." His entry for this day states, "Rose at half past 6. Rode. Busy counting house. H's certificate. City. Wrote some chess rules for Eleanor. To Joseph's for goods. Mems. Blue devils—they always follow reflections on present situation. Retire to rest past 11."[40] Two days later Lyon noted going to "Holborn etc with H's certificate" and added, "Such repulses [and] insinuations as I witnessed [do] not make me astonished at the despairs of many a man when he finds himself valued. This has been a [ ] lesson and I trust I shall always profit by it."[41] He understands—is not astonished—to learn how men feel despair when "valued" based on their economic standing. This lesson is not simply learned but is described as itself a source of profit—a word chosen perhaps with a sense of irony. On June 15, 1826, Lyon anticipates his outcome in another worrisome entry:

> Again the agonizing task of examining the books, but I fear to no purpose. The bright prospects they held forth at the commencement of the year is over-shadowed by so thick a cloud that I fear the sunshine of prosperity

> will never again pierce [ ] thro it to illumine its leaves with the prospect of pleasing termination. A long subject with George on the subject [*sic*], so often agitated, of my quitting England for Barbados. Altho happen what will, I shall always leave England with regrets. Yet another scene is absolutely necessary for my future establishment in life, and every day the present presents more images of frightful despair which almost threatens the seat of reason. Indeed, I cannot deserve the agony my reflection occasions.[42]

The choice to leave England for the West Indies marks a rising level of intensity linked to concerns about his homeland and sense of belonging.[43] "Reflection" is a persistent thread in the diary; in 298 entries and 21,000 words, Lyon uses the words "reflect," "reflected," or "reflections" 31 times. And in many more diary entries he engages in acts of rumination in moments where the word "reflect" is absent. The writing is clearly an attempt to measure and deduce, as he uses writing acts to help him intellectualize his declining circumstances.

Lyon traces a growing awareness of his identity and circumstances in descriptions of the unfolding of events through which his character emerges as a dynamic personality caught in a web of struggles. Along with entries about his money troubles, Lyon writes about his hopes and joys in experiences with family and friends. Throughout the second diary, in particular, Lyon presents human life as a path, a journey, or an unfolding sequence of events. Anne-Marie Millim notes that nineteenth-century literature in general became increasingly interested in the "emotional make-up of its characters." A related "consciousness" emerged among diary writers in this period who saw themselves as investing "a deliberate 'literariness'" into their work.[44] In several entries, the writing creates distinct characterizations and consciousness. In one entry from July 12, 1826, just after A. S. Lyon and his brother realize they face grave financial ruin, Lyon escorts Henrietta, a child and relative, to Margate where he meets up with family for a brief vacation. In this entry Lyon uses figurative language and wonder to describe his joy in the moment that makes him "another being" and far apart from the horrors he faces at home:

> Off at 9 with Henrietta. A most delightful day and much amused with the delight the novelty of the scene occasioned little Henrietta. May her heart, unacquainted with real sorrow as is at the present moment, remain in that blessed ignorance, which I fear is denied the most pious, for that path of human life has never yet been discovered strewn with roses,

> but that thorns have sprung up to sting the most perfect of mortals, and happy they who can be content with the good they receive. The same time the accompanying evils are looked upon as lessons[?] to check our frailties. May my little Henrietta possess the happiness I wish her, with as few of the evils of life that ever were experienced by the most happy. Arrived at Margate at 4. Set off immediately for Ramsgate and found all out. Leaving Henrietta, I posted down to the pier, where the sight of so many for whom my bosom burnt with the sincerest emotion of friendship. To say I felt another being, too much happiness to think it real and never did my wondering imagination, sunk in the most profound slumber, agitated with revels, too happy to be real, so entirely efface the past as the happiness of the present moment.[45]

Here Lyon constructs his character as having an effaced past overtaken by the joy of the present. But in wishing Henrietta life without thorns, he also remembers a time of innocence when he knew nothing of the sorrow he has pushed away in this moment. Again, he refers to his pain as a lesson, "to check our frailties." While we're never quite sure what he has learned, this passage suggests that he processes his current pain as a kind of lesson or opportunity from which to become a better kind of person. Such moments are not written for us. Carried with him across the ocean and saved during the years of his life, the entry addresses the only one capable of returning to earlier passages from a distant future to reflect on the voice that long ago anticipated the diarist's return. While we may witness characters in novels narrating events with an awareness of their future and past and lessons learned, such moments of perspicacity are rare in extant writing by East Enders from this period. Between the silk-lined covers of his private diary, Lyon preserved a rare instance of an individual carving out a path through difficult circumstances with flashes of clarity and levity that echo the style of writing used in literature from this period.

In *Spaces of Modernity*, Miles Ogborn offers a familiar description of East End residents during the very period in which A. S. Lyon kept his diary. According to Ogborn,

> The poorest areas north and east of the City were densely populated, dirty, and dangerous. People were crowded into poorly built and decaying houses in a labyrinthine cluster of courts and alleys that covered any spare ground behind the main streets. Short leases and the absence of guild restrictions meant that foreign immigrants crowded into areas like

> Spitalfields, while the dominance of the docks and wharves in the east's riverside parishes made them into a separate urban world, as well as one of the places where the world entered London.[46]

Lyon and Polack would have fallen into Ogborn's classification of "foreign immigrants." Ogborn constructs cultural or ethnic difference as an outgrowth of the environment, manifested by "poorly built and decaying houses" spread out in "labyrinthine" clusters. Certainly, many East Enders from this period struggled with poverty, just like residents living in other parts of London. What makes Ogborn's narrative uniquely disturbing is the construction of East End residents as flattened characters, universally abject and frightening. Lyon's diary entries challenge this view by acknowledging one individual's expressions of desire to belong and grow roots, to become educated, to succeed in business, and to be counted as an Englishman and insider. There's no room in Ogborn's version of the East End for a dynamic character like Lyon.

With few exceptions, the dominant historiography of the nineteenth-century East End has been written by those who never lived there.[47] In passing down A. S. Lyon's diaries from one generation to the next, the Lyon family preserved a rare vision of what it was like to build a life in London as a child of a struggling immigrant father. Lyon's writing recounts his failure to thrive and his subsequent feelings that he's been exiled to Barbados and later Jamaica.[48] Diary passages articulate his attempts at rooting himself in a homeland, and his desire to create permanent connections and a sense of belonging. Anne McClintock and others have traced the significance of young English men making their way to the colonies to establish professional and familial ties and to expand the work of empire building. However, Lyon's situation doesn't quite square with this model.[49] Many diary entries reflect the complexities associated with Lyon's migration. On May 14, 1829, for example, Lyon mentions a fellow passenger on his ship to the Caribbean who "made some illiberal reflection on my being a Jew."[50] Although brief, this diary entry offers a reminder that migrations from metropole to colony were various and individualized. Not all young men immigrating to colonial outposts identified fully as Englishmen or as proud custodians of British culture. The inclusion of this comment underscores the fact that national and religious affiliations often created intersectional identities that fail to adhere to simplistic nation/colony categories. Lyon's entry offers a call to consider how his sense of Englishness might have been inflected by his identity as a Jew, and how his reasons for migrating have something to do with his feelings of being a failure and outcast in England and a child of immigrants who fled anti-Semitism in Bohemia.

Indeed, the diary functions as more than a migration narrative detailing Lyon's path from London to Jamaica. It's also a written account of a Jewish family's diaspora story that began with Solomon Lyon's migration in search of greater religious freedom. A. S. Lyon's inability to support himself in London and his subsequent move from the East End to Kingston, Jamaica, in 1839 marks a new stage in the family's diaspora story. A. S. Lyon arrives in a British colony just after slavery has been abolished and the apprenticeship system has begun.[51] Scholars have noted that nineteenth-century Jamaican Jews sat at a cultural crossroads.[52] According to Jane Gerber, Jamaican Jews did not achieve full civil rights until 1831, "six months after the free blacks and three years before the general abolition of slavery."[53] Holly Snyder and Kay Dian Kriz describe Jewish divergences from dominant Jamaican society in this period. While Jews held a position higher than slaves, they were still treated as a separate class from the British.[54] Holly Snyder adds that "although Jews [in Jamaica] were nominally free [and were] of European origin and therefore experienced neither the utterly degraded position of the enslaved nor the undesirable condition of those who arrived under indenture of servitude, they were nonetheless stigmatized as non-white by the Anglo-Jamaican elite."[55] It's as if Lyon moved from a position of uncertainty in London to an in-between position in Jamaica. In his feelings of regret for leaving England, Lyon hints at his sense of exile, of his perception that the move constitutes an undeserved or forced displacement.[56] Records of his Jamaican life are not known to exist. Our knowledge of his migration, however, shapes what we come to understand about the diaries, for every description of a personal failure recorded in the diary brings Lyon closer to his final destination in Jamaica. At the same time, the diaries hint at the gravity of what Lyon believes he is leaving behind, signaling his deep ties to a world that spanned the Atlantic, emanating from his family and social ties in Whitechapel.

From Cedar Chest to Digital Archive

Photographs, manuscript materials, and books passed from one generation of the Lyon family to the next have been preserved by Annabel Foster-Davis, the great-great-granddaughter of A. S. Lyon. The Lyon Archive contains digital objects that draw from Annabel's archive, including digital surrogates of the manuscript diaries; transcriptions of the diaries; student exhibit essays; a soundscapes map depicting the sounds and sights A. S. Lyon might have encountered in London; and copies of podcast interviews I conducted with three of his descendants: Diane Lyon Wead in Florida, Annabel Foster-Davis in California, and Naomi Cream in London. In aligning and blending primary sources and interpretations of those sources, the Lyon Archive gestures toward a form of analysis that unfolds continually with each new contribution to the archive. The boundaries of the space expand to accommodate new content, as the meaning of the records shift in response to the broadening array of materials and forms. The Lyon Archive might be read as a cognitive assemblage, or what Katherine Hayles describes as "a flexible and constantly shifting network that includes human and technical actors" and that is "characterized by the circulation of information, interpretations, and meanings by human and technical cognizers who drop in and out of the network in shifting configurations that enable interpretations and meanings to emerge, circulate, interact and disseminate throughout the network."[57] Similarly, the Lyon Archive captures and puts into play shifting relations among the digital objects placed on the archival stage.[58]

The publishing platform Omeka.org and the theme I've selected, along with the choice of plug-ins and embedded tools, affect every object's meaning and identity. As with physical archives, objects in a digital archive are never neutral or objective, never raw or untouched by the medium, creator, or relations with other objects in the archive. Digital archives function as an extension of the physical archive's form rather than a disturbance of truth. With its exposure of multiple actors and structuring tools, the Lyon Archive does not just display its wares (the Swahili meaning of *Omeka*) but puts multiple visualities into interactive play. The following discussion shows how this archive's shape-shifting parts draw from the affordances of the digital sphere to challenge prevailing assumptions about East End people and cultural expressions. The version of the East End constructed by this archive emerges through the actions, chance interplay, and human responses prompted by content housed on the site. The Lyon Archive is therefore part of a continuum where objects move from physical archive (the cedar chest) to digital space while simultaneously inviting future encounters.

The digital copy of my podcast interview with Naomi Cream, the transcriber of A. S. Lyon's diaries, includes a discussion of the problem of silences in the physical space of the archive. Naomi reflected on her experiences working in archives and record offices throughout London:

HK: What was that like? Going around to different record offices?

NC: It was very interesting, but it was very expensive and time-consuming when compared with modern days when you just have to look at lists on the internet. . . . I think that in general, record offices are a much more, um, much more attractive places than they used to be. . . . They used to be [places where] somebody . . . told you to be quiet, for example, and not to disturb anybody, whereas now they are quite keen to help you. And also, I think at first it was considered rather shameful to want to research your past, whereas now it is quite a common thing to do that.

HK: That's interesting. Why was it shameful?

NC: Well, I had to, I concealed it from some people who are rather scornful of the fact that people were interested in their families. I don't know why that was.[59]

Naomi was reticent upon further questioning about shame associated with her archival research. The conversation turned to other subjects, but in this short exchange Naomi exposes the influence of cultural norms or social pressures in the creation of archival silences or gaps. Naomi's voice and words recount her resistance to such norms; for, despite feelings of shame or pressures not to conduct research, she persevered. Her published work on the Lyon family establishes important groundwork for the study of nineteenth-century Anglo-Jewish culture through the experiences of one family's story of migration, education, and literary production.

I could hear the rustling of paper throughout my interview with Diane Lyon Wead, the second Lyon family member I interviewed.[60] When the recording ended, Diane expressed frustration at my choice to ask questions out of order, since she'd prepared answers to my pre-circulated questions. Asking the questions out of order was unplanned; I was simply following the flow of the conversation. But I realized too late that my actions led to Diane's confusion—a confusion I hadn't noticed in the interview. From the start, Diane displayed a warmth and enthusiasm about the diaries and her family research. She has tracked down rare copies of many of her family's publications, including a rare copy of Emma Lyon's *Miscellaneous Poems.* I was struck by how well Diane prepared for the interview. I was both surprised and pleased by the sound of the rustling papers. They reminded me of Derrida's point that "there is no archive without . . . a technique of repetition, and without a certain exteriority. No archive without outside."[61] Photographs of nineteenth-century diary pages now sit in a digital archive alongside recordings of the sound of Diane's rustling pages of notes. It was only once I heard her rustling that I remembered the silent operation of turning digital pages.

My work on the diaries preceded the creation of podcast interviews with family members. Shortly after my visit to Jamaica, I asked the family if they would grant permission to let me teach the diaries. I explained my vision of placing digital copies of the diaries as a centerpiece on the Lyon Archive site. Students would create interpretive exhibits and maps that, if done well, would be made "public." Work would only be made public, however, if they earned an A on the assignment. Those who earned lower grades had the option to revise their work for publication on the site. All three cousins were excited about this initiative. I offered the course, New Media and Digital Culture, in fall of 2016. In addition to examining other period diaries and contexts in the East End and Jamaica, my class considered how digital exhibits and surrogates of paper objects re-form texts to address latencies in content and context. Using Omeka's exhibit plug-in, my students created Digital Exhibit Essays, or multimedia projects in which they presented their interpretations of the diary. One ambitious student, Mai-Ling Maas, focused her exhibit essay on Lyon's repeated references to the "blue devils." She found evidence in the *Oxford English Dictionary* that this expression recalled a "harmful or malignant demon, *esp.* one that causes melancholy."[62] The term first appeared in 1616 and was used by popular eighteenth- and early nineteenth-century authors. Lyon's inclusion of this expression alongside confessions of dullness and despair are hard to ignore. Mai-Ling studied the following passages as evidence of Lyon's declining mental health:

> 24 Wednesday May: Rose at 8. Into H's. W. End with him to Lindos etc. Indeed *very bad spirits* in consequence of the bad times, and in fact whenever I reflect on our present situation to what it really might happen, it *makes me dull* indeed. (emphasis added)

> June 11, 1826: Exceeding low in spirits nor did the conversation of James add a single instance to relieve my unhappiness. His looks are sufficient to indicate his situation and if my outward appearance is not witness *of a disease within,* yet I am fearful there reigns one that is not easily to be indicated. (emphasis added)

> June 22, 1826: *Blue devils in abundance.* Where will all this end, and how, is left for time to reveal, but *its prospects are most appalling.* (emphasis added)[63]

Following her examination and further research, Mai-Ling concluded that Lyon may have thought he was suffering from a form of depression. To be clear, Mai-Ling's goal was not to diagnose Lyon medically. Rather, she sought ways of analyzing the significance of Lyon's choice of words and use of figurative language. She wondered if correlations existed between his declining health and failed business ventures and the popular use of the expression "the blue devils." Mai-Ling was also curious about Lyon's mention of specific doctors. Her exhibit essay used Voyant, a text analysis tool, to explore Lyon's affective responses to economic insecurity. And she connected her analysis to a longer discussion about Lyon's medical treatment and contemporary concerns about disease and filth in London. This body of work led her to conclude the following:

> Lyon's depression and anxiety seem to hold a large role in how he lives his life and the changing style of writing we see in the latter half of the diary, but our modern concept of mental health is very different from the way it would be approached in Lyon's time. This exhibit will explore nineteenth-century views of mental health and how Lyon responds to his own battle against the "blue devils."[64]

Mai-Ling's exhibit essay was published on the Lyon Archive in December 2016. In our podcast interview the following summer, Diane expressed concerns about Mai Ling's exhibit essay.

> HK: If you could add anything [to the Lyon Archive] what would it be?
>
> DLW: There's one thing on the, on the Lyon Archive, that I don't like. I know you didn't ask this question, but I don't really like the article about the blue devils. I wish it wasn't on the archive because I don't see A. S. Lyon as suffering from depression in the true sense of it. He was going through a hard time. He admitted it. When someone was cruel to him or he fought with his brother or a girl would not return his affection, he felt it. He, he did get sick a lot, got those headaches as you say. I don't see him as wallowing in depression. You know, he took action, he tried, when business was hard in Britain he tried going to Paris for a year. Then he got himself together to go to the West

Indies. And notice that when he arrived, after he was in Barbados for a year, he mentioned that his health was still good. Several times he mentioned, "my health is still good." And so perhaps the British climate was a little, maybe he had a little bit of, um, a bronchitis problem, or something like that. Because, he, this happened to me in my own childhood. When I was a little girl in New York I was constantly sick and after I got to Jamaica I just blossomed. So, I don't think of him as, um, as we think of a depressive person. Um, and I know that Naomi has um, kind of raised her eyebrows about it as well, by the way. We never saw it that way. And being that it's one of the prime stories on the site it was kind of, sticks out.

HK: What do you make of his own references to having the blue devils? What do you think he meant by that?

DLW: Well, just, you know, the thinking, I think of people as being in a blue mood. I don't regard it as chronic depression. There's a difference. I mean, I get into blue moods myself. I dare say, a lot of people do. But, you know, the fact is that I get up and go again.

Part of the complexity of this moment stems from the variety of audiences contributing to the Lyon Archive and the contexts they drew from in their interpretations of the diaries. I welcomed Diane's counter-reading of Lyon's descriptions of his health. By registering her dislike of Mai Ling's exhibit, Diane exposed one of the central tenants of my project: the productive work of archival dissonance brought about by the players on the archival stage. Diane's response to Mai-Ling's essay succeeded in making dissent legible to the public, while underscoring the stakes of disparate stories and perspectives in a noisy archive. Materials housed in archives never achieve closure. The boundaries of the archive and finding aids may create the illusory promise of such, but in the end the narrative tensions evoked by each item, the selection of materials, the happenstance of survival, and silences or gaps bring us back to an endless array of interpretive possibilities and uncertainties.[65]

I came to understand Mai-Ling's and Diane's differing approaches as illuminations of their distinct and equally valid interpretive lenses. As a member of the family, Diane interpreted Lyon's comments about his dullness as part of an extended narrative about her connection to her family. She noted that Lyon's symptoms aligned with her own experiences of feeling blue. And she further emphasized connections between ailments and her place of residence. Once she moved to Jamaica, her symptoms vanished. She reasoned that Lyon's would have followed suit. Thus, Diane read her own feelings in light of Lyon's; and she read Lyon's in light of her own—an act many of us perform when we gaze at artifacts from family archives. We might notice our hair color or nose shape matches what we see in an old family photograph. Or we might cherish images in family archives that not only help us find ourselves, but connect us to a longer past, a past rooted in evidence and artifacts rather than memories. For Mai-ling, however, the diary was a window into an unknown nineteenth-century figure. Lyon was a young man about her own age who struggled to find his way in the world. She read the expression "the blue devils" as one that tied Lyon to another time. It's not surprising that a student enrolled in a literature course would notice the use of popular figurative language in a text she studied. For her, Lyon's mention of the blue devils tied him to popular phrases. She reasoned that his diction may even indicate his sense of playful levity about his feelings by expressing them through popular cultural associations.

Diane, Naomi, and Annabel signed waivers that allowed me to display student work alongside the rest of the Lyon Archive's content.[66] I asked students to sign another waiver indicating whether they wanted their work displayed to the public and/or if they preferred to use a pseudonym on their contributions to the archive. All members of the Lyon family and Mai-Ling have read and approved this chapter. I understood these permissions and approvals as a gesture of inclusion and a desire to represent the work of the archive as a collaborative exchange rather than a repository of objects silently borrowed from a family archive or taken from a student assignment. Naomi had already transcribed three of the diaries when I began working on the project. One of my students and I collaborated on the transcription of a fourth. I later created digital surrogates of Emma Lyon's *Miscellaneous Poems* (1812) and a book by her granddaughter Lucy Henry titled *The Roll Call, and Other Stories* (1891). By explicitly consenting to the creation of the archive and the use of the diaries in my course, the family enabled students to learn from Lyon's rare, unguarded account of life in London. Consent forms were adapted from those used in the Special Collections department of my university's library. I worked with the family members to revise some of the language on the form to address their specific interests in retaining intellectual copyright over the diaries.[67]

In the end, I made the decision to include both Mai-Ling's digital exhibit and Diane's critique of that exhibit. Complying with Diane's request to remove Mai-Ling's essay would have meant reneging on my promise to my students to publish A-level work on the project site. Including Diane's dissenting view, however, gave me a way to honor her concerns while still following through on my commitment to my students. The digital archive's job, after all, is not to put forward a single narrative, but to make space for users to consider the rich interpretive possibilities raised by archival records. And my goal in building the archive was to inspire reflection, collaboration, analysis, and speculation about archival sounds and silences. It was also an occasion for considering why we yearn for narrative coherence and completeness in the first place.

Travels through London

While the diaries describe Lyon's experiences of travel to distant places in Scotland, Paris, Barbados, and Jamaica, they also capture his daily excursions through his home city of London. In rare moments, Lyon recounts the experience of movement through London streets or his observations about his experience of travel. I created a soundscapes map to extend these moments by imagining sounds Lyon might have encountered along the way: a bird chirping, the scraping of a pen as it moves across a piece of paper, and the soft rumbling of crowds gathering in the street. The map does not record what Lyon mentions seeing or hearing; rather, it uses voice and sound to speculate about Lyon's experience of traversing the city from East to West and back home to the East at the close of the day. And while Lyon made a point of including Hebrew words, references to visits to synagogues, observance of Jewish holy days, acts of prayer, and expressions of belief in God in his diary, readers seldom learn what he sees or sounds he hears. Moreover, readers have limited access to his thoughts about occupying two worlds—the secular world in which he strives to become an Englishman, and the Jewish world where he participates in communal religious activities. Yet the writing gives the impression that on any given day, Lyon moves effortlessly from opera to synagogue; from a family friend's gathering on the occasion of a circumcision to a day of work in his West End counting house. Readers are left to speculate about his thoughts of the experience of place, and of the ways that sounds and sights might signal important turning points in his life. The integration of sound and image in the digital soundscapes map addresses this gap, while suggesting that Lyon's apparent ease of movement across local or cultural boundaries anticipates his future migration to the West Indies. Readers of the diary know what's coming, of course, but the diarist, writing in real time, describes his beloved world of London through the fear of loss rather than its inevitability. It's not until the final years of the diary that his fear is realized in his migration to Barbados and later Jamaica.

Indeed, the move to the West Indies appears in the diary as a problem Lyon describes with regret and frustration. Did he see his move as a rupture of his hoped-for English identity? Was it another experience of Jewish exclusion, one that replayed his father's departure from Bohemia to England? As someone who identified as both English and Jewish, and a first-generation child of immigrants, Lyon's mention of his migration concerns underscores the complexity of place for those who experience the force of exile. The fact that Lyon identified as Jewish, and found a welcome home among residents of his East End Jewish community, however, situates that feeling of exile as an extension of a longer Jewish diaspora history. Bryan Cheyette notes that migration and diaspora are often Janus-faced operations complicating the conditions of belonging:

> At one end of the spectrum, diaspora is on the side of impurity and hybridity (and points in the direction of emergent or lost cultures) and, at the other end, diaspora is conservative and "roots defined" and has as its end point a return to an autochthonous (pure) space. The celebratory version of diaspora tends to foreground a transgressive imagination and precolonial histories made up of intertwined cultures (and is associated with Postcolonial and Diaspora Studies), whereas a victim-centered version tends to stress particular communities of exile with specific and unique histories of suffering (and is associated with Holocaust and Genocide Studies).[68]

Lyon's diaries are obviously written before the Holocaust, but the Bohemia of his father's youth was tied to the longer history of European racial, ethnic, and religious persecution. We hear hints in the diary of feelings of victimhood in his reluctance to leave England or his worry that emigration was a punishment for his business failures. While we can't know if he remained bitter throughout his life—since later diaries don't exist—Cheyette's articulation of a split between "a celebratory version of diaspora" versus a "victim-centered version" offers context for Lyon's stated apprehension about his migration. We'll see further evidence of this concern among members of his community in the epitaphs in Kingston's Elletson Road Cemetery where Lyon is buried. Ties to place and nation clearly mattered to this community. In expressions of broken ties, they preserved a record of their feelings of longing and loss as well as of hope for a sense of connection.

The soundscape map presents Lyon's writing about his sadness upon leaving England for the West Indies. Everyday dramas and disappointments are threaded through the diaries. In many cases his writing expresses a sense of belonging to people and institutions throughout London. One benefit of the soundscapes map is that it provides a platform for imagining a version of the East End that was both changeable and energized by the people who lived there. Rather than presenting place as static, the soundscapes map works toward a construction of place that evokes the dynamic nature of Lyon's urban arena. The diary entries I selected for the map were recited by a student and recorded using Audacity, an open-source audio software used to make podcasts. The movies integrate the sound recordings with images uploaded to iMovie. Each movie was then linked to a pin on the map where Lyon traveled. The cluster of sound and visual objects was further enhanced by the Ken Burns tool—a feature in iMovie that grants frozen images the illusion of movement. A deliberate fabrication and interpretive experiment, the movies in the soundscapes map reach beyond the limits of what we can know in order to consider what might have been lost in Lyon's diary writing. Like any other archival object, the movies create a narrative that leverages the archive's fiction-making qualities as opportunities for speculation. The pins on the map mark Lyon's paths or pauses in particular places. Users of the map glimpse his decline in slow motion by watching one short movie at a time. The dynamic soundscape map gives us a way to imagine Lyon's poverty as a gradual process of becoming rather than a fixed state of being.

In one diary entry, written September 14, 1823, Lyon describes a typical pattern of juggling religious and secular experiences. He writes,

> Rose at half past 7 o'clock. Wrote a French lesson. Read. Went to my French Master's, took a French lesson. Busy in the counting house. Went up to dress for Synagogue, being the evening of the fast for our sins. Went to Synagogue, prayed there till 10 o'clock. Went to Enthoven's. Played a game of chess with Keyser, won it. Went to the Spanish Synagogue and also to the Great Dutch Synagogue. Retired to rest at quarter to 12 o'clock.[69]

Lyon recalls his activities on the evening of Yom Kippur. At sundown observers of this holy day fast in atonement and resume eating at sundown the following day. The period between sundowns is typically spent in prayer. Although Yom Kippur is observed variously around the globe, chess playing marks a bold departure from common practice. Indeed, in some circles such activities would raise eyebrows, given that Yom Kippur is considered by many to be the holiest day in the Jewish calendar. Lyon not only admits to playing chess on Yom Kippur, but cheekily boasts to having won the game. This moment, in fact, seems both noteworthy and unexpected. For while numerous entries in the diary depict Lyon's observance of Jewish religious rituals, they simultaneously chart religious expression in transformation, as acts that bridge rather than separate his secular and religious life.

Missing from Lyon's diary entry is a detailed description of his experience of prayer in the synagogue. What would he have seen or heard in religious services during the high holy days? Whom would he have met on the walk to synagogue? The movie for this entry addresses such absences by recalling the ways that archival silences derive as much from what's been lost as from the idiosyncratic choices writers make about what to include in their work. In the movie depicting Lyon's experience of prayer, I've integrated moving images and music. My goal was to find a way to present nineteenth-century synagogues as bustling places infused with talking, music, and prayer rather than the empty buildings suggested by old photographs of these spaces. The movie further dramatizes the diary by the selection of Max Bruch's composition for cello, *Kol Nidre,* named after the prayer by the same name recited at the beginning of the evening service on Yom Kippur. Bruch, who was not Jewish, completed the composition in 1880, long after the 1823 diary entry. Yet Bruch included a section in the piece that draws from Isaac Nathan's arrangement of "O Weep for Those That Wept on Babel's Stream," an adaptation of Byron's poem published in *Hebrew Melodies* (1815).[70] The composition's place in the movie positions the diary as anticipatory of a future unknown to Lyon (Bruch's composition) while including a detail reminiscent of the Lyon family's friend—Isaac Nathan, Solomon Lyon's student who also set Emma Lyon's poetry to music. The inclusion of Bruch's cello piece in a movie about A. S. Lyon's experiences observing Yom Kippur recalls Lyon's London social circle, and the blending of poetry and music in his lifetime. A. S. Lyon remained friendly with Nathan and his relatives during the period he lived in London. In one diary entry I transformed into a movie, Lyon describes the experience of attending Miss Nathan's and Mr. Braham's wedding. In speculating about the experience of prayer, I've situated the movie at a crossroads between events that precede and extend beyond it.

Maps never operate as objective statements of fact. They offer a perspective or facilitate articulation of an argument or agenda. Similarly, I created the soundscapes map on the Lyon Archive as a kind of deep map, or what David J. Bodenhamer, John Corrigan, and Trevor M. Harris describe as a map that includes "the discursive and ideological dimensions of place, [as well as] the dreams, hopes, and fears of residents." They add that deep maps also have the ability to reveal "the ties that places have with each other" and to reflect "networks that span scales and range from the local to the global."[71] In depicting Lyon's experience of place, I sought ways of imagining and signaling his unstated affective responses or speculating on what he saw but never recorded in the diary. Indeed, Lyon doesn't simply describe his movement from point A to B in the diary; he depicts strings of destinations, forging connections among places along the way. I've wondered about his dreams, hopes, and fears expressed on days when he visits significant sites, and about moments of pause that punctuate his travels or reflect thoughts carried from one place to the next. The map and movies are designed to use digital tools to reflect dynamic and relational meanings of place while registering Lyon's accumulated experiences or progressive states of mind. Thus, the map does not attempt to fix the East End by constructing it as a static place. Rather, it was created to signal the ever-changeable contexts Lyon encountered on his walks, defined as much by architecture and landscape as by his mindset that shifted as he traversed urban spaces.

Cut off from database searches, card catalogues, and finding aids—tools found in physical archives—the digital objects housed in the Lyon Archive have been created with a desire to connect the past with the future. The family archive is not entirely unlike the digital archive and the cemetery archive in its endless exposure of silences and gaps or its attention to lost objects. Hints of utterances and silences show how print and media cultures forge and reflect connecting threads among people and places. The Jamaican cemetery where Lyon is buried extends that work by connecting Atlantic kinships and economic affiliations with epitaphs and grave markers. Just as the soundscapes map illuminates the writer's developing vision, the graves in the cemetery where he is buried offer a similar story about his place within a community in transition.[72]

Voices in the Cemetery Archive

Our culture has trained us to think of cemeteries as spaces for the dead, as morbid sites of ghosts and hauntings. Buffy the Vampire Slayer does her best work in moony cemeteries. Silly, we may think, but such dominant cultural narratives try to define the cemetery's rows of dead bodies as a sign of its abjection, or what Julia Kristeva describes as that which "disturbs identity" and stands as an emblem of the "in-between, the ambiguous, the composite."[73] I suggest that we might instead read cemeteries as an archive of memory acts whose function is both to memorialize the dead and to address future audiences. Derrida explains in *Archive Fever,* "The question of the archive is not . . . a question of the past. . . . It is a question of the future, the question of the future itself, the question of a response, of a responsibility for tomorrow. The archive: if we want to know what that will have meant, we will only know in times to come."[74] Derrida draws our attention to the perspective of archive creators who imagine future readers as their audience. They create archives and finding aids with an eye toward those who will someday arrive to study the past. Alexandre Joseph Lindo's Jamaican epitaph makes this clear: "And far away thy memory shall be blessed, By children of the children of thy seed."[75]

Derrida recalls some of the reasons why we cannot read archives as empty boxes filled mindlessly by archivists or stories stashed in neutral repositories. Archives are crafted, created platforms that mediate relationships between the past and future. They enable and intervene in cultural continuity. And they serve as platform for both exchange and erasure. When the archive is a cemetery, the platform expresses itself through its display of headstones, epitaphs, and memory rituals performed by audiences and readers. In addition to connecting people from different time periods, however, cemeteries also sometimes reflect ties across disparate geographical spaces. Adam Mendelson observes that in the 1840s the "twin revolutions in printing and transportation tied the dispersed outposts of English-speaking Jewry into a transnational intellectual and cultural community."[76] As we'll see in the following discussion, cemetery archives facilitate both spatial and temporal communal connections in the way Mendelsohn suggests. It's in the cemeteries and their archive of epitaphs where we find evidence of ethnographic print and literary objects that capture a world otherwise unrecorded, a Jewish world in Jamaica anxious about the continuation of Judaism and interested in aligning Jewish memorial writing with Protestant tropes of grief.

As the nineteenth century marched forward, memorial culture shifted in response to literary writing about death. Richard Etlin explains that during the late eighteenth century, a period marked by the rising popularity of the picturesque landscape, "the tomb entered the garden."[77] In a direct move away from the grim horrors of gothic representations of churchyards or public burial grounds visited by body snatchers, the early nineteenth century began to see burial space as one better dressed with flowers, columns, and ornate fountains. James Stevens Curl adds that Solomon Gessner, the Swiss writer and artist, had an enormous influence on the development of English funerary art:

> In Gessner's world the tomb in the garden was a place where the living could weep moderate tears, recall the dead to mind, reflect, remember, and keep the departed 'alive' in some way in thought and spirit. Gessner's *Idylls* have many references to graves in beautiful landscapes, surrounded with honeysuckle, willows, and creeping ivies, where the living could pour libations and remember their dead in a way that almost suggested their continuing presence. The Gessnerian tomb in the Arcadian landscape therefore stood as an evocative and potent marker between two worlds [. . .] where the living could derive inspiration, happiness, moral uplift, and tender feelings from visits.[78]

Headstone design and epitaph writing in historic Jamaican cemeteries suggest that Jamaican Jews were eager to participate in this movement. Moreover, headstones from the mid-nineteenth century were often used as a platform for complicating their identification of homelands. Moses Abendana's grave states, "Sacred to the Memory of The Rev Moses Abendana of *London.*" Henry Solomon Samuel's epitaph states, "Sacred to the Memory of Henry Solomon Samuel, *Born in England.*" And an epitaph for Solomon Charles Ansell states, "In loving memory of Solomon Charles, eldest son of the late Moss and Mary Ansell *of London England,* who departed this life April 17th, 1891–5661" (emphasis added). This last example not only situates the dead in England, but also blends Christian and Jewish calendars. Many Jamaican Jewish graves preserve similar evidence of a complex sense of belonging or blended religious traditions. Collectively, these tombstones document concerns by and about a community in formation, one that drew from multiple cultural registers in a process of inventing distinct Jamaican Jewish memorial traditions.

Including the birthplace of the dead was not the only interesting spatial delineation on headstones. In many cases, the engraver's stamp was still visible (see fig. 10). This common feature of Orange Street Cemetery's grave markers functioned as both a form of marketing and a sign of communal ties between Jamaica and London. James Robertson explains, "It's likely that most of the island's pre-emancipation memorial stones were imports, and would have made good ballast on trans-Atlantic ships. Many of the post emancipation monuments in Orange Street Cemetery would have been made and engraved in London."[79] I've long wondered if the inclusion of addresses signaled the use of cemetery space as a genealogical site aimed at preserving the community's family records. And I've mused at the use of gravestones for marketing purposes, or the choice to include advertisements by the company responsible for the engraving.

Dates on the rows of headstones organized archival content chronologically, while differences among the various shapes and writings created unique identifying marks. No two markers were alike, and yet each was linked to the rest by people and place names. Engravings sometimes included Hebrew prayers or a blending of Hebrew and English languages, while garden-like monument designs, ornate calligraphy, and lavish poetry in English became increasingly common with each passing decade of the nineteenth century. Other epitaphs creatively integrated Jewish and

FIG. 10. A grave in Orange Street Cemetery, Kingston, Jamaica

non-Jewish death announcements. For example, one states, "Sacred to the memory of Jacob Jesurum Lindo, born in the Island of Saint Thomas, D.W.I. [Danish West Indies] on the 20th Sivan 5581, 20th June 1821, departed this life 25th Tebet 5646, corresponding with 1st January 1886." This particular stone encodes translation assists, for it not only tells the reader that the Hebrew dates correspond to secular dates—in case that's unclear—but also includes both a Hebrew prayer and a transliteration of that prayer in English. Hence, Hebrew readers and nonreaders alike are able to recite the prayer aloud. Such interpretive aids, which appear on many of the grave markers, hint at a concern about the legibility of the epitaphs for future audiences. In their anticipation of our arrival, epitaph writers of the past not only preserved evidence of death traditions in flux but also shared signs of their anxiety about the future of Judaism.

While literary scholarship has embraced interdisciplinarity as a concept and common practice, fieldwork has, until recently, mostly remained the purview of social scientists.[80] Shalini Puri has detailed some of the challenges literary scholars face when they move into this mode of knowledge creation and analysis. Puri notes that fieldwork is not just a different mode of investigation than traditional literary research, but is a practice of study that creates access to distinct materials for study. In her own work, she adds, "I turned to a kind of improvised fieldwork, one that offers an important route to knowledge and expression unavailable in print; to disallowed or delegitimized knowledges; to localized or vernacular rather than globalized knowledge and memory; to transient expressions of popular opinion; and to exploration of controversial issues about which people were not willing to speak publicly."[81] Print records for Lyon's community are scarce. Burial spaces are therefore among the very few extant historical materials I was able to consult in my research. My challenge was to find a way to read the artifacts in the cemetery and their spatial arrangement as a form of local and vernacular culture. I'd participated in the cemetery inventory for many years before learning about A. S. Lyon's diaries. However, reading the diaries in light of my experiences in Jamaica helped me to interpret the cemetery's encoding of cultural references that tied Jamaican Jewish culture and Atlantic memorial rituals and poetic traditions. In particular, each row of stones in the cemetery archive bore the mark of their origins in London and their inscriptions by East End Hebrew engravers.

My fieldwork introduced me to many Jamaican cemeteries with a broad range of epitaphs and translation help. Gradually I learned that many of the headstones were designed to educate cemetery visitors about how to translate Hebrew dates or how to recite Hebrew prayers. At the same time, graves from this era frequently turned to Christian culture for aesthetic inspiration. Not only did this community design monument stones in keeping with Christian garden cemeteries, but they composed epitaphs that mimicked those found in Christian memorial poetry. David Brandon's grave in Orange Street Cemetery draws from the following poem written by Henry Ware Jr. (1794–1843)—a Unitarian theologian and member of the faculty of the Harvard Divinity School. Ware's poem reads:

> Kneel down at the couch of departing faith,
> And hear the last words the believer saith.
> He has bidden adieu to his earthly friends;
> There is peace in his eye that upward bends;
> There is peace in his calm, confiding air;
> For his last thoughts are God's, his last words prayer.[82]

The poem appeared in American poetry anthologies from 1827 through 1877. Most of the anthologies had explicitly Christian titles, including *The Church Register Devoted to the Interests of Religion in the Protestant Episcopal Church* (1827) and *Hymns for the Christian Church and Home* (1840). A few had less obviously Christian titles, such as *The Monthly Traveller, or Spirit of the Periodical Press* (1830); *New-York Visitor and Parlour Companion* (1840); and *A New Library of Poetry and Song* (1877). Brandon's family produced this epitaph by removing the first line of Henry Ware's poem, "kneeling down at the couch of departing faith," presumably because kneeling is a practice Judaism associates with idol worship. Stripping the poem of its Christian connections, Brandon's mourners transformed Christian expressions of loss into Jewish memorials. A section of his epitaph states,

> Hear the last words the believer saith.
> He has bidden adieu to his earthly friends;
> There is peace in his eye that upward bends;
> There is peace in his calm, confiding air;
> For his last thoughts are God's, his last words prayer
> [in Hebrew and translated as]
> May the Spirit of God Lead him into Paradise

The passage opens with a powerful homonym—hear/here—and a concluding emphasis on spoken prayer, while the invitation to listen is a call to action, to follow the response of the dead through prayer. Like many nineteenth-century epitaphs, the celebration of accomplishments is followed by mention of a sacred life to honor and inspire readers. This one is unusual, however, in that it unites a Christian death prayer with an untranslated, un-transliterated Hebrew prayer—"May the spirit of God Lead him into Paradise." Any questions about the religious identification of the dead are clarified by the inclusion of the concluding Hebrew inscription.

Middle-class graves in America and England in this period frequently aspired to be places of learning. As Mark Taylor has noted of the rural cemetery movement originating in 1831 in Cambridge, Massachusetts, the living placed lessons on gravestones in an effort "to educate survivors in the art of living rather than the art of dying. The dead are remembered so that we might live better lives."[83] Yet in addition to listing Brandon's accomplishments, the monument also acknowledges his family's pain of loss. And while the epitaph never mentions heaven, the poem suggests that Brandon's departure is a soft exit from his earthly life. For the speaker implies that the dead man placed under the tombstone has peace in his bending eye and confiding air *because* his last words were prayer—the concluding Hebrew prayer. The Christian heaven has been excised by the epitaph adaptation, but the power of prayer remains one of the chief edifying features of the memorial. And the two forms of prayer—Christian poem and Hebrew concluding prayer—are linked by the work of God. If Brandon's last thoughts in the poem are of God, the details of the Hebrew inscription ensures that they are not wasted, as God will lead him not to a Christian Heaven, but to a Jewish paradise.

Similarly, the epitaph of Sarah Lindo Lyon, A. S. Lyon's wife who died in 1908, adapts two popular poems united as one on her grave marker:

> A precious one from us has gone
> A voice we loved is stilled
> A place is vacant in our home
> Which never can be filled
> God in his glory has recalled
> The boon his love had given
> And though in peace she slumbers here
> Her soul has soared to Heaven[84]

The first stanza was published in the *Railroad Trainmen's Journal* in 1891, although this was possibly not the first appearance of the poem.[85] A version of the second stanza appeared in several periodicals including the *Happy Home and Parlor Magazine*, a Boston periodical edited by the Reverend A. R. Baker in 1857.[86] The periodical version of the poem included the final lines "And though the casket moulders here, / The gem is sparkling now in heaven," which the Lyon headstone adapts to "And though in peace she slumbers here / Her soul has soared to Heaven." In the Jewish version of the poem inscribed on Lyon's gravestone, Heaven is not a place, but the direction toward which her soul points. And despite the fact that the two stanzas of Lyon's epitaph come from different poems, the engraver has included quotation marks around the entire section of the epitaph, thereby blending them into a single poem.

While it's tempting to see Jewish cemetery rituals as a sign of muted expressions of Jewish culture in a process of becoming secular or assimilating to American or Jamaican culture, I suggest that these texts and their expressions of anxiety about the future of Judaism should be read as signs of Jamaican Jewish diasporic identity performed between and through multiple Atlantic cultures, including Protestant literary culture. It's difficult to know the immediate sources of these poetry adaptations, since the originals were so broadly reprinted in the American periodical press. However, their repeated use in Jewish cemeteries suggests that Jamaican Jewish communities were avid readers of American Protestant poems and periodicals. Their reception of these works has not—to my knowledge—been recorded. But the recycling and adapting of Protestant death poetry on Jewish headstones signals their appeal to Jamaican Jewish readers and a sustained interest in extending that appeal to future cemetery visitors.

In their discussion of Jewish cultures in the diaspora, Jonathan Boyarin and Daniel Boyarin helpfully note, "This is the paradoxical power of diaspora. On the one hand, everything that defines us is compounded of all the questions of our ancestors. On the other hand, everything is permanently at risk. Thus contingency and genealogy are the two central components of diasporic consciousness."[87] The Jamaican cemetery archive preserves such signs of continuity and risk. While gravestones contain many sources of information about the lives of the dead, their place of birth, family histories, and accomplishments, the choice of poems, transliterations, and translations signal the community's knowledge of the kind of performances that take place in the cemetery. The mounds of crumbled stones unable to be read recall the archive's preservations of lost records and silenced perspectives. The archive of epitaphs speak to Atlantic world intellectual exchanges while also, perhaps paradoxically, expressing communal cohesion and continuity rooted in Jewish memorial traditions that drew from Protestant poetry.

Every stone in the cemetery archive toys with our desire to uncover, to identify a name and date, to find hope of a lost history preserved by dust-covered words on crumbling stones. As I stood at the foot of each grave alongside volunteers, ruminating on the journey the stones took from London to Kingston, I was struck by the ways the built environment and culture of print integrated multiple histories and aesthetic forms. Many of the graves were cracked fragments, scattered on the ground amid rocks and trash. In the long hours spent puzzling the headstones back together, I found numerous stone fragments that began their life in the East End, in the very streets where Lyon walked before coming to Jamaica. However, our job as volunteers was not to lead us back to London, but to piece together shards of information and to carry those identities forward for future generations. In most cases, records of the dead were gone. The only evidence of their lives was on the headstones. Our failure to assemble the pieces of broken stone meant that not only could the grave *not* be read, but the name and identifying details of the person marked by that headstone would be lost forever.

My encounter with these objects was shaped by the people and cultures tied to the cemetery—people who influenced my record of thought and the range of my thinking. This form of literary-studies fieldwork was new to me, and notably different from every other form of archival research I'd undertaken in my search for Polack. My cemetery work took place a great distance from my desk and library. My hands were covered in dirt as I kept notes on a clipboard with loose pieces of paper—tools seldom used in my research at home. I misplaced my pencil frequently as my attention shifted between listening, searching for broken stones, and writing. I used my hands not to type on a computer, but to dig in the dirt. When I found a stone, I worked flour onto its incisions—the shallow, cracked trenches visibly transformed by the pressed white dust. This was an old historic preservation trick that allowed the writing to come clear without damaging the stones. Rain washes away the flour, unless goats grazing in the cemetery get there first. Individual stories emerged one letter at a time. And through these activities I came to understand fieldwork as less an activity than a mode of inquiry made possible by the surrounding artifacts, landscapes, animals, and voices. Over the course of each day, my attention moved from the objects before me to those that remained buried but announced themselves through suggestive mounds pushing against the rubble. White paper pages on my clipboard darkened as the hours passed, absorbing stains from pencil lead, dirt, flour, and bug spray. I kept reflections in a personal diary, just like A. S. Lyon, and hoped I'd be able to interpret my thoughts under the hotel's dull lighting later in the evening.

Even as I struggled to connect fragments, I was aware that my impressions and integration of stories was imprecise. I was an outsider in Jamaica. And just like nineteenth-century wanderers who made their way into the East End, I would always be a stranger in the cemetery archive. Still I continued the work of assembling stones, translating fragments of text, and transcribing memories, as I wrestled with my hope of finding names, stories, poetry, and signs left by the living so that we could learn from their memories of the dead. My fieldwork experiences in Jamaican cemeteries shaped my understanding of the island and its people. I held hands with children as we steadied ourselves across rocky grave sites. I worked in a historic cemetery buried in a jungle and tangled up with hundreds of stray vines. I swung a machete to carve a path through thick green prickly brush in search of unrecorded names on headstones. And I witnessed Diane Lyon Wead make her way over mounds of debris to find the graves of her ancestors, lopsided, chipped, but intact—with names that matched those scattered throughout the diary pages tucked inside her suitcase.

A vernacular invention, nineteenth-century graves offer evidence of Atlantic writing traditions. A. S. Lyon's English epitaph echoes the spatial networks of his community in its recounting of a life lived in many places across time:

> Sacred to the Memory of
> Abraham Septimus Lyon
> Born Cambridge England
> 22 August 1804
> Died
> 10 October 1872
> May his soul be bound in the cradle of life everlasting.

A. S. Lyon's grave is far less ornate than others in the Elletson Road Cemetery where he's buried. But noteworthy in its simplicity is the inclusion of the place of his birth in Cambridge that renders his Kingston identity eternally foreign. And mention of the "cradle of life everlasting" expresses a hope for a permanent home elsewhere. It's difficult to see these choices outside of the diary passages describing his uneasiness about leaving England and his desire to find and make a home for himself in London.

The practice of creating a cemetery inventory entails a form of archival work aimed at individuating the dead through the reconstruction and recordings of memorial objects, including those whose lives are frequently absent from public records offices or library archives. On several occasions we worked with local volunteers. We exchanged stories with local volunteers, religious leaders, educators, and descendants of the people buried in the graves. When our work concluded, we walked away with our notebooks and cameras, leaving the graves to nature and other fates. We recovered nothing. But through our work we've created and shared stories about the material conditions of the cemetery at the moment when we arrived. In some cases, we studied headstone fragments for an hour or more, searching for a missing word or year with hopes that we might be able to find or decipher identifying information. We experienced tremendous relief and joy whenever we found chunks of stone that helped us decode fragmented names of the dead or their birth and death dates. And we felt an equal sense of loss when the pieces failed to surface. We like to think that our paper records will become more permanent than the tilting and fractured grave markers. Before leaving the cemetery, we gathered in a circle of remembrance to say Kaddish, a Jewish prayer for the dead, surrounded by hazy mountains and local observers, as we watched the goats lick flour off the stones.

Antoinette Burton has urged us to "talk frankly and openly about the archives and the encounters that we as scholars . . . have with them." She explains, "All archives come into being in and as history as a result of specific political, cultural, and socioeconomic pressures—pressures which leave traces."[88] One of our biggest challenges is to account for those pressures, or to find a way to recognize or hear them. Facing a sea of lopsided stones didn't always offer clues about the cultural and political forces that shaped their form and content. And searching for evidence of spatial networks from names and locations inscribed on headstones was not always possible given that so many stones were destroyed beyond recognition. During the period I worked in the cemetery, I focused on the confusion, the subtle traces of Jamaican-London ties that would help me to understand Polack and the appearance of *Fiction without Romance* amid a broader world of East End writers and Jamaican readers and subscribers. It was in the cemetery, in fact, where I began to understand the tapestry that bound Polack to her community in Jamaica.

A. S. Lyon's diary and the cemetery archive illuminated one of the most understated facts about the nineteenth-century East End—its identity as a cosmopolitan space with literary and print connections to Atlantic world communities. East Enders may have struggled economically, and many may not have had access to formal education. Yet they were still readers and participants in global print culture. Their East End was not confined by ghetto walls. It was formed through the crossing of borders and opportunities for cultural exchange in music, prayer rituals, epitaph writing, and literature. Ultimately, the work of piecing together stone fragments preserved evidence of migrations, a longing for lost lands among writers in the diaspora, and the creation of communal ties that reached across oceans. The element of surprise—of learning about diaries previously unknown to me—served as a reminder of what can happen when we make ourselves open to discovery; when archive encounters make room for acts of speculation and wonder, for listening and speaking. Rather than reach back, the digital archive and the cemetery archive connect old and new voices as they anticipate future encounters with the past.

Studying the names on Polack's subscription list revealed glimpses of details about the people who supported her work. I could begin to construct their geographical relations and to sketch contexts that illuminated the significance of the gender or geographical distribution of subscribers. But in the end, the names on the list revealed little about the thoughts or identities of the subscribers. In contrast, reading A. S. Lyon's diary entries—the private thoughts of a single subscriber—touched on a range of emotions, reactions to events, and personal struggles. Indeed, Lyon's elaborations on what he read or how he felt about a play recall what has been lost in the absent Maria Polack archive. His entries evoke the missing story of how Polack came to see herself as an individual with a past and future, as a writer responding to her community's emerging interests in secular literary culture. My good fortune in meeting Diane Lyon Wead and working with a family willing to share their private archive underscored the serendipitous nature of the search within and beyond the walls of archives.

4

An Archive of Lies

EVIDENCE AND THE JEWS' ORPHAN ASYLUM INVESTIGATIONS

THE 1841 census is one of the only public records to mention Maria Polack's name. From that single source we learn Polack's approximate age of fifty-five, her address on Mansell Street in the East End, and her profession as a "teacher of M"—an occupation the census taker declined to interpret. We also learn that Polack's husband, Lipman, was a tailor, and someone named Elizabeth, age twenty-five with the occupation "author," lived with them on Mansell Street. Such details invite speculation of all sorts. An aspirational narrative—totally unfettered by evidence—renders the Elizabeth Polack of the census record the same one known to have written five plays. An even more ambitious narrative makes her the daughter of Maria Polack. On days when I was struck by archive fever, I imagined mother and daughter writing together in a candle-lit room, an urban Jewish version of the Brontë sisters writing at their living-room table in Haworth. The Victorian historian James Picciotto offers a vague biographical theory about the family, noting that Ephraim Polack was "the father of Maria Polack, an authoress, and grandfather of Elizabeth Polack, also a writer."[1] Picciotto does not cite sources. We're left wondering if the Elizabeth he mentions is Maria Polack's daughter or niece. Polack was a common Jewish name, after all. In fact, even Maria Polack's maiden name was Polack. More recently, David Conway has claimed that Elizabeth Polack is Ephraim's niece and was a cousin of Sir Francis Palgrave, author of *The Golden Treasury* (1861). Once again, the origin of this information is unclear, making it impossible to know for sure if he's alluding to some other writer by that name.

Especially curious is the musical thread connecting members of this family and household. Ephraim is believed to have been a chorister of the Great Synagogue. A woman named Elizabeth Polack created musical works for the stage. It's unclear if this playwright is the same person as the woman named on the 1841 census record. Ephraim would have been dead by the time of the census, but his daughter, Maria Polack, carried on his interest in music in her novel. Indeed, I've long suspected that the reference to "teacher of M" signaled Polack's interest in music. When I began looking for evidence, I noted the emphasis in *Fiction without Romance* on theatre and music and overlapping debates about female education. In a discussion of Eliza's education, her uncle Desbro explains the following to her adopted parent, Mr. Howard:

> Be assured, Sir, the female mind is equally strong and capacious with our own; and when a woman is ignorant, it is the fault of man that she is so. It is a sort of vanity, or conscious superiority in our sex, that disdain to acknowledge an equal in the other. Many a brilliant imagination is cramped, and its finest ideas destroyed, for want of encouragement from those beings whom they are taught to love and look up to. And I firmly believe, that the frivolity, so often depreciated in women, would cease to exist, if they were properly encouraged in the pursuit of more rational amusements.[2]

An example of such amusements takes place during Desbro's visit to Mr. Zachariah's home. The narrator describes Desbro as "very much pleased by the rational and intelligent manner in which they [Zachariah's children] answered the several questions put to them." The narrator later adds, "[T]he two little girls amused their father's visitor, by a display of their 'musical talents'" whereupon they played "several beautifully arranged Hebrew melodies, some of which their brother accompanied with his voice, producing, as it were, so sacred a feeling, that Desbro felt himself completely at home."[3] As I noted in the last chapter, Byron provided the words to *Hebrew Melodies* (1815) while Isaac Nathan composed the musical score. According to David Conway, "The three most remarkable Anglo-Jewish musical careers of the late eighteenth and early nineteenth centuries—those of Michael Leoni (Myer Lyon), John Braham and Nathan—began firmly in the Synagogue" in London's East End.[4] Emma Lyon's poem "The Soldier's Farewell" was set to music by Nathan, one of her father's former students. And the poem was performed by the famous tenor Braham, whom Picciotto describes as having "experienced much kindness from Ephraim Polack."[5] Braham's name appears on Polack's subscription list and recurs throughout A. S. Lyon's diaries. These contexts reflect a culture of music education, mentorship, and performance within Polack's East End circle and across generations of her family and community.

Early in my search for information about Maria Polack, I struggled to determine the relationship between Maria Polack's interest in music and Elizabeth Polack's musical plays. Was Maria Polack the mother or aunt of Elizabeth Polack? And was the person living with Maria Polack in 1841—the one listed as "author" in the census record—the same person as Elizabeth Polack the playwright? Frustrated by dead ends, I made the decision to abandon musical questions and to focus instead on the other clue in Polack's census entry: the word "teacher." Eventually, as the conclusion to this chapter makes clear, my unexpected discovery of announcements in a local newspaper would illuminate some of these mysterious family connections. Prior to finding these clues, however, I turned to the subject of East End education. I reasoned that I might be able to learn about the contexts in which Polack taught by studying archival records from local charity schools. Despite my later revelations, the school thread was indeed a helpful guide in exposing East End efforts to redress social problems through educational initiatives.

I dove into school records preserved in the London Metropolitan archives. It was here, in these dusty volumes, as I recalled in the introductory chapter, where I located Maria Polack's name among the papers of the Jews' Free School. I learned that Polack was a writer of passages used for student recitations at fundraising dinners. Beyond this one lead I found nothing. After winding my way through numerous boxes of books, folders, and envelopes, I came to the reluctant conclusion that evidence of Polack's teaching probably didn't exist. I decided to change my approach by considering broader questions about charity schools and educational initiatives in the East End. I sought information about the kinds of students Polack might have taught and the classroom resources available to those working in charity schools. I wondered what her students were educated *for?* What kinds of subjects prepared working-class Anglo-Jewish children, many the children of immigrants, for religious or civic life in England?

Behind these questions lurked the larger problem of finding and reading archival materials. Folders and filing cabinets hadn't been structured in ways that addressed my questions. Hence many of the record books were stashed in boxes, organized not by chronology but by efficiencies of size. Smaller books sat atop larger books from earlier generations because they allowed more material to fit inside shared preservation boxes. As I read across the boundaries of box labels and book covers, I searched for patterns of thought and organizational systems. I scrutinized educational debates from one set of secretary's notes to the next. I sometimes read three or four meetings ahead to see how the issues played out or where disagreements cropped up.

One day I stumbled upon a reference to investigations at the Jews' Orphan Asylum, a charity orphanage and school located in Polack's neighborhood. The reference mentioned a curious collection of writing from the middle decades of the century about three investigations—in 1853, 1856, and 1857—relating to the abuse of the students. The Jews' Orphan Asylum was located in the shadow of Polack's home (fig. 11). She died in 1849, before the investigations, but as a local educator and neighbor she likely knew about the school and its stories of abuse. She might even have offered classes in "M" to student witnesses. I therefore made my way to the University of Southampton's Hartley Library, which houses archival materials relating to all three investigations at the Jews' Orphan Asylum. In addition to testimony from students, school reports, and letters from community members, the archive includes a bold personal testimony from the newly appointed headmaster, Myer Davis (1830–1912), who later became a scholar of medieval history. His memoir, which remains unpublished, is one of the few autobiographical texts written by an East Ender in this period. In the archive I found references to people known to Polack, names that appeared on the subscription list of *Fiction without Romance.* I was never able to prove whether she taught at the school, but the archive's holdings provided ample and illuminating contexts for Polack's career as an East End educator and author.

All three investigations in the 1850s were undertaken with the explicit purpose of rooting out child abuse. But reactions to the second investigation of 1856 got in the way of this goal. The concluding report made three recommendations: first, the school's headmaster, Myer Davis, should be "superseded in his duties"; second, the superintendents of the asylum, Mr. and Mrs. Franklin, should be placed on probation; and third, a few difficult children should be expelled.[6] A torrent of criticism from the community in response to these recommendations led leaders to initiate a third investigation in 1857. While extant records are incomplete, it's still possible to see that nearly every witness in the second and third investigations accuses others of lying. What's been preserved in the archive, then, are *not* records of events or actions, but evidence of what individuals *claim* to have happened as a corrective to "false" statements made by other witnesses. While we may be used to thinking of archives as repositories of truth-telling primary source material, the Jews' Orphan Asylum archive troubles that characterization, reminding us that as the

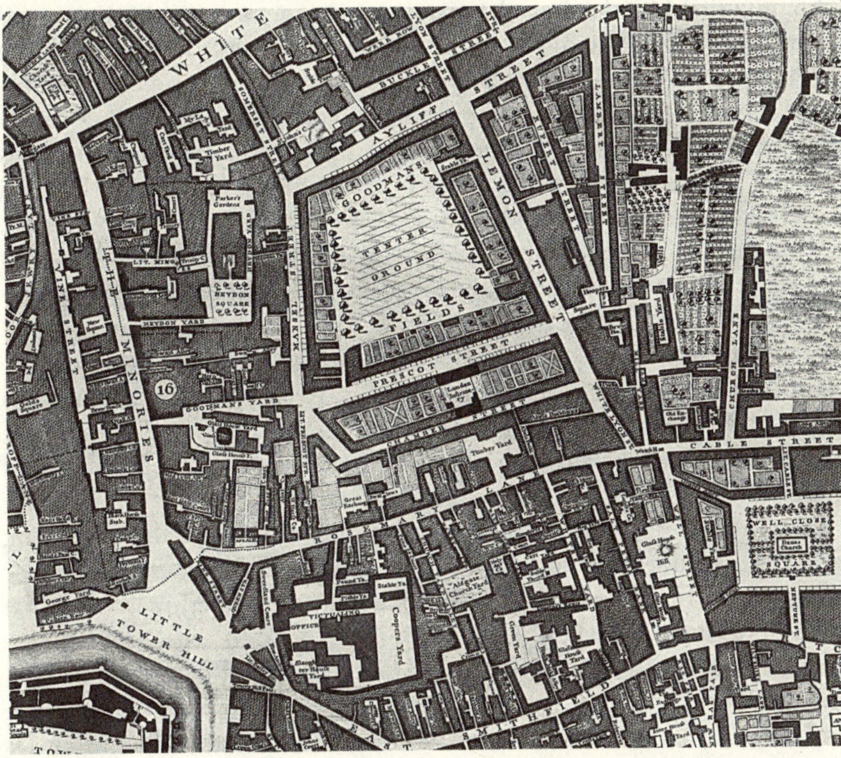

FIG. 11. Map of the East End. The Jews' Orphan Asylum was situated on Tenter Ground, in the center of the above map. Maria Polack lived on Mansell Street in 1819 and in 1841, located on the western edge of Tenter Ground. By the year of her death in 1849, Polack had moved to 84 Lemon Street, on the eastern edge of Tenter Ground. For better orientation, note that the northeast corner of the Tower of London is visible on the bottom left of this map. *A Plan of the Cities of London and Westminster, and Borough of Southwark; with the Contiguous Buildings; from an Actual Survey, Taken by John Rocque, Land-Surveyor, and Engraved by John Pine* (London: John Pine & John Tinney, 1746). (Wikimedia/Library of Congress, Geography and Map Division, G5754.L7 1746.R6)

eponymous hero of the television show *House* puts it, "everybody lies."[7] In this case, lies seem to have emerged not just from those who sought to deceive the investigators, but by those who attempted to keep truths hidden. As I suggest in the following discussion, in these lies we find evidence of truth in the witnesses' offhand statements of reason, in their expressions of vulnerability, and from narrative tactics that structure their lies.

The nature of the accusations and extent of the violence against children make this archive unsettling on a number of fronts. A collection of handwritten confessions, letters, memoirs, memos, justifications, and summary reports initially inspired me to read every trace of evidence with my twenty-first-century knowledge of child abuse and crime detection. I moved through the pages slowly and copiously, surveilling details from an unfamiliar world. Papers summarizing the investigators' findings seemed most compelling of all both because they have the last word and because of their privileged identity as *saved documents.* For all we know, their conclusions may be accurate. But the fact that they've been saved by school archivists not only has the power to diminish or block other narratives, particularly those that were not saved, but gives the impression that the saved records—above all the rest—exist because they were more worthy of being saved. The fact that the archive is missing pages muddled my decoding efforts. Moreover, repeated signs of the way the investigation was tainted by its own frightening methods of interrogation raised unsettling questions rather than answers.

Faced by these interpretive challenges, I began my work by translating and transcribing each document, converting Hebrew dates into secular dates. From there I assigned each document a number, reasoning that bread crumbs would help me find my way back to cross-check pages and statements. In this newly transcribed state, I still had trouble keeping track of the names. I added explanatory notes in the margins, such as "This is the child with a sister who has a different last name" or "Is this the same child mentioned in document 22 with the name spelled differently?" My inability to see faces or learn backstories confused me as I made my way through mounds of pages containing conflicting accounts and accusations of lies. At one point I tried organizing testimony into columns titled "true" and "false" but quickly abandoned this method when I realized I had no way of knowing the difference. This led me to wonder, If I can't determine which sources are credible, what am I looking for? And what can I learn from such an archive? Initially I considered the similarities between evidence in the archive and fictional narratives in novels like *Dracula* or *The Moonstone*—texts with multiple or unreliable narrators. I learned quickly that I needed help from a narrator or editor to slow the pacing of plot or to introduce personality traits that differentiated characters. I struggled to understand how authority worked in a world where orphans had no advocates, where corporal punishment was legal and commonplace in the classroom, and where adults manipulated children by giving them black eyes. What was justice in such a world?

In her reading of sixteenth-century pardon tales, Natalie Zemon Davis approaches a similar set of problems by focusing on the fictional qualities of archival records, or as she puts it, evidence of the way each witness would "shape the events of a crime into a story."[8] Reading the archive as fictional, Davis explains, entails focusing on the writers' "forming, shaping, and molding elements: the crafting of a narrative."[9] By adding falsity or embellishing the truth, written archival records "might well bring verisimilitude or a moral truth" or they might show evidence of "what they thought a good story was, how they accounted for motive, and how through narrative they made sense of the unexpected and built coherence into immediate experience."[10] Davis's approach worked for some parts of the testimony, leading me to an increasing awareness of the ways in which the statements reflected evidence of motive, justice, ethics, and human-created narratives. Case by case, testimony yanked individual characters out from the cacophony of voices. I read their statements as literary evidence of their powers of persuasion and fears spoken through metaphor. And I was able to identify material evidence of violence and manipulation through the written materials left behind. Although the archive is incomplete and fractured, I came to understand that the records nevertheless preserved evidence of the rhetorical flourishes and signs of vulnerabilities leaking out of otherwise guarded narratives.

My work on this archive also leans on Arlette Farge's helpful observation that "even if the discourse [in the archive] is muddled, mixing lies and the truth, hatred and cunning, submission and defiance, it does not diminish the 'truth' that it carries. The archives do not necessarily tell the truth, but, as Michel Foucault would say, they tell *of* the truth. Namely, the unique way in which they expose the mode of speech of an individual, wedged between the relationships of power and herself, relationships to which she is subjected, and that she actuates by expressing verbally."[11] Indeed, the Jews' Orphan Asylum archive operates as a stage upon which insecurity, gossip, public outcry, secrets, and eavesdroppers produced testimony that animated narrators through their stated desires for justice and acts of self-silencing. The voices from the archive exposed the logic behind defensive poses or acts of subterfuge. It was in these fleeting withholding acts where I was able to hear flickers of truth propelling their stories.

The following discussion focuses on evidence in the Jews' Orphan Asylum archive produced by four people: a student, Myer Levy, who testified against Mr. and Mrs. Franklin, schoolteachers at the asylum; a second student, Simon Phillips, who offered inconsistent evidence; P. Abrahams, the older sister of Simon Phillips who submitted an unsolicited letter containing damning evidence against the Franklins; and Myer Davis, the headmaster of the institution, whose memoir was written in defense of his impending character assassination. While discussions in the previous two chapters explored the use of digital or physical archives to process or contextualize signs of East End literary culture, in this chapter I turn to a more conventional physical archive made of scraps of evidence from a crime scene.[12] I approach these materials by teasing out traces of self-silencing, or the story behind or under the one recorded in the official record, what Nancy K. Miller calls the "understory" as opposed to the backstory.[13] I'm interested in what these speech and silencing acts convey about life in an East End charity school in the neighborhood where Polack lived and worked. I have no reason to believe she taught at this school, but details about the children and their culture of learning illuminate features of her intellectual and professional world. The evidence I discuss below underscores the challenge of hearing voices against and through the authority of the investigation that prompts and frames them. I do not conclude that the Jews' Orphan Asylum archive lies. My point, rather, is that in preserving incomplete and partial records, the testimony in this archive is incapable of providing absolute truth. I therefore offer a model of reading aimed at registering the lived contexts that give rise to archival fictions, including those articulated by so-called liars.

Jewish Education

The Jews' Orphan Asylum was one of many East End charity schools formed in the wake of Patrick Colquhoun's 1795 exposé of London street crime, *Treatise on the Police of the Metropolis.* Picciotto describes Colquhoun as "an able and philanthropic magistrate, who for many years presided at the Westminster Police Office."[14] It was a report that included "matters of essentially Jewish interest." In a later edition of the work, Picciotto adds, "Mr. Colquhoun drew so severe a picture of the malpractices habitually committed by some of the foreign Jewish poor, and painted their sufferings and their general conduct in such gloomy colours, as to attract the attention of some of the most enlightened members of the Askenazim" [*sic*].[15] Colquhoun detailed what he perceived to be the forces of violence wreaking havoc throughout the city:

> A Class of Cheats of the Society of Jews, who are to be found in every street, lane and alley in and near the Metropolis, under the pretense of purchasing old clothes, and metals of different sorts; Their chief business

> really is to prowl about the houses and stables of men of rank and fortune, for the purpose of holding out temptations to the servants to pilfer and steal small articles, not likely to be missed, which these Jews purchase at about one third of the real value.—It is supposed that upwards of fifteen hundred of these depraved people are employed in diurnal journeys of this kind; by which, through the medium of bad money, and other fraudulent dealings, many of them acquire property, and then set up shops and become Receivers of stolen Goods.[16]

The "depraved people" identified in this passage were the very same living in Polack's community. The problem, Colquhoun surmises, was rooted in Jewish community leaders' willingness to allow children to be "[e]ducated in idleness from their earliest infancy" and to "acquire every debauched and vicious principle which can fit them for the most complicated arts of fraud and deception; to which they seldom fail to add the crime of perjury, whenever it can be of use, in shielding themselves or their associates from the punishment of the law."[17]

Evidence of interest in Jewish education in London dates as far back as 1664, but it was in the late eighteenth century when discussions turned to educating the Jewish poor.[18] Colquhoun's report energized efforts to address poverty and education. The Jewish community worried about the impact of constructing "the Society of Jews" as a universally "depraved people."[19] In a letter dated March 24, 1801, communal leader Joshua Van Oven noted, "The constrained and deplorable state of these poor gives ground for the continuance of the prejudice against them."[20] It was their failure to address Jewish poverty, Van Oven reasoned, that had the unwanted effect of bolstering negative stereotypes. John Marriott recalls that Colquhoun's *Treatise* "went through four editions in two years." Readers were shocked to witness the degree and forms of poverty described on its pages.[21] Marriott adds that Colquhoun wasn't just noting a social problem; he was constructing urban poverty in "strikingly novel ways. Whereas previously the London poor had been seen as a motley collection of underworld characters, classified according to types of fraud and trick used to dupe the bourgeois pedestrian or householder, Colquhoun defined them as an endemic and predatory body, organized in confederates, and operating to defend what they considered customary rights of access to moveable property."[22] Under the leadership of Van Oven, London's wealthier Jewish leaders responded by developing new schools and curricula. Despite the increase of educational opportunities for Jewish children, narratives of East End deviance and crime persisted, as chapter 1 of this study explained. And as the Jews' Orphan Asylum archive attests, apparently schools didn't always succeed in addressing the problem of juvenile crime.

To make matters worse, Jewish East Enders grew concerned over the simultaneous rise of Christian Evangelical conversion efforts. Michael Ragussis notes that "missions to convert the Jews became the subject of public scandal in the opening decades of the nineteenth century [during which] . . . English national character and its reputation for tolerance were called into question."[23] He adds, "What had been throughout most of the eighteenth century a steady (if somewhat negligible) stream of literature on the conversion of the Jews and their restoration to Palestine became nothing short of a torrent in the 1790s. In the tumultuous events of the French Revolution and the Napoleonic Wars, millenarians saw the signs of the Second Coming, which, according to biblical prophecy, was to be preceded by the restoration of the Jews to Palestine and their conversion."[24] The East End experienced the effects of this trend, as conversion efforts intensified in the early decades and likely inspired writers like Polack to argue for respect for religious difference. In the end, as I later discovered in events covered in this chapter's final pages, even Polack's anti-conversionist bulwark would fall.

Polack's community grew anxious from the rising pressure. In the absence of alternate educational options, many Jewish families had no choice but to enroll their children in Christian charity schools where they received food and clothing in addition to lessons on Christian subjects. Gerry Black explains that "eventually the Ashkenazi community bestirred itself" in response. School would be a bulwark against Christian conversion efforts in the Jewish regions of the East End. The Jews' Free School curriculum was poised to help, given that they had already transformed in the late decades of the previous century, when educators moved "away from treating mastery of rabbinic texts as the only foundation of a Jewish education. Pride of place was given to more 'practical' and elementary subjects. English reading, writing and arithmetic were added to the curriculum, and the time devoted to Hebrew was reduced."[25] According to Todd Endelman, by the early nineteenth century "the prospect of losing children to the missionaries alarmed communal leaders and, in tandem with their interest in making the poor respectable, helped to loosen their philanthropic purse strings. That same fear galvanized the community to open the Jews' Hospital in 1807, the Jews' Free School in 1817, and the Jews' Infant School in 1841."[26]

Additional East End Jewish charity schools emerged in subsequent years to accommodate a growing population of the Jewish poor and the persistent threat of conversion. This second generation of schools included the Jews' Orphan Asylum, founded in 1831. Edward S. Conway cites a local legend that explains its origin: "In 1830 there was a great cholera epidemic. A poor couple, Assenheim, died within a short time of each other and left 3 children. At that time there was no provision for such cases. A poor cucumber-seller, Abraham Green, whose sense of pity was aroused, left his stall and went round the streets and private houses and shops in the Jewish quarter to find help. Carrying two of the children in his arms and leading the third by the hand, he appealed for money until he had collected the nucleus of a maintenance fund. This was the origin of the Jews' Orphan Asylum."[27] In 1846, ten years before the first Jews' Orphan Asylum investigation, forty students were enrolled in the asylum.

The Jews' Orphan Asylum archive contains forty documents from all three investigations, some as long as ninety-two pages.[28] It wasn't until my third or fourth reading of the records that I began to understand how the missing pieces of evidence pointed to the archive's structure of cover-ups. In some cases, the archive was silent about its gaps, leaving me to wonder if the loss was intentional or the result of an accident. Even more curious at first—although this point would later become clear—I wondered why the 1857 investigation chose to ignore but deliberately save the body of testimony labeled "Appendix F" produced by the 1853 investigation. Why would they create an intentional hole in the story, but save remnants from that hole as disqualified testimony? They offered the following statement to account for this strange decision: "Your Education Committee thinks it but fair that as the statements (in appendix F) are so conflicting, every opportunity should be afforded to the Steward [Mr. Franklin] and Matron [Mrs. Franklin] for rebutting charges which if not brought under their notice and, as your Education Committee has good reason to hope, wholly disproved by them, would leave them open to suspicions which should never be allowed to rest on parties whose situations require so implicit a trust as must be confided to the directors of an Orphan Asylum."[29] The justification was baffling. The committee ignored testimony, they claimed, because it was internally conflicting, but then moved on to say that the Franklins should be allowed to defend themselves against the allegations found therein. If this evidence was not credible, why would the Franklins need to defend themselves against its accusations? And if the Franklins were guilty—that is, if the evidence reflects the truth—why would the investigators invite the Franklins to disprove the evidence in order to secure trust?

In my mind, appendix F constituted damning evidence against Mr. and Mrs. Franklin. In fact, one of its longer and most detailed records is a transcription of testimony by Myer Levy, a student from the Jews' Orphan Asylum. Children and servants from the institution were called into a room to testify in front of members of the committee. As the witnesses answered questions, a transcriber would record their responses. It's unclear if they ever saw their written transcripts or if they had opportunities to fact-check them for accuracy. Transcribers of the children's testimony had uneven writing abilities and levels of transparency. Some neglected to use punctuation or routinely misspelled names. Others inserted commentary or corrections. When, for example, Simon Phillips shared his recollections about his teachers, the transcriber altered his testimony, explaining, "Langworth he means[;] he is called Mr Byers by the boys."[30] These offhand moments in the transcriptions led me to conclude that they were not replicas of spoken testimony. The transcribers' identities do not appear in the documents. Moreover, these written documents were mediated not only by the potentially flawed technology of production—speaker and transcriber—but also by power disparities between the adults grilling children, often sternly, and the students they interrogated. To complicate matters further, allusions to eavesdroppers and gossips suggest that even if the doors were closed, witnesses were aware of the fact that they were speaking to hidden audiences lurking outside the interrogation room. It's impossible to know for sure how a witness's awareness of eavesdroppers might have affected their spoken testimony.

One thing that is clear, however, is that children were abused and neglected, and the community wanted to put an end to the violence. The children most vulnerable had no advocates or protectors. Any evidence they disclosed could be used against them in the wake of the investigation. Myer Davis, the headmaster, also lacked power, but of a different kind. At the point when he began his new job in 1856, the school was unable to control difficult students. Standard methods of school discipline in this period included corporal punishment. When questioned, Myer Davis notes that starting with his first day on the job, students met him with "grimaces, and then offensive expressions and Exhibitions—by offensive epithets calling me a liar."[31] Following such incidents, Davis forbade students from leaving the classroom during the first hour of instruction. Immediately following this new rule, several male students acted out by urinating on the floor of the classroom, an event described as especially horrible because it was "passed in the presence of the girls."[32] Student testimony affirms these accusations. While it's difficult to know the exact sequence of events, it's clear that the students were challenging their new teacher. He scrambled to assert his authority. Clearly Myer Davis felt unsupported by his colleagues, Mr. and Mrs. Franklin. The cast of characters he faced—though victims—ought not to be read as a variety of weeping, darling street urchins or virtuous teachers. Indeed, many of the students arrived having developed scrappy methods of self-preservation that included defiant provocations. Their survival at the school depended upon a toughness of spirit that might have struck Myer Davis as disrespectful noncompliance. The incomplete extant records document a battle waged between rigid, unsupported teachers and orphan children unprepared for claustrophobic Victorian classrooms.

Testimony of Myer Levy

Myer Levy's 1856 testimony sounds strikingly persuasive, perhaps *too* persuasive. He speaks with a confident ease that sets him against other student voices in the archive. We'll see evidence of this disparity in the following discussion of Simon Phillips's testimony. Before proceeding further, however, I offer a caution against believing a word of Myer Levy's story, not because I think he's lying but because he's a good storyteller whose account is impossible to verify. I suggest that we approach his narrative instead by listening for oblique statements, unspoken but implied admissions, or his own brand of subtle logic suffused within his narrative. It's important to note that Myer Levy's 1853 testimony was discounted in the last investigation of 1857 because it contradicted other evidence. As I read his account, I was struck by his keen understanding of the subtleties of power and his emotional intelligence. His testimony demonstrates his awareness of the psychological triggers that motivate children living in powerless situations. Our reaction of horror to his stories, I suggest, is a response to the effectiveness of Myer Levy's storytelling abilities. Indeed, his crafted expressions are the very place where Myer Levy challenges his audience's stereotypes of East End depravity; for in these passages he draws from an awareness of Jewish ethics that pushes against narratives of universal East End social deviance.

When asked to provide basic autobiographical details, Myer Levy states that he was a former inmate of the asylum. At the time he delivered his testimony in 1853 he was 14½ years old and lived at 8 Princes Place St. Georges where he worked as an apprentice to Mr. Solomons of

38 Great Prescott Street. He adds that he was 11½ when he "was taken into the orphan Asylum" and remained for 2½ years during the period when Mr. Franklin served as a schoolmaster.[33] Myer Levy moves on to address questions about a fellow schoolmate named Joel Lyons put under his care:

> I had to wash and dress and keep him clean in every respect[.] I liked him[;] he was obstinate but would do anything on talking to him. Two or three days after he came in he was observed to have a dirty head[.] Lice were found in the bed by Leah Joales [Joels][,] a girl about 14 who made the bed[;] she told me of it[.] I had already observed it and was trying to get rid of them without saying a word to any one because if a boy comes in with anything it is always thrown in his face afterwards[.] Leah Joel told me of it and that Mrs Franklin wanted to see if I was going to keep it secret and I then told the other boys[.] I should have been punished had I kept it secret[.] I was ordered to comb his head ½ an hour every morning with the small tooth comb[.] Leah Joel told me she got several cuts on the hand from Mrs Franklin for telling me[.] Mrs Franklin went up one day to examine the bed and she asked Leah Joel if there was anything the matter with the boys bed[.] Leah Joel sayd what boys bed? Mrs Franklin replied you know very well[.] Leah Joel said Joel Lyon has a dirty head[.] Mrs Franklin said "I wanted to find out if Myer Levy was deceitful[.]" [W]e were called deceitful if we kept anything secret and were bribed by having things left at dinner given to us or things taken from another boys share and put to ours[.] After this Joel Lyons was generally very wild in school and disturbed the classes and would sometimes be reported to Mr Franklin and go without his tea and be locked in the washhouse.[34]

Mr. and Mrs. Franklin taught classes and oversaw the dormitory, clothing, and medical care of the children. When Myer Davis arrived in 1856 to serve as headmaster of the institution, tensions arose instantly among the teachers. Myer Levy's statement details a great number of disturbing revelations about the authority figures in the school. He notes that children actively used deception to secure a sense of their own safety or that of other students. Myer Levy's observation that Joel Lyons was "obstinate but would do anything on talking to him" reveals his awareness of logical, rational individuals who fail to respond to the manipulations of teachers and caretakers. In reporting the event, Myer Levy characterizes children pegged as "difficult" to be capable of empathy and reason. And by acknowledging such points, Myer Levy shows his understanding of human motive. He deduces that children who are harassed and intimidated will become obstinate. Alternately, those treated with fairness are more likely to comply with instructions.

In the moment of delivering this narrative, Myer Levy's challenge is to persuade his adult audience that his former teachers, the Franklins, are corrupt and violent and that the students were mistreated. He was no longer living at the asylum at the time he delivered his statement. It stands to reason that he probably felt less intimidated than students offering testimony who were still under the care of the Franklins and Myer Davis. Myer Levy's narrative expresses confidence and a desire to establish credibility as a witness cognizant of human motivations. He suggests that lying was a strategy used in the asylum for self-preservation and inmate solidarity—the very traits his teachers might interpret as insubordination. Such an admission helps to contextualize every other accusation or admission of lying expressed under a punishing system of power.

Levy's testimony continues:

> Joel Lyons was several times reported to the Committee and once had a severe thrashing with a birch—a birch broom was sent for was put up stairs into a cistern of water until wanted that it should not rot some of the switches would be taken out tied together[.] Joel Lyons was flogged by Mr Franklin on his bare back held by Mrs Franklin and one of the boys I think Israel Cohen over Mr Franklin's knee he was quite sore afterwards and unable to sit[.] [M]arks left for weeks[.][35]

Clarifying questions followed this statement, leading Myer Levy to add, "Abraham Cohen was sent for the birch. He used to like to see the flogging. The little boys would be birched for wetting the bed. Abraham Cohen's brother was done so and Emanuel Cohen a little Dutch boy also."[36] This passage reveals one of the most unsettling tensions in the archive—the asylum's failure to distinguish between corporal punishment and child abuse. Given that this is a point that later haunts Myer Davis's testimony, it's curious that the investigation disqualified Myer Levy's statement. Concerns about physical violence as a mode of punishment pulse through this archive. One wonders if the sordid nature of the details exposed in this passage may have led investigators to disqualify it. Perhaps the depiction of the Franklins' severity matched with Abraham Cohen's sadistic pleasure in watching children being birched suggested a form of deviance too troubling for broad public consumption.

According to Myer Levy, violence was not the Franklins' only crime. In his final account of the death of a fellow student, Lipman Hyam, Myer

Levy narrates with a focus on the ethical implications of the Franklins' abandonment and neglect of the children. In the following statement Myer Levy creates a chronology of linked events while drawing from high-Victorian sentimentalism in his descriptions of orphan children gathered around a child's deathbed. The combination of logical and emotional rhetoric once again demonstrates both his narrative skills in capturing the attention of his audience and his emotional intelligence. We cannot know if he's telling the truth. But we can discern evidence of his thinking and reasoning powers in his choice to tell the story in this way. Myer Levy's description of Lipman Hyam's death begins,

> When he was dying he was not used as he ought to have been used[.] [H]e had no proper care taken of nor any kindness shewn him[.] [H]e was separated from the other boys but a boy would go up to him if the door was open[,] unknown to Mrs Franklin[,] and ask Lipman[,] do you want anything[?] Lipman Hyam would be afraid to ask[.] I can't explain all for I was not there long during his illness[,] only a little before he came from Margate[.] Lipman Hyam would be afraid to ask because it would be denied him if a boy was ill and wanted anything[.] [H]e would have to get it out of his own money and Lipman had none[.] [I]f he was sick he would have to wipe up his mess himself although he had scarcely any flesh on his body[.] On the morning he died at about half past three or four o'clock he was calling some of the boys—he slept in our room[;] he was only separated in the day time he kept his bed—I went to him and asked what he wanted[;] his mind wandered[.] I went to call his sister[;] she immediately came[.] A little before five I went to call Mr Franklin[;] he said he would come [but] instead of doing so—as he promised—he never came into the room until about twenty minutes to nine and the child died about fifteen minutes to nine[.] There was no doctor and no watcher. Mr Franklin gave S Phillips [Simon Phillips] orders to say if any gentleman or other person knew of it and asked if proper attention was paid to say Mr Franklin was attending on him before four in the morning[.] Simon Phillips was told first because he was going about to fetch the watcher and others and Mr Franklin told the other boys the same afterwards[.] Simon Phillips told Mr Dias so.[37]

Levy's account of neglect and illicit confidences between teachers and students echo throughout the investigation records. Lipman Hyam was afraid to seek help for reasons Levy cannot explain. He admits that he only knew Lipman for a short time but is still certain that his schoolmate fails to ask for help because he has no money, and hence no power. Myer Levy frames his litany of events as a sequence of failures: adults fail to care for the young; children are powerless to protect their loved ones; appropriate religious figures and doctors fail to support children in need; and an innocent orphan child dies helpless. As the story unfolds, Myer Levy embeds flashes of detail about life at the asylum, insinuating the health implications of the children's neglect, in this case of a child's inability to pay someone to clean up his own mess. In mentioning the indignities of neglect, Myer Levy exposes his understanding of how children should be cared for and what he believes ought to have occurred on the night of Lipman Hyam's death. In his opinion, Mr. Franklin should have made an appearance, along with a doctor or a watcher to guard over the body between death and burial, a common Jewish religious practice. The absence of a watcher points to Myer Levy's understanding of the importance of religious ritual, of the Jewish ethics of dying and care for the body of the dead. Mr. Franklin, Myer Levy claims, was wrong not to have come to the bed of the dying child; equally wrong, however, was Mr. Franklin's lie about his actions and bribery to conceal his neglect. Myer Levy moves on to express further outrage at the conspiracy of silence that protected teachers from punishment while granting special privileges to students susceptible to manipulation by those in positions of authority.

Why should we believe Myer Levy? Children often don't understand the complexities of adult choices. We might assume Mr. Franklin's innocence and interpret this narrative as a child's mistaken understanding of another child's misfortune. Perhaps the doctor visited hours earlier to say there was no hope of recovery, which would explain Mr. Franklin's decision not to come to the bedside in the middle of the night. Alternately, another sick child may have drawn Mr. Franklin away from Lipman Hyam's deathbed. Or maybe we're better off reading the subtext of Myer Levy's testimony as an admission of fear and helplessness. It seems logical, after all, that an eleven-year-old child would desire the presence of an adult on the terrifying occasion of witnessing another child's death.

In her study of eighteenth-century fictional orphan narratives, Cheryl Nixon notes that frequently "the orphan signals the ability of the self to achieve order by organizing his or her narrative; the orphan plots success by plotting the self. The orphan must not only take control of his or her life, but must take control of his or her story. . . . Ultimately, the orphan may have few resources, but proves to have one source of power—narrative—that cannot be taken away."[38] Myer Levy's account is not a novel, of course, but he engages in a similar kind of plotting in his presentation of the memory of fear, injustice, and helplessness. He speaks on subjects of his choosing. He boldly offers—at the young age of fourteen—a scathing critique of a teacher's refusal to grant dignity to a dying child and then of the teacher's cover-up. Myer Levy's articulate, well-plotted testimony, banished to appendix F, provides evidence of the investigators' belief that his words carried weight. Even if he was lying, his narrative presents an understanding of neglect as an unsettling example of mistreatment. And with his observations of human motives, Myer Levy expresses his understanding of the way corruption works, and the power of stories about dying children abused by adults. For these reasons, it's a rare and important example of one East End voice that pushes against a louder narrative of lost, wild Jewish children waging war against an otherwise stable society.

Testimony of Simon Phillips

Appendix F preserves Simon Phillips's statement about the events that took place on the night of Lipman Hyams's death. Phillips's narrative diverges in style and content from Myer Levy's. Simon Phillips's clipped responses and repeated words and phrases sound like undeveloped answers to questions rather than a cohesive narrative structured by chronology or cause and effect. It's unclear if his style of testimony is the result of a failure in his storytelling abilities or if his reticence signals an emotional retreat brought about by fear or the pressure to divulge secrets. His account begins:

> Remember Lipman Hyams was in the Asylum before me[;] recollect him being ill[;] Recollect his returning from Margate[;] Mr Franklin kept him in the parlor and was very kind to him[;] used to give him what he wanted I think[;] he used to sleep in the boys bedroom[.] This continued until he died[.] Cant recollect at what time he died.
>
> Remember Joel Lyons coming into the Asylum[.] He was always a very bad boy[.] [H]e would not do what Mr Franklin told him[.] He was striking, fighting, quarreling with the other boys and disturbing the classes[.] Recollect Abraham Cohen[;] he was generally a good boy[.] He was liked by the boys[.] I believed I liked him very well.[39]

Whereas Myer Levy's account connects emotional dots, and weaves together relations between events and human responses to those events, Simon Phillips speaks in bullets, refusing to linger on details or descriptions.

These two remarkably different accounts of the same event offer a stunning example of the way the meaning of archival records emerge through the relations of parts, for each of these accounts would tell a different story if read in isolation from the other. According to Myer Levy, Abraham Cohen is a deviant child who takes pleasure in the humiliation and punishment of other children. Simon Phillips's claim that Abraham Cohen is "generally a good boy" calls the earlier narrative into question. Their differences of opinion guide our reading of these passages, leading us to notice details we might otherwise never think to question.

Simon Phillips's brief account from appendix F is complicated by four additional documents written in 1857: a letter submitted on February 11, 1857, by his sister, P. Abrahams; and three additional pieces of evidence written by Simon Phillips over the course of a few hours. In her letter, P. Abrahams offers one of the most direct recommendations of all: The Franklins are violent and corrupt and her brother, Simon Phillips, is a compromised informant. Before reading these criticisms, however, it's helpful to begin by focusing on the way she expresses her motives for composing and submitting an uninvited letter:

> I hereby forward you the following. I do this, not out of revenge or animosity against Mr or Mrs Franklin, but for the truths sake only + if possible to put an end to their usual conduct toward the children. . . . I have heard continued complaints of ill treatment + wickedness going on, but took no further notice, after the treatment of Mr Franklin to me on a previous occasion, + there being the younger 3 children left [her siblings enrolled in the school] who would have suffered had I interfered [earlier]. . . . I am the mother of 5 children + do this in the hope that the poor orphan children will be put under better protection + teaching. I have often mourned the condition of the children, being brought up to lying, knavery, falsehood, spying upon each other, bad language + trickery of every description. . . . I have no fear of the three [siblings] telling the truth, but Simon is yet under Mr Franklins influence, and I would wish you not to rely on any statement he might make in Mr Franklins favour, as should he appear before you, it is only again by means of bribery. His appearance would be contrary to my wishes. I am his older sister by 20 years, + would have come forward myself but that my household duties keep me entirely at home.[40]

P. Abrahams characterizes herself as seeking only the truth and the creation of a better, safer environment for the children. As evidence of this point, she admits to withholding information for fear that it would cause harm to her three younger siblings. She adds that as a mother of five she must prioritize her household responsibilities. Instead of an in-person testimony, P. Abrahams submits a letter. Yet her written performance shows signs of strategic crafting. Assuring readers of her compliance with social conventions lends credibility to her concern for the well-being of the children. Her acknowledgment of "the condition of the children, being brought up to lying, knavery, falsehood, spying upon each other, bad language + trickery of every description" seems on the surface to corroborate Colquhoun's impressions of the Jewish community. At the same time, her articulate style of writing suggests that Colquhoun's claims were not universally true of all East Enders. P. Abrahams's advanced rhetorical skills and her fortitude in defending children in the asylum construct a character both honorable and brave rather than criminal. The letter is savvy and erudite, indicating that this East Ender has learned how to compose a persuasive narrative.

Abrahams's letter moves on to discredit her brother and to restore credibility to Myer Levy's account. In fact, her letter showcases one of the most important features of the archive: the weight of the 1853 investigation seems to have rested upon the competing testimonies of these two boys, Simon Phillips and Myer Levy. The later 1857 testimony—which includes the letter from P. Abrahams, the three letters from her brother Simon Phillips, and statements by Montague Leverson—proves what earlier investigators were unable to determine definitively. P. Abrahams continues,

> The 2 boys Abraham + Simon were apprenticed to the shoemaking [trade] [.] Mr Franklin repeatedly called upon them about 3 ½ years ago, and by inducements, promises, + bribery they were induced to make false statements + writings such as they had always seen practiced in the school, they have since acknowledged that Mr Franklin owes his being in his present situation, wholly + solely to them, papers were written which counteracted true evidence given by a boy named I believe Myer Levy. Mr Franklin has acknowledged this kindness, by repeated invitations, presents, +c +c, + by tapping them on the shoulders in acknowledgment of services done. Now to the present affair of Mr Franklin. My younger brother Simon Phillips, has been repeatedly called upon by Mr Franklin + *once* also by a lady named Mrs Sol[omon] Joseph of the Crescent Minories.[41]

This letter may explain why the Franklins were exonerated in 1856, and why a subsequent investigation took place in 1857 as a correction. In her account of a sequence of events missing from the framing documents and other reports in the archive, P. Abrahams suggests Myer Levy's earlier testimony was true. In contrast, she suggests that counterevidence supplied by her brother Simon Phillips and his friend Abraham was the product of Mr. Franklin's bribery.

Eight days after the date of P. Abrahams's letter, Simon Phillips wrote three of his own. This trio of documents speak to a chaotic context for their composition. In his first 1857 letter Simon Phillips accused the Franklins of misconduct. In the second partial letter he wrote what seems to be a draft copy of the first letter that somehow, strangely, found its way to the archive. The third piece of evidence retracted statements made in the previous two documents, arguing instead that the Franklins have been kind; and it was his sister Esther and her husband who forced him to write false statements. Together the three documents exhibit a level of confusion and distress far more disturbing than earlier allegations of lies. It's worth examining each document in order to address the contours of his confusion or complicity—depending on how we read them. All three letters were composed within a period of a few hours. In his first letter, dated February 19, 1857, Simon Phillips wrote:

> Sir
>
> Mr Franklin has asked me to come up to the Committee + speak for I promise to do so but since then I find he has been telling me falsehoods to mislead me he has endeavored to make my sisters out to be thieves which he + I know to be false[.] [T]hey have spoken the truth + now I wish to support them in their statements[.] I gave Mr Franklin a good character before because I was under his influence + was forced to do it[.] Any questions you may ask me I promise honestly to tell the whole truth. Don't think me a liar as what I did before was by Mr Franklins direction + knowledge.
>
> I am your obedient Servant,
>
> Simon Phillips[42]

The second letter in the same handwriting, with the same date and address as the above letter, states:

> Sir
>
> Mr Franklin has asked me to come up to the Committee to say what both Mr Franklin + me knows to be false, I did so once before.[43]

The remainder of the page is blank. However, a third document—a transcription of Simon Phillips's testimony—contains his name with the same date as the previous two letters—February 19, 1857—but has the time stamp of "12 Oclock Midnight Thursday night." The transcription reads:

> I, Simon Phillips, formerly an Inmate of the Jews' Orphan Asylum, have come to the Asylum to make the following statement.
>
> I have always been treated in the most parental manner by Mr. and Mrs. Franklin both while I was in the Institution and since. I have left it; and I had promised Mr. and Mrs. Franklin to make a statement to the Committee to that effect. This promise I made without any inducement being held out and merely from motives of gratitude to my former benefactors.
>
> Since then, my sister Esther Davis and my brother-in-law Henry Davis have been endeavoring to poison my mind against Mr + Mrs Franklin by telling me that they have stated the most disgraceful untruths against my two sisters Esther and Hannah and have tried to prevent me from speaking the truth to the Committee. They excited my feelings conjuring me by my dead parents to speak against my benefactors. Henry Davis brought me a document for me to sign and I twice refused to do so. He however so worked upon my feelings that I in a moment of madness signed the paper at last. Since then I have not had a moment of peace of mind, and I have now come down here to speak the truth and to express my deep regret for the rash act which I have committed.
>
> This statement is perfectly true in every respect and I intend to state the same to the Committee.[44]

In the first document Simon Phillips's writing seems disjointed and confused. He mentions an earlier case of supporting Mr. Franklin, presumably his testimony in appendix F. But several hours later he tells another version of the story transcribed by someone more adept with punctuation and pronouns. The document in the middle—a tiny, incomplete fragment—leads us to believe he revised his work in an effort to get the story right. The three documents offer a suspicious protest. The understory of the three contradictory letters reveals a child's vulnerability in the face of heavy-handed adults. Indeed, his letters offer disturbing evidence not just of children overpowered by adults, but of the dangerous effects of the trauma of reliving earlier painful experiences in their testimony and letters.

Ann Laura Stoler, Antoinette Burton, and Anjali Arondekar, among many others, remind us that the terms by which archives have been created, organized, saved, and housed mediate every facet of the archive's content and production in known and often unknown ways.[45] Evidence from the Jews' Orphan Asylum archive follows suit, but is further complicated by the fact that it was filtered through the divided loyalties of children. One additional record, a single letter written by Montague Leverson, president of the Jews' Orphan Asylum, reminds us of the impossibility of treating the investigation as an arbiter of truth. In his letter dated February 16, 1857, Leverson forwards another letter received from Myer Levy. He reminds his audience that Levy was "one of the boys examined between three and four years ago by the Committee of Investigation."[46] Leverson recalls that Myer Levy's 1853 testimony, the very part discussed above and saved in appendix F, was "clamored down by the General Committee on the statement made by Mr. Alexander Levy" because Myer Levy confessed to lying, albeit under pressure.[47] Leverson explains that Mr. Alexander Levy was wrong about Myer Levy's lying. His proof is a missing letter written by Myer Levy explaining that he was *not* bribed and that his evidence in 1853 was true. The letter validating Myer Levy's testimony was lost. The 1853 investigators, therefore, had no way to determine whether Myer Levy spoke the truth. This fact led them to disqualify his testimony. When Leverson recalls the existence of a missing letter from the earlier investigation, he implies that evidence was tampered with by the very people charged with leading the investigation. According to Alexander Levy's account, which remained part of the archive, Montague Leverson paid Myer Levy to lie. According to Myer Levy, Alexander Levy invented this story about the bribe. In the end, we're left with three inconsistent accounts that speak truthfully about the tragic corruption of the investigations. The 1857 investigation overturned the 1856 recommendations by sacking the Franklins and acquitting Myer Davis. In so doing, they sided with the statements by Myer Levy, P. Abrahams, and Montague Leverson rather than those by Simon Phillips, Alexander Levy, and the Franklins.

From my position outside this world, gazing at missing evidence, accusations of lies, tampered evidence, and child abuse, a coherent or legible reading is impossible. I'm suggesting instead that we're better off approaching these archival records by focusing on individuated voices or each speaker's rhetorical strategies. Despite its limits of legibility, testimony from the Jews' Orphan Asylum still manages to reflect a culture of the East End absent from popular published accounts, such as those discussed in chapter 1. Moreover, offhand comments about school life, learning, and religious observance offer a thoughtful intervention and sense of context on Polack's writing and teaching career. In passages where young East End children speak about the importance of religious practice and of treating children with respect, the myth of universal East End depravity is challenged by a more complex narrative created by child witnesses—criminals, as Colquhoun calls them—speaking, or perhaps lying, through trauma and abuse.

Testimony of Myer Davis

The 1853 investigation at the Jews' Orphan Asylum left a trail of accusations and lies. The fact that two investigations followed in 1856 and 1857 points to the ineffective gathering of facts. At the point when Myer Davis assumed the role of headmaster in 1856, the school was already burdened by ill-behaved students and administrative corruption. At the young age of twenty-six, Myer Davis took on the leadership of the Jews' Orphan Asylum. He'd been trained by the legendary Moses Angel, headmaster at the Jews' Free School, an older institution with a well-established record of strong leadership. Moving from the Jews' Free School to the Jews' Orphan Asylum would have been difficult for anyone, but for a young man unfamiliar with school corruption it turned out to be a disaster. Moses Angel was called upon to testify in the 1853 hearing.[48] In the pages of that report, Angel defined the purpose of corporal punishment in schools, claiming, "Punishment should be adopted less as a means to hurt the offender (to make him feel) than with a view to awaken in him a sense of the wrong he may have committed. No child should be degraded physically but he should be made to feel the moral degradation which his own error has inflicted on himself: he should be made to blush less at being found out than at the mental obliquity which preceded the misdeed & led to it."[49] While the line between punishment and abuse was clear to Moses Angel, others at the Jews' Orphan Asylum seemed less sure. Even by Victorian standards, an age in which corporal punishment was common in schools, punishments at the Jews' Orphan Asylum alarmed the community. To compound matters, Myer Davis was ill-prepared for student and faculty challenges to his authority. He entered a school that failed to delineate violence from discipline, and he faced a community ambivalent about his arrival. It's no wonder he became a target.

The archive preserved seven letters written by Myer Davis, one spoken testimony transcribed by a member of the 1856 investigation, and one incomplete ninety-two page "statement" that he describes as "a narrative of my connection with the Jews' Orphan Asylum," produced on the occasion of the 1857 investigation.[50] While letters and memos offer evidence of his life in the institution, his 1857 memoir stands out for its raw blend of confession, vindication, explanation, and feelings of terror. The writing hints at his sense of vulnerability and fears about the accusations leveraged against him. In his early days in the job, Myer Davis makes helpful suggestions in his letters to administrators relating to books or the curriculum. In the first extant letter, five pages in length, dated January 14, 1856, his voice is positive, hopeful, and delighted to take on the challenge of improving the asylum.[51] The second letter of January 16, 1856, begins, "I have pondered over the suggestions proposed on Monday evening, and have somewhat amended my manual so as to embrace your opinions without trenching upon the general principles I recommended."[52] The gap between these documents points to institutional resistance to his first letter. In his second letter Davis continues with a conciliatory, professional tone as he attempts to strike a balance between his aims as master of the school and the committee's wishes. The tone of the third document, dated April 17, 1856, offers a jarring contrast. It begins, "Mr. Meyer Davis called in and examined."[53]

The 1856 investigation arrived at the conclusion that Davis should be fired, and Mr. and Mrs. Franklin should be placed on probation. When members of the community protested, a subsequent investigation followed in 1857. In the wake of dissent, letters written by Davis and addressed to the president of the Jews' Orphan Asylum offered daily status reports in a tone suggesting he was under some kind of surveillance. In one, for example, dated May 20, 1856, Davis writes, "This morning, as agreed on, I took the boys to instruction, and passed with them a few quiet hours, while the girls were at needlework with Mrs. Franklin, and the rest of the time at Hebrew with Mr. Franklin. The boys conducted themselves with propriety."[54] In materials written after the contentious 1856 report, including Myer Davis's incomplete ninety-two-page memoir written to defend himself, his voice alternates between indignation, fear, and frustration. From our vantage point, the memoir may seem overwrought or melodramatic. After all, we know he was acquitted of charges made in the 1856 report. But at the point when it was written, Myer Davis was clearly feeling vulnerable. The archive's missing documents and accusations of lies suggest that he had reason to be afraid. Composed on forty-six pages folded in half and sewn together, the memoir recounts his desire to vindicate himself from accusations of inappropriate behavior toward the students. The pages are oddly disheveled—odd, that is, given the collection of his carefully written letters preserved alongside the memoir. Myer Davis's writing in the memoir displays crossed-out sentences, changed words, corrected spellings, and insertions of missing phrases. In other words, it looks like a rough draft. Indeed, Davis claims that "[t]he report I furnished to the Com^{ee} on February 18th was destroyed, & has not been entered on the minutes; it is for others to attribute this to its right cause: I had adopted the precaution of measuring my draft copy."[55] This brief statement, if true, explains why the extant narrative looks so rough. The polished copy is not part of the archive. Whether it was lost purposefully or accidentally is anyone's guess.

Davis writes his narrative in his usual deferential tone: "Gentlemen, In obedience to your suggestion, I have prepared a statement for your consideration, which I have thought it best to present in the form of a narrative of my connection with the Jews' Orphan Asylum, giving particular answers to the questions you put to me, and abstaining as much as possible from incriminating others, seeing that the matters to be dis[?] of are the *charges against myself.*"[56] The efficient and direct opening gives way to an anxiety-driven narrative. As Davis puts it, he's forced to respond to charges that "assume no shape more substantial than vague rumours, and I am still fighting with a shadow."[57] While Colquhoun would find only crime and danger in his assessment of this community and Watt Phillips would describe greasy thieves, Davis's narrative imagines the individual experience of self-improvement and intellectual acumen drawn through the metaphor of the shadow.

Davis structures the remainder of his narrative around a sequence of events that detail how he came to teach at the asylum, his previous work experience, and his educational philosophy. He tells numerous stories of children's misconduct and of betrayal by Mr. and Mrs. Franklin. Even as he offers a chronological account of events in the asylum, Myer Davis roots his defense in the construction of his good character. Lies, he claims, are waged against his record of character and professional propriety. By his own admission, Myer Davis engages in numerous forms of corporal punishment. He reasons that these actions were warranted as a reaction to bad behavior by students. It's the subsequent claims by students, or what he classifies as lies rendering his violence worse than it was, that make him vulnerable. This logic may seem strange to readers less tolerant of corporal punishment. But within the context of Victorian schools, hitting a child was considered a perfectly acceptable form of discipline. Myer Davis doesn't feel compelled to deny his violence. Rather, his challenge is to defend himself against accusations that the abuse was a sign of his bad character.

This rationale appears in the following passage in which Myer Davis describes his abuse of Rachel Solomons. He explains,

> You ask me did I give a black eye to Rachel Solomons[.] I answer most decidedly in the negative. I *did* box her ears for repeated insolence of the most vulgar and offensive description. She and other inmates have had black eyes, partly owing to their habit of pugnacity, which I have not only witnessed but read of as incessant, in the report of 1853; partly owing to other causes, you may judge what, than their own combativeness. I have seen this girl and others subbing their faces with their cotton handkerchiefs, and even inflicting personal chastisement upon each other for the purpose of making it appear I ill used them.[58]

According to Myer Davis, Rachel Solomon was at fault for his violence against her. The slide from one form of violence—boxed ears—to another—a black eye—leads Myer Davis down a dangerous path. The girls, he claims, see in one form of violence an opportunity to implicate him in another. If true, then the children have adopted the very forms of violence the investigators attempt to root out. If false, then Myer Davis has to find a way to prove his innocence. Later passages point to additional examples of Myer Davis's violence against the children. He states of Elizabeth Blumenthal, "[I]t is *quite* probable that I boxed her ears, in consequence of her systematic and daring insolence: but, I am quite certain I was specially forbearing in her case, having *pity* on her for her weak eyes."[59] In another striking instance Davis claims, "That Michael Raphael's knee was cut is *true:* for the facts connected therewith I refer you to my letter to the Pres. of Nov 26th last. To the observations contained in that letter I will only add, that for about 3 weeks previously, the inmates had repeatedly provoked me to *strike* them in return for their incessant insolent invective and had frequently made use of the following remark: 'We'll make you hit us but you mustn't: we'll force you to do it' and the like."[60] Davis's defensive position is to censure the children for provoking him to violence. Rather than deny his acts, he shifts the blame. Through his tangled logic, he stops short of calling them liars. He insinuates instead that they bait him to engage in acts that will lead to his downfall. The concept of lying takes a strange turn in these passages. In Myer

Davis's statement, lying isn't merely a false statement or a withholding of information; it's a setup, a provocation to act on false pretenses.

In the conclusion to his narrative, Myer Davis makes one final argument in defense of his actions. It's a plea based not on his treatment of the students but on his reputation and character. He explains,

> I further submit for consideration the fact that no man becomes either brutal or dishonest at one plunge. Is it likely that having during nearly 20 years established a character for mildness and probity, & sustained such character up to 23rd January 1856, it is likely that I should suddenly on 24th have become "a rogue" "a monster" "a —— butcher" and merit the stigma before *one* year has passed over my head of being "a —— who deserved to be quartered." And while I can proudly refer to my past character and career at the [Jews'] Free School, I fearlessly appeal to you, as to whether you believe of me the unsubstantial shadows which have been hung around my reputation at the Orphan Asylum.[61]

The passage moves from absolute certainty to the anxiety about his inability to convince everyone of his innocence. Arriving at the asylum on the heels of "nearly 20 years" working as "a pupil, master and teacher"[62] at the Jews' Free School, Myer Davis claims that he offers "proof that during the whole of the above period I was enabled to earn and retain a character for industry, probity and humanity."[63] Put differently, he uses his good character as evidence of his innocence. A man with such character could not become a monster overnight. The use of a character-based argument is historically resonant. H. S. Jones notes "the central importance of the concept of character, which was itself intimately related to the equally pivotal concept of manliness" in the Victorian period. Jones adds, "It was a commonplace in Victorian moral discourse that character was tested and strengthened by adversity."[64] Samuel Smiles, the well-known author of *Self-Help* (1859), argues that character "is one of the greatest motive powers in the world. In its noblest embodiments, it exemplifies human nature in its highest forms, for it exhibits man at his best. . . . Although genius always commands admiration, character most secures respect. The former is more the product of brain-power, the latter of heart-power; and in the long run it is the heart that rules in life."[65] While Myer Davis borrows from these ideas of character, he doesn't imply that the challenges he faces will strengthen his character. Rather, his point is that his past character should render such accusations unnecessary. He shouldn't have to be burdened by such accusations.

Myer David Davis was born in the East End to a father who worked as a tailor. His grandfather, Jacob Myer, was a Hebraist and teacher at a Whitechapel school. Myer Davis was tutored by Angel Moses, the headmaster of the Jews' Free School, and later worked as a teacher at the Shaare Tikvah School. He married Frances Wolfson, who served as headmistress of the Westminster Jews' Free School.[66] Davis developed an interest in studying medieval history after reading d'Blossiers Tovey. Over the course of his life, Davis worked with legal papers relating to Anglo-Jewish Medieval history from the Public Record Office, the British Museum, and Westminster Abbey.[67] It's noteworthy that a man so interested in archives would have his own letters and memoir preserved in one. It might also explain why he was compelled to record his experiences in such detail. Davis wrote an archival study in his foundational monograph *Shetaroth: Hebrew Deeds of English Jews before 1290* (1888), which was published for the Anglo-Jewish Historical Exhibition.[68] Later Davis worked as editor of a prominent London paper, the *Jewish World*, and as one of the people involved in founding the Jewish Historical Society of England in 1893.[69] In short, this man born and educated in Whitechapel became a local hero of London's Anglo-Jewish community for his advocacy of Jewish history, his record of exemplary teaching at a number of prominent schools, and his advances in the scholarship of medieval culture.

The Jews' Orphan Asylum archive preserves evidence that can never be verified. The fact that Myer Davis became a well-respected scholar may influence the way readers of the archive interpret his narrative. Indeed, his fame as a local hero grants him a last word of sorts. It's possible that the Franklins moved on to similar kinds of fame. But because their work was not included in well-known historical records, all we know of this couple comes from the Jews' Orphan Asylum archive. The collection of evidence we encounter as strangers gazing into a foreign world is thus always uneven and partial. Missing or biased evidence skews our analysis of extant records—a fact that drives the stakes of archival creation and destruction. In a fortuitous twist of fate, Myer Davis's reputation from work performed long after the 1850s investigations—his public persona and character as a famous scholar—has the power to reframe what we learn about him in the pages of the school archive.

The Scholars' Feast

In all likelihood, Montague Leverson's missing letter vindicated Myer Davis in the 1857 investigation. In another letter dated November 5, 1856, just after beginning his new position, Myer Davis writes to Montague Leverson, president of the Jews' Orphan Asylum: "Friday is 'the Scholars' Feast' and with your permission we shall have a holyday as at other establishments."[70] The Scholars' Feast, a holiday still practiced in some Ashkenazi communities, takes place in the eighth month of the Hebrew calendar. This event is described by the nineteenth-century Reverend John Mills as "instituted to commemorate the tradition concerning the plague that raged amongst the scholars of the celebrated Rabbi Akkivah, which, after destroying a great number (24,000, according to the Talmud), ceased all of a sudden, as by a miracle, on the eighteenth of this month."[71] The event was simple in practice—it was a feast commemorating the miracle that brought an end to the killing of scholars. When I first read this line, I was fascinated by Myer Davis's request to hold such a feast at an East End charity school. He doesn't explain why he cares about this celebration, but he does mention it was celebrated by other East End institutions. Its basic premise drew me in. The Scholars' Feast is a celebration of the end of the death of scholars, the end of the death of scholarship. Was Myer Davis suggesting that his students should see their own schoolwork as scholarship, worthy of a celebration? Or was he interested in nourishing in the students a reverence for the work of other scholars, or for scholarship? As I reflected on his request for permission to hold a celebration, I considered how this tradition of a Scholars' Feast stands as an emblem of work in the archive and the winding paths through stacks of papers, rows of tombstones, and cryptic accounts of missing evidence and abuse. I've engaged in a kind of intellectual feast in my forays into archives, libraries, and communities that preserve and celebrate the work of East Enders. We will not recover the voices lost by the plague, but we know *of* their stories and the miracle of preservation that brings absolute loss to an end.

Along with Davis's testimony and the profuse collection of statements and letters produced by members of the committee, the archive contains one undated document written by an unnamed archivist that creates a paratextual threshold in its framing of the Jews' Orphan Asylum archive:

> 14.1.1856–8.6 1858 and n.d.
>
> Material rel. to a dispute between Myer Davis, headmaster of the O.A., and Mr. and Mrs. G. Franklin, second master of the O.A. and his wife, concerning discipline.

[For Davis see obit. notice in J.C., 19.1.1912. Mention is made of Davis' teaching at the Jews' Free School and his headmastership of the Shaare' Tikvah Schools; no reference to his career at the O. A.]

1830–1912[72]

Davis's prominent position in the community led to the publication of an obituary in the *Jewish Chronicle,* one of the most important Jewish periodicals in the nineteenth century. The presence of this statement by the archivist elevates Myer Davis's status. It signals to readers that this man who was once forced to defend himself against accusations of child abuse was important enough to have been included in one of the most important Jewish periodicals of his era. The archivist continues by mentioning that while Myer Davis's work at other Jewish institutions received glorious attention in his obituary, his work at the Jews' Orphan Asylum was never mentioned. Readers are left to interpret the significance of this critical silence. But the archivist has an important hand in shaping our thinking. For the archivist insinuates that omissions in the obituary are attempts to hide secrets from Davis's past. In the end, it's the archivist's voice that transforms the content of the investigation into a salacious event.

The archivist's insertion recalled to my mind Maria Polack's understated obituary published in the *Jewish Chronicle,* which reads, "Died. On Monday the 8th inst., Mrs. Lepman Polack of 86, Leman Street, Goodman's Fields; deeply lamented by her Family and Friends."[73] The inclusion of an obituary in the well-respected *Jewish Chronicle* suggests that Polack, like Myer Davis, had some degree of prominence at the time of her death. I copied the obituary many years ago, prior to writing the chapters of this book. Mention in the Jews' Orphan Asylum archive of an obituary for Myer Davis prompted me to purchase a day-pass to the *Jewish Chronicle*'s digital archive. Eager to witness her name in print one more time, I ran a quick search for Polack. She was already dead by the time the Jews' Orphan Asylum events took place. But looking for evidence of her life had become a habit of thought. Every time I used a database or digital archive, I searched for Polack's name first, even though most of the time I was supposed to be searching for other subjects. On this occasion I found several references to people named "Polack." The first on the list was dated 1855 and stated, "Lecture at Malton—On Tuesday evening last, the members of the Literary Institute were gratified with a long-expected lecture, by

Miss Polack, on the 'Women of Israel.' Founded on the work of that name by Grace Aguilar, and illustrated by a succession of Hebrew melodies, sung with great taste and feeling, in the full, deep, rich voice which the lady possesses, and accompanied by herself on the pianoforte."[74]

The passage moved on to discuss details of the performance and the audience's "loud applause." I wondered why a story from Yorkshire about a woman's performance of Hebrew melodies and Grace Aguilar's writing would find its way into London's *Jewish Chronicle.* I searched further by opening the other Polack articles that came up in my search. One from the year before noted "Malton.—Musical Lecture.—The meetings of the Literary Institute for this season, were wound up on Tuesday evening last, with a brilliant lecture on 'The Ancient Music of the Hebrews,' by Miss Polack, a lady of the Jewish persuasion, who, in a rich, deep voice, gave several illustrative specimens chiefly from Lord Byron's 'Hebrew Melodies,' set to ancient airs, and accompanied by herself on the pianoforte."[75] I paused over mention of the "Hebrew Melodies." I wanted to believe there was a connection between Miss Polack in Malton whose performances were announced in the London Jewish press, and Mrs. Lepman Polack from Whitechapel, Maria Polack the novelist, who died a few years earlier. Could this Yorkshire Miss Polack be the elusive Elizabeth Polack, the granddaughter of Ephraim Polack? And was she Maria Polack's daughter? Could she be the playwright? Another *Jewish Chronicle* hit from my search offered a clue. The editor published the following article titled "Our Synagogal Music" on January 30, 1857:

> Our readers will remember a letter which appeared in our columns some time ago, and in which the community was informed that the Portuguese synagogal music would soon appear in print. This communication elicited a letter (no 1) to us, which we submitted to H., the writer of the original letter. Our correspondent, in returning the note, made several remarks which, in conjunction with Miss Polack's observations, appeared to us calculated to excite interest in so desirable an object as the publication of the German synagogal music. We therefore asked the permission of both writers for inserting such portions of the communications as were fit for publicity. Having premised this explanation the order and purpose of the subjoined correspondence will become clear.[76]

The first letter, signed by Elizabeth Polack from Malton, Yorkshire, January 7, 1857, states,

> Dear Sir,—I was delighted to see in a recent number that our sacred music is about to be published; such ought to have been done long ago. From the admiration and interest shown by my Christian friends here when I play and sing our ancient Jewish melodies (to which I adapt English words), I am sure such a work would sell well amongst Christians everywhere; and for ourselves, what so right and consistent as that we should humbly imitate the "sweet Psalmist of Israel," and sing the praises of God, not on the Sabbath only, but in the evening gatherings of every domestic circle?[77]

The article continues with a discussion of the religious feeling evoked by such music. Elizabeth Polack explains, "I know a great many airs which, from their antiquity are not much known now; I learnt them from my mother and if they would be acceptable will, with much pleasure, send copies to whoever has the work in hand."[78] Who was her mother? Could this be the very same Maria Polack listed on the census record as "teacher of M"? I want to believe that Elizabeth Polack's mother was responsible for teaching her synagogue music, perhaps even music passed down from Ephraim Polack, Maria's father. Maybe Maria Polack had helped Elizabeth develop "a rich, deep voice" carried all the way to Yorkshire.

This book should have ended with these questions. But on a lark while revising the final manuscript, I made the decision to check one last lead—the reference to Miss Polack, the singer in Malton who learned Jewish music from her mother. I reached out to archives in Malton with little understanding of their holdings. The first archive forwarded my email to another local archive. Two days later I received a helpful note from Nicholas Hatton, a volunteer at Woodhams Stone Collection at the Malton and Norton Heritage Centre.[79] A highly skilled researcher, Nicholas was able to track down further details about Elizabeth Polack and Maria Polack. Nicholas not only added nuance to my readings of census records but also found additional evidence that compelled me to rethink every assumption I'd made about Polack's life and cultural contexts.

I knew that Maria Polack died in 1849, followed by her husband the following year. Nicholas found census records detailing Elizabeth's residence every decade until her death in October 1889. In the 1841 census, Elizabeth was approximately twenty-five years old and living with Maria, Lipman, and Martha along with a family servant. In the 1851 census Elizabeth was living in Aldgate, a region that abuts Whitechapel, as an "Annuitant."

Later, her name appeared in in the *Jewish Chronicle* and Yorkshire papers for her musical performances. This work might have earned her some money, but not enough to survive as an unmarried woman. Nicholas discovered that in later records she's listed as a "fund holder," which affirms that she earned money from an annuity. More specifically, Elizabeth was living on a "Consolidated Loan Annuity" from Ephraim Polack of Mansell Street, who had invested in the Bank of England. In October 1812 dividends on this loan stopped being claimed, presumably because of his death. The money continued to grow and by the time Lipman passed away, Elizabeth inherited her grandfather's annuity.[80] While living in Malton, Elizabeth became involved in local church fundraisers but later moved to Birmingham. Her name appears in the *Dudley Castle Miscellany,* which Nicholas describes as "a fundraising book for a Bazaar to raise funds for the Coseley Church Repair Fund." Elizabeth's poem "Dreams," which was originally published in the *New Monthly Belle Assemblée* in 1834, was reprinted in the *Dudley Castle Miscellany* in 1860.[81]

Nicholas and I continued to correspond about our further quest for details about Elizabeth Polack. After a week of multiple emails, I received a strange note in my inbox. Nicholas wrote, "I think I might have stumbled on something this afternoon that might be significant to the Ms Polack story. (It might simply be a strange coincidence, but please read on.)" The remainder of his email included a bulleted list of findings. I was amused by his choice to detail evidence in the form of a list, given my interest in East End list-making:

- I was searching Malton records for Hebrew names; came up with a surgeon by the name of Zebulon Mennell living here in the 1840/50s.
- Zebulon is married to a woman named Mary Marks who was born in Jamaica.
- It looks as if Mary Marks' full name was actually Mary Marks Polack, daughter of Marks Polack.
- Zebulon and Mary had several children one of whom moved to London and became an eminent doctor.
- Could it be that Elizabeth Polack is a relative of Mary Marks Polack and comes to Malton to be with relatives after the death of her parents?

At this point in our collaboration Nicholas knew nothing of my work on the subscription list, detailed in chapter 2, which included an entry for "Marks Polack, Jamaica"; nor did he know about Maria Polack's other subscriber, A. S. Lyon, who moved to Jamaica and whose story became the focus of chapter 3 of this book. With Nicholas's help, I learned that the Jamaica branch of the family had not simply supported Maria Polack's novel; over the years they remained in contact with the family, and by the early 1850s Elizabeth made the decision to leave her London home to live with Jamaican cousins in Malton. This welcome fact was both surprising and helpful, for it led to further questioning about her relationship with her East End community following her move to Malton.

In 1853, Elizabeth Polack was involved with the Vegetarian Society in Malton. This growing society stretched from Malton to Leeds to Birmingham. This connection might have been the prompting for her later move to Birmingham. Nicholas tracked down three additional addresses: 178 Bristol Street, St. Martins, Birmingham (1871); 17 Sampson Road, Aston, Birmingham, Warwickshire (1881); and 31 Sampson Road, Camp Hill, Birmingham, Warwickshire (1889)—all within spatial proximity of the Singer's Hill synagogue. With this information we consulted probate records and found that Elizabeth Polack died on October 18, 1889, and was buried in the Witton Old Jewish Cemetery. I've tracked down several poems and short stories published in the *New Monthly Belle Assemblée* from the 1830s to 1840s, but have failed to find additional records of her writing beyond her letter to the editor of the *Jewish Chronicle* in 1857.

While these details interested me, particularly Elizabeth's involvement with Methodists, none prepared me for the most significant revelation that followed. Nicholas found a record indicating that Maria Polack was baptized in 1840 by William Weldon Champneys, the famous rector of Whitechapel St. Mary's parish church, located just a few blocks from Polack's home in Whitechapel. Nothing in my search for Polack prepared me for this information. As the first Anglo-Jewish novelist and the author of an anti-conversion narrative, I had assumed she remained Jewish throughout her life. But in this sliver of a record just a few lines long, I learned her birth date—January 31, 1787—and the names of her parents, Ephraim Polack, a tailor of Mansell Street, and Cecilia Polack. Appointed in 1837, Champneys was well known for his charity work in London's East End and his efforts to convert Jews to Christianity. Maria Polack's baptism record suggests that she was among his converts. Records of another member of the household, Martha Polack, support this claim. Martha's occupation was left blank on the 1841 census, which aligns with those who are the wives or children of households, or those who do not earn a salary. It was difficult to know the exact nature of her relationship to Maria and Lipman Polack. Martha died at the age of seventeen in 1842 and was buried on June 16, 1842, at St. Mary's Whitechapel. The burial was performed by Edward F. Champneys, the son of William Weldon Champneys—the rector responsible for Maria's baptism.

The baptism record raised crucial questions about both conversion pressures in the East End and Maria Polack's understanding of Jewish-Christian relations. In an effort to find out the identities of Martha Polack and Elizabeth Polack living with Maria and Lipman in 1841, I ordered death certificates for the entire family. It was here, in these official documents of death, where I found the connections uniting these family relations. The records clarified the birth and death dates of all members of the family, and verified that Elizabeth Polack was the daughter of Lipman Polack and thus, presumably, his wife, Maria Polack. Martha's death record notes that she was the daughter of Jonas Polack, and Lipman Polack's niece, suggesting that either Lipman and Jonas were brothers, or Maria and Jonas were siblings and Lipman was Martha's uncle by marriage.

I have no way to explain Maria Polack's baptism. All I know is that she was born into a Jewish community; she learned Jewish music and published an anti-conversion novel in 1830; she belonged to London's Great Synagogue; she educated her daughter in Jewish music; and she now lies buried in a Jewish cemetery in London's East End. Somewhere along the way she made the decision to be baptized. Her daughter, Elizabeth Polack, was not only a poet and fiction writer but also performed Jewish music for Christian audiences and charities in Malton. I suspect that Maria Polack's heroine in *Fiction without Romance*, Eliza, was named after her own daughter, Elizabeth. And I know that it was through Elizabeth's performances that East End Jewish music made its way to Christian audiences in Malton and Birmingham.

The pieces didn't line up. Or perhaps they did, and the bullseye lantern that led me to see religious identity as fixed or straightforward prevented me from considering that for Maria and Elizabeth, involvement in education, music, and charity was not religiously specific. Perhaps they understood their activities with Christian groups as an extension rather than a break from Judaism, or as a version of "rational morality" tied to their belief in educating the poor or helping the needy. Or perhaps Maria Polack regretted her baptism and returned to Judaism in time for her own burial in a Jewish cemetery in 1849. Or maybe she kept her baptism a secret from her family. The archives are silent on these possibilities. But in resistant sources that seem to suggest contradictions and paradoxes, I'm led back to a version of Maria Polack's life that refuses legibility. I had to wonder upon finding this information so late in my work, What kind of book might I have written had I learned of Polack's baptism early in my research? The late revelation that this Jewish author was also a Christian was both a discovery and a tease; for while it shifted my thinking about religious identity in Whitechapel, it complicated rather than clarified my understanding of East End Jewish culture.

Derrida has famously defined the archive or arkhē as both a source and a system of law, or a commencement and a commandment. The word *archive,* he explains, "coordinates two principles in one: the principle according to nature or history, *there* where things *commence*—physical, historical, or ontological principle—but also the principle according to the law *there* where men and gods *command, there* where authority, social order are exercised, *in this place* from which *order* is given."[82] Original manuscripts preserved in the archive claim to tell the truth and to call out others who lie. Approaching these materials as a place of origins and truth is a trap, as I'd learned from Maria Polack's baptism records. Yet the search for origins and sources can distract us from the archive's other meaning—as a narrative of authority and law, or an investigation, a stage upon which order might be restored and exercised. The investigators were not spouting anti-Semitic rhetoric at lowly East End Jews; rather, they were wealthy Jews from the West End—detached and objective outsiders—trying to help fellow Jewish people put their school in order. Despite their common religious ground, it is *their* visuality—as outsiders occupying a position of power and authority—through which evidence was generated and saved. In preserving primary documents from the Jews' Orphan Asylum, the archive also preserves evidence of the very system of law and order that granted authority to those in charge, those who believed the process would lead them to truth. This fact doesn't make the archive's content true or accurate. But it does mean we're better off reading evidence in the archive not as statements of fact but as reflections of the conditions under which ideas of truth were created and tested.

CONCLUSION

Strangers in the Archive

THROUGHOUT THIS study I've argued that archival records preserve traces of creative and intellectual industry among residents of the East End. Each chapter raises questions about how archival records challenge stereotypes of the nineteenth-century East End and how we might understand our reading acts in the archives. I've argued that archival materials create contexts and "understories," producing narratives about the East End that can *only* be written by the distinct forms and histories that shape archival records.[1] Like any narrative, archives hide and preserve truths. They give voice to some perspectives, while silencing others. In response, I've sought methods of approaching archival narratives of East End cultural and intellectual activities. And I've considered how we might expand our thinking about the way we read archives now, as speculative sites of learning or as a kind of fiction born from material fragments situated in both public and private spaces. Part of my goal has been to inspire future archival work on marginalized communities in the East End or elsewhere. I've argued for a sharper focus on women writers and educators, literature from below, or ethnic, religious, or racial communities often positioned in the margins of nineteenth-century literary and print culture. The version of the East End to emerge from these chapters is one characterized by social justice movements, educational initiatives, and vibrant efforts to preserve Jewish cultural activities in the face of threats posed by assimilation, conversion, and systemic poverty. Learning about Polack's existence made me more aware of these forces and of competing narratives of East End depravity.

My interest in this project began when I learned about Maria Polack and her absence in the archives I consulted. I was amazed by that loss, just as I was befuddled by the existence of an East End author in 1830 whose presence defied everything I'd assumed to be true about this region of London. Over time I've developed methods of reading archival records through those absences, a sideways approach of looking for evidence of what's gone missing or was never saved. While Emma Lyon and the unnamed author of *The Jewish Preceptress* published books on Jewish subjects, the latter demonstrated interest in using the publishing market for the explicit purpose of educating Jewish children. It was in the context of these two obscure texts that Polack wrote and published *Fiction without Romance,* a novel situated between the emergence of Jewish secular literary activities and the rise of women's professional writing. I've long suspected *Fiction without Romance* was produced for the education of young women. Fueling my hunches were comments in the Jews' Free School Lady's Visitor's Book about female students under the tutelage of the schoolmistress, Miss Arnold. While there was no mention of Polack in these school records, the voices belonged to members of Polack's own community, people similarly concerned with the education of children and literature's power to teach morality.

I was struck by the reappearance of one name in the visitor's book—Amelia Solomon, who visited several times over a multi-year period. In an entry dated July 1812, Amelia Solomon of Clerkenwell writes,

> [M]uch credit is due to Miss Arnold for having taught the children the 13 Creeds which some of them know extremely well—particularly Catherine Lazarus and Eve Solomon—however their *moral education* is certainly still very deficient—they have no English books (the Sacred Writ excepted). Miss Arnold as well as myself regret this extremely—and I shortly hope to submit to the Committee a plan whereby the above [unreadable word] may be remedied in some measure for the girls many of them possess good capacities—and a *moral* education is absolutely indispensable to render them fit members of Society and a credit to this excellent institution.[2]

The "13 Creeds" recalls Maimonides's Thirteen Principles of the Jewish faith detailing the basic tenants of Judaism. This comment reflects an expectation that children would not only learn about Jewish subjects in school but would be exposed to a form of moral education. Admittedly, Amelia Solomon doesn't explain what she means by "a moral education," but her quip nevertheless resonates with the assertion in *Fiction without Romance*'s preface that Polack has "confined" herself to "that rational morality which many, I hope, will admire, and which all can comprehend."[3] In her return to the Jews' Free School in April 1815, Amelia Solomon noted the continued deficiency of books in the school. Other visitors, in contrast, commented on the careful use of particular books, including *The Book of Trades,* a dictionary, and *Baldwin's Fables,* children's tales written by William Godwin in 1804 under the pseudonym Edward Baldwin. Such comments led me to wonder about Polack's choice to write an anti-romance tale, a novel designed for moral instruction that borrowed 1790s phrases and concerns about female education. As a longer work, the novel would perhaps appeal to older students, those more advanced than readers of *Baldwin's Fables.* During the 1790s, Suzanne L. Barnett and Katherine Bennett Gustafson explain, "didactic writers" used a realist style in writing for children or for educational purposes. Many of the writers alluded to in *Fiction without Romance,* such as Mary Wollstonecraft and Maria Edgeworth, though different from one another on issues of pedagogy, "were united in their distrust of so-called imaginative fiction (such as fairy tales and romances)," which these authors viewed as "wasteful, self-indulgent, and confusing to children."[4] The very title of Polack's novel—*Fiction without Romance*—recalls such concerns.

The visitor's book didn't include evidence of a response to Amelia Solomon's request for more schoolbooks. If the school administrators offered one, it has been lost. However, the minute books, kept by the committee overseeing the Jews' Free School, hint that such concerns about books were either addressed or shared by school leaders. In the minute books I found evidence of literary activities in copies of Hebrew odes delivered by boys and English odes delivered by girls at the annual anniversary fundraising dinner. Other general references to the curriculum are threaded throughout the institution's archival records, suggesting that the wish for books was shared by many members of the community. The entry for September 19, 1837, notes, "The President read a letter from Miss Lindo, presenting to this Institution Two Dozen Copies of her Hebrew Vocabulary for the use of the Boys, and one Dozen for the Girls." A copy of Lindo's response appeared in the next entry alongside the school's thank-you note to the author. It's noteworthy that Lindo and Polack lived on the same street. Another entry in the minute books, dated April 6, 1846, alluded to Lindo's donation of four copies of her Hebrew lexicon.[5] Abigail Lindo (1803–1848) was the child of David Abarbanel Lindo, a well-known leader in the East End's Jewish community.[6] She published a Hebrew-English vocabulary in 1837 followed by a Hebrew-English dictionary in 1846. Her well-known Sephardi parents had eighteen children. They would not have attended Maria Polack's Ashkenazi synagogue, but the two women could have been acquainted, especially given the close proximity of their homes in the East End and their communal ties.

Entries in the visitor's book and the minute books record not only Solomon's pleas for literary instructions and books, but also further evidence of East End women engaged in writing activities and teaching (Miss Arnold) as well as children studying poetry, fables, and languages.

The combination of books mentioned in Polack's novel and in the pages of institutional records reveal the centrality of literary arts—recitations, reading, and ethical reflection—in the school's curriculum. As writers, teachers, and visitors to local schools, East End women performed or assessed educational initiatives. Frequently they functioned as informal public servants, overseeing or monitoring the content and style of instruction of the young. Though fleeting and fragmentary, such details create a rich context for Polack's novel. They also challenge stereotypical accounts of the region's ubiquitous crime and danger. They allow us to tell a different kind of story about the East End and the leading role of women writers in shaping educational initiatives that addressed poverty.

Fiction without Romance fit in well with these contexts, filling out the list of school subjects by adding the importance of teaching music and geography. Grace Aguilar (1816–1847), who lived in the East End region of Hackney, published several books that became wildly successful among both Jewish and Christian audiences throughout England, the United States, and the West Indies. Beginning in 1841, Charlotte Montefiore and Aguilar collaborated on a book series titled "The Cheap Jewish Library." As Michal Shahaf has noted, "The 'little books' that comprised the Cheap Jewish Library were a series of fictional works written in English, sold for pennies and designed to speak to the hearts of humble members of the Anglo-Jewish community, with realistically drawn heroes belonging to their world. Between 1841 and 1849, ten serial stories were issued in 17 or 18 booklets, later assembled in two volumes."[7] This collection offered working-class children affordable books with realist stories aimed at moral instruction. It was precisely the kind of writing that defined Polack's venture eleven years earlier. Miriam Mendes Belisario (1816–1885), the granddaughter of the well-known Jamaican illustrator Isaac Mendes Belisario, undertook a similar literature-for-education project by working at a school for Jewish girls in Hackney established by her mother in 1807. She later completed *Sabbath Evenings at Home; or, Familiar Conversations on the Jewish Religion, Its Spirit and Observances* (1856)—books modeled after Aguilar's writing about the Sabbath.

Locating these authors and their shared intellectual interests from two regions of the East End—Whitechapel and Hackney—ties them to a larger community and to one another. It also recalls the existence of East End literary culture decades before it was thought to exist. Typically, scholars note the rise of East End literary works by later-century authors, such as Arthur Morrison (1863–1945) or Israel Zangwill (1864–1926). Situating Jewish women's publishing activities in the East End and as evidence of a network of women writers compelled me to wonder about the possibility that Maria Polack or her daughter may have continued to publish their writing, perhaps under cover of a pseudonym. While Amelia Solomon's plea for classroom books may have provided a clue about why these women turned to writing in the first place, I had no idea what led to the end of the publication trail and Polack's apparent silence following the appearance of *Fiction without Romance*. Her preface clearly indicated her hope that reviewers would play the part of teacher to help improve her writing. Didn't this suggest a wish to continue writing? Perhaps she persisted, along with her daughter, by writing under a pseudonym? Evidence of the Polacks' writing life could be anywhere, or nowhere. After ten years of research in archives, I made the decision to abort my search. I might have been one archival box away from discovery. Or I might have been one hundred boxes away. Despite this decision, the late discovery of her daughter's writing suggests that further work on this literary family and their East End community remains unfinished.

The chapters of this study do not offer a comprehensive account of all aspects of East End literary and cultural arts from Polack's era. A. S. Lyon's diary entries about his own education and cultural interests attest to the value of manuscripts in the study of literary culture.[8] Indeed, the ephemeral qualities of personal diaries mean that it's possible many more diaries were written and are now lost. Not only did Lyon include detailed records of the books he was reading, the plays he attended, and the social encounters he experienced, but he also commented on raw details about the physical and emotional fallout of his social and economic traumas. Lyon wasn't as poor as many others in his community. Indeed, he had the ability to take riding lessons and French lessons as a young man—luxuries in comparison with opportunities available to many East Enders from this period. In time, however, his formal learning opportunities receded just as fears about poverty intensified. In contrast to the profusion of accounts characterizing the Jewish poor as incapable of self-redemption, Lyon offers evidence of one who attempted and failed to raise his social standing. Diary entries suggest that he felt his only option was to leave London for economic opportunities in the West Indies where he could become involved in family business opportunities.

The Jews' Orphan Asylum archive is littered with evidence of the plight of the East End's most vulnerable population—children living in poverty lacking appropriate adult protection. In records detailing disease, physical and emotional abuse, neglect, and the hardships of poverty, archives have preserved evidence of communal and individual commitment to ethics and education. Myer Levy and Myer Davis wrote about their desire to live a Jewish life. Myer Davis's letters, written in his early days as headmaster, recall his enthusiasm for teaching children about Jewish history and culture. Though still a child when questioned by investigators, Myer Levy expressed his belief in students' rights to protection and safety and teachers' responsibility to preserve the well-being of children. His statements add context to Colquhoun's view of Jewish children as thieves—a view that fails to account for the systemic social problems that might have prompted their criminal behavior. Myer Levy's testimony, in fact, offers numerous examples of the complexity of children's thought. His account of their struggles captures strategic obfuscations in response to feelings of powerlessness. These differing accounts by Colquhoun and Myer Levy do not disqualify either. Rather, their dissenting views enables us to focus on the conceptual frameworks that tend to silently shape unquestioned perceptions of the East End. The version of the East End to emerge from the archives is one of people striving to improve their lives through closer adherence to religious expressions, literary engagement, the study of languages, charitable acts, and a commitment to morality. In these accounts, instances of crime and violence are offset by evidence of individuated motives and desires that resist sweeping generalizations. Presented from insiders with intimate knowledge of local culture, the archives preserve and narrate a world in pursuit of improvement, and—school politics notwithstanding—a culture actively seeking a better life for the next generation.

I conclude by turning to Brady Street Cemetery, Polack's burial site that lies hidden behind a wall in London's East End. The cemetery was created in 1761 to bury members of London's New Synagogue and Great Synagogue. Like every other archive I've discussed in the pages of this book, Brady Street Cemetery resists closure of every kind. When it was declared full in 1855, the community poured six feet of dirt over one section of the graveyard in an effort to create more space. This raised plot, now called "the Strangers Ground," was modeled after the more famous Jewish cemetery in Prague where thousands of graves overlay one another. Unlike the Prague cemetery, however, Brady Street Cemetery grew only one level taller before its "official" closure in 1858. Many years later Nathaniel Mayer Victor, 3rd Baron Rothschild, successfully petitioned the government to be buried next to the remains of his ancestor, Nathan Mayer Rothschild, the earliest member of the English branch of the family. His petition was not aimed at a family or religious attachment. According to his biographer Kenneth Rose, "Victor left instructions that his remains were to be buried next to those of Nathan Mayer Rothschild." He adds that "to re-open its gates, where his great-grandfather had been buried in 1836, involved him in several years of negotiation with authorities."[9] English cemeteries closed for more than one hundred years are vulnerable to relocations to make room for urban development. Victor Rothschild's petition, which grew from a fear of removing the cemetery from its location, keeps Brady Street Cemetery in its current site until 2090. Given the cost of land within the city of London, the cemetery will likely be moved after that year to some shady side of a highway or an inexpensive patch of land deep in the countryside—someplace far from the cemetery's urban surroundings in the East End.

Relocating Brady Street Cemetery is controversial for a number of reasons, including the fact that it violates Jewish burial laws stipulating that a grave should never be exhumed. However, the removal is significant for other reasons as well. The cemetery artifacts—incised imagery, epitaph writing, a boundary wall, and the spatial geography of the graves—are an essential part of the story of the past and future life of the East End. To move the cemetery from its current location limits opportunities for shared narratives from disparate historical trajectories and cultures, just as it prevents emergent narratives or future visitors from developing relationships with older artifacts. Pearl Binder's illustration of Brady Street Cemetery emphasizes the interlacing qualities that bind together objects within the East End's built environment.[10] Buildings don't simply border or align with one another in Binder's image; they appear to have melted into one another, fused as one unit. The cemetery space braids together histories and creators, as the architecture casts shadows over the graves, tall towers with windows from which residents anchor themselves within the particularities of place.

The wall of the cemetery teases us, as it fails to separate the living from the dead. Here lie the dead, we are told repeatedly—here, in the East End, are the mortal remains of the living, buried by East End dirt, commemorated by writing and performances of remembrance. Here we lie buried in this spot of earth, they insist, just up the road from our synagogue, at the end of the path where we were carried from our earthly homes to our final resting place. "Here," in *this* context, is where you will find evidence of our lives. Each headstone in the Brady Street Cemetery, each contour of the writing space, the epitaph subject, choice of languages, and dates convey both something about the dead and something

FIG. 12. "Jewish Burial Ground," by Pearl Binder. (Reproduced courtesy of Pearl Binder's three children)

about those who chose to bury the dead in this way so that we could learn about their lives. The cemetery artifacts may want us to believe it's a place for the dead, but the rituals of mourning remind us continually that they are created for us, the living audience.

Brady Street Cemetery was one of the first archives I visited in my search for information about Polack. A senior scholar advised against the trip. He was convinced I'd find nothing more than unreadable stones, cracked by time and sooty air. He added that, since everyone in the East End was so poor, tracing their lives in epitaph fragments was an absurd waste of time. I listened to his admonishments while sitting at my desk across the ocean from the cemetery. He explained, "Poor people couldn't afford tombstones. Don't even bother visiting the cemetery. You won't find what you're looking for." I scribbled these words on a page from a notebook I carried with me to London. I've been haunted by his prophecy. At the time I reasoned that while many people living in the East End were poor, until the middle of the nineteenth century middle-class people lived in Whitechapel. Surely it was possible that one might have a grave marker. Was it accurate to say that *no one* would have a headstone in Brady Street Cemetery because the East End was universally poor? I insisted stubbornly that traces of Polack's life might still be legible in her burial space. I reasoned that finding her headstone might help me to identity of her family, her birth date, and perhaps other biographical details included in her epitaph.

I arrived many months later. Brady Street Cemetery was small and easily managed. And my mission was targeted—find and photograph all the graves with the name "Polack" engraved on the headstone. In addition to tracking down every extant fragment of information on Polack's life in preparation for my trip, I tracked down articles on London cemeteries, which led me to Hugh Meller's description of Brady Street Cemetery's stunning beauty:

> The old Jewish cemeteries are small secretive places, a few acres hidden by high walls and locked doors, often cheek by jowl with new buildings and identified from outside only by the trees that overhang walls topped with broken glass. Brady Street is typical, an oasis in a wilderness of East End urban desolation comprised of waste land and forbidding council house blocks. Originally it was a brickfield adjacent to Ducking Pond Lane but was leased to the New Synagogue in 1761 for an annual rent of twelve guineas. Like the other Jewish cemeteries in Whitechapel it is now closed to burials (since 1858) but it is still crowded with tombstones.[11]

"An oasis in a wilderness" in the middle of the East End? How could that be? My maps indicated that Brady Street Cemetery was sandwiched among schools, shops, apartment buildings, and rows of private homes. I assumed Meller was confused, until I saw this wilderness for myself. I was greeted by a few acres of land packed with headstones that stood in the shadow of an old brick wall. The space was overwhelmed by large apartment buildings. A kind man, jangling his keys, welcomed me at the gate and spent a lot of time answering my questions before leaving me to wander on my own. I expected to find decay, graffiti, headstones marred by moss and trash. Instead I found deep shadows cast by broad branches and a brilliant sun pushing its way to the damp green grass. It was a space of whispers and wily tree roots wound over and around and under the graves.

An hour of searching led to nothing. I turned back to my host, the man with the keys meandering from one row of tombs to another. He listened patiently before blurting with a wry smile, "You're looking for a needle in a haystack. I'll give you an hour to find it." My work continued against this prediction of failure. The headstones had darkened with stains of time. I noticed the writing in the older section was uniformly Hebrew. Later stones created after the 1830s were carved with elaborate art and displayed a mix of Hebrew and English. I was drawn to every object conveying individuated details of family loss and signs of the lived experiences of people unknown to me. I searched anxiously with my limited time, darting from one stone to the next, observing dates, names, iconography, and mention of addresses and professions. Much as I longed to find the epitaph with Polack's name, it failed to materialize. Feeling desperate, I enlisted the man with the keys to help. I emptied the contents of my backpack on one of the horizontal stone slabs as I held up a copy of the novel, the subscription list, the single line from the census record. I pointed and made large waving motions with my hands, expecting to coax him into excitement by the intensity of my curiosity. I'd come all this way, over the ocean, across the city of London, to find my lost writer. How could he not be enticed to stay a few more minutes? He shook his head, knowing full well—and he was right—that I would never find Polack's grave. He explained that her family probably couldn't afford the cost of a headstone; or perhaps they could, but it fell and cracked. Or maybe it's there, but the letters had worn away by time and years of sooty East End air. I continued searching, refusing to believe that Polack's grave might be irrevocably lost. I photographed the trees, the iron gate, and as many graves as I had time to record. I used my camera to trace the curving wall point-by-point. Maybe if I stood taller or looked sideways leaning to the left I'd find a clue? Another hour passed and the man with the keys informed me that it was time to pack up my belongings. He had another appointment.

To move the cemetery structure, to alter its dwelling space and form, to ignore its provenance as a still-growing body of memorial activities, is to miss seeing how memorial space speaks, how it affirms, reconstitutes, and politicizes Polack's social world, even, as I have learned, as it forecloses the possibility of finding evidence of her life amid the field of graves. Months later, working my way through records from one of the archives, I came across a familiar-sounding name. It matched the name from one of my cemetery photographs. I checked the subscription list next, and there it was. Each scrap of evidence led to another name, a street, a record, a list, an archive. Upon turning to my photographs from Brady Street Cemetery, I began to see fuller connections. I've since wondered about the possibilities of mapping Brady Street Cemetery, of creating a digital archive like the one in Jamaica created for Lyon's community.

What could we understand about the nineteenth-century East End if we read cemetery writing as evidence of cultural and intellectual rituals?

After studying the grave markers, consulting my subscription list, reading the synagogue burial register against the names on the graves, and scrutinizing the language from obituaries published in the *Jewish Chronicle* and the *Voice of Jacob,* I could piece together an idea of Polack's East End far richer than any single headstone would provide. A faint social network revealed shared communal values, memories, and histories that pushed against familiar narratives of East End blight. I've returned to Brady Street Cemetery many times since that disappointing first visit. On these occasions I roamed through the markers of time, trying to construct an impossibly fluid narrative that bound one fragment of text to another. I saw clues and wanted to believe they reflected upon other clues. I saw common names and wondered how family events might have tied them together. The cemetery walls protected me from the bustle of urban life on the other side, creating a thickening quiet and stillness. I never stopped searching for Polack's tombstone during visits to Brady Street Cemetery, even though I'm certain it doesn't exist. With each visit, I was confronted by remnants of a world in which I was a stranger facing memory stones left by those who believed someone from the future might come to find them.

NOTE ON SOURCES

Early in this project I faced a wall of stereotypes that became increasingly suspect with each archive I consulted. Below I've compiled a list of cultural references mentioned in these archives. My list is by no means a complete record of cultural activities referenced by East End artists, writers, teachers, and readers. Yet even as a small sample taken from the incomplete archival remains of Polack's community, the length and breadth of the list underscores the importance of questioning sensational narratives that often feed dangerous and misleading stereotypes. Many archives not included in this study offer further evidence of the rich and varied forms of nineteenth-century East End cultural production. Readers interested in learning about additional examples of nineteenth-century East End cultural life may wish to consult records from the *Voice of Jacob* (1841–46) and the *Jewish Chronicle* (1841–present), which contain abundant references to cultural activities Polack and her community would have experienced firsthand. Similarly, the East End Theatre Archive (https://www.elta-project.org/) includes rare and valuable evidence of nineteenth-century playwrights, actors, and theatre culture.

Cultural References Mentioned in Archival and Other Sources Consulted in This Study

Books, Authors, Book Series, and Composers

Grace Aguilar, *The Women of Israel* (1844)
The Bible
Johann Friedrich Blumenbach, *The Institutions of Physiology* (1787, translated 1828)
Lord Byron, *Hebrew Melodies* (1815)
Miguel de Cervantes, *Don Quixote* (1605/1615)
William Cobbett, *Grammar of the English Language* (1818)
George Crabbe, *English Synonyms* (1816)
Maria Edgeworth, *Moral Tales for Young People* (1802)
James Fordyce, *Sermons to Young Women* (1766)
John Gay, *The Beggar's Opera* (1728)
Richard Glover, *Leonidas* (1737)
Oliver Goldsmith, *Vicar of Wakefield* (1766)
William Godwin, *Things as They Are; or, The Adventures of Caleb Williams* (1794)
William Godwin, *Fables Ancient and Modern* (1804; pseudonym, Edward Baldwin)

Thomas Gray, "Elegy Written in a Country Churchyard" (1751)
Georg F. Handel, *Jephtha* (1752)
William Hazlitt, "On Modern Comedy," in *The Round Table* (1815–17)
Felicia Hemans, "Italian Girl's Evening Song to the Virgin" (1829)
Lucy Henry, *The Roll Call, and Other Stories* (1891)
David Hume, *History of England* (1754–61)
Hyman Hurwitz, *Hebrew Tales from the Writings of the Hebrew Sages* (1826)
Samuel Johnson, *The Rambler* (1750–52)
Alain-René Lesage, *Gil Blas* (1715–35)
Abigail Lindo, *A Hebrew and English and English and Hebrew Vocabulary* (1837)
Emma Lyon, *Miscellaneous Poems* (1812)
Maimonides, "Thirteen Principles of Faith" (1138–1204)
Bathsua Pell Makin, *An Essay to Revise the Antient Education of Gentlewoman, in Religion, Manners, Arts and Tongues* (1673)
Jean-François Marmontel, *Moral Tales* (1813)
Thomas Middleton, *The Phoenix* (1603)
John Milton, *Paradise Lost* (1667)
Thomas Moore, *Irish Melodies* (1807–34)
Sholto and Reuben Percy, *Anecdotes* (1823)
Elizabeth Polack (playwright), *Esther, the Royal Jewess; or The Death of Haman* (1835)
Elizabeth Polack (poet and fiction writer), "Dreams" (1839)
Maria Polack, *Fiction without Romance* (1830)
Alexander Pope, "An Essay on Man" (1733)
Charles Rollin, *Ancient History* (1730–38)
Walter Scott, *Guy Mannering* (1815), *The Well of St. Ronan* (1824), and *The Betrothed* (1825)
William Shakespeare, *Merchant of Venice* (1597) and *Henry IV* (1597)
Tobias Smollett, *The Adventures of Ferdinand Count Fathom* (1753)
Laurence Sterne, *Tristram Shandy* (1759–69) and *A Sentimental Journey* (1768)
John Thelwall, *The Peripatetic; or, Sketches of the Heart, of Nature and Society* (1793)
James Thomson, *The Seasons* (1730)
Mrs. Cornwall Baron Wilson, *Hours at Home: A Collection of Miscellaneous Poems* (1826) and *The Cypress Wreath: A Collection of Original Ballads and Tales in Verse* (1828)
Edward Young, *Night Thoughts* (1742–45)

Artists and Events

Henry Bishop, performance in *Virgin of the Sun* and *Guy Mannering*
John Bull Festival
John Braham and Thomas Dibdin collaboration, *The Cabinet: A Comic Opera in Three Acts*
David Garrick

William Macready and Miss Maria Foote in James Sheridan Knowles's *Virginius,* performed at Drury Lane Theatre
William Moncrieff, *The Cataract of the Ganges; or, The Rajah's Daughter*
Wolfgang Amadeus Mozart, *Marriage of Figaro*
"The Mutiny of the Bretianna," performed in London
Elizabeth Polack, *St. Clair of the Isles*
Account of Royalty Theatre burning on April 10, 1826
William Shakespeare, *The Winter's Tale*
George Soane, *Rob Roy* (based on Scott's novel), performed at Covent Garden Theatre
Giovanni Battista Velluti, performance of Giacomo Meyerbeer's *Il Crociato*
Lucia Elizabeth Vestris, 1779–1856, London performance of Wolfgang Amadeus Mozart's *Don Giovanni*

Museums, Schools, and Synagogues

Bevis Marks Synagogue, Sephardic Synagogue in the East End
British Gallery of Painting
Burton Crescent, Cartwright Gardens
Covent Garden
Gray's Inn Coffee House
The Great Synagogue, Ashkenazi Synagogue in the East End
Hatton Garden
Highgate School
Literary Society, Aldermanbury (the City of London)
London Institution
The Mansion House, London
M. deFontain Riding School
Regent's Park, London
St. Peter's Gardens, London
Society of Hebrew Literature
Somerset House, London
Tower of London
Vauxhall Gardens, London
Willis Rooms

Social/Family Activities

Lyon attends the Lord Mayor's Ball
Lyon travels to the West End to see Mr. Graham in his balloon over Soho Square
Lyon plays loo, backgammon, and chess multiple times throughout the diaries
Lyon took riding lessons and French lessons in 1823
Lyon has tea at Hornsey Wood House
Lyon visits Ramsgate and Margate
Lyon visits Furnival's Inn
Lyon visits Mrs. Youen's Ball

Authors and Artists with Known Family/Cultural Ties to the East End

Grace Aguilar
Miriam Mendes Belisario
John Braham
Myer Davis
John Hollingshead
Hyman Hurwitz
Abigail Lindo
A. S. Lyon
Daniel Mendoza
Arthur Morrison
Isaac Nathan
Elizabeth Polack (poet, fiction writer, and daughter of Maria Polack)
Maria Polack
Abraham Solomon
Rebecca Solomon
Simeon Solomon
Bernard Van Oven
Joshua Van Oven
Israel Zangwill

Archives and Libraries Consulted in This Study

Annabel Foster-Davis Family Archive
Brady Street Cemetery
British Library
Devon Records Office
East London Theatre Archives
Elletson Road Cemetery, Kingston
Guildhall Library
Hartley Library, University of Southampton
Jamaica Institute
London Library
London Metropolitan Archives
National Library of Jamaica
Orange Street Cemetery, Kingston
Plymouth & West Devon Record Office
Rothschild Archive
Tower Hamlets Archive
Victoria and Albert Museum and Archives (records of Spitalfields School of Art and Design and East End Theatre materials)

Related Works

The East End Digital Library (https://eastendarchives.net)

NOTES

Introduction

1. "*Illustrated Police News,* 8 September, 1888," Casebook: Jack the Ripper, https://www.casebook.org/press_reports/illustrated_police_news/il880908.html.
2. Numerous studies have examined Victorian London and the construction of the East End as a dark or threatening space. See, for example, L. Perry Curtis, *Jack the Ripper and the London Press* (New Haven, CT: Yale University Press, 2001); Drew D. Gray, *London's Shadows: The Dark Side of the Victorian City* (London: Bloomsbury, 2010); Simon Joyce, *Capital Offenses: Geographies of Class and Crime in Victorian London* (Charlottesville: University of Virginia Press, 2003); Seth Koven, *Slumming: Sexual and Social Politics in Victorian London* (Princeton, NJ: Princeton University Press, 2004); and Judith R. Walkowitz, *City of Dreadful Delight: Narratives of Sexual Danger in Late-Victorian London* (Chicago: University of Chicago Press, 1992).
3. Tim Barringer, "Land, Labor Landscape: Views of the Plantation in Victorian Jamaica," in *Victorian Jamaica,* ed. Tim Barringer and Wayne Modest (Durham, NC: Duke University Press, 2018), 281–321, 285.
4. Sander Gilman and Chaim Bermant have both examined the anti-Semitic lens and racial profiling used in the Ripper investigation. See Chaim Bermant, *London's East End: Point of Arrival* (New York: Macmillan, 1975), especially chap. 9, "Jacob the Ripper"; and Sander Gilman, *The Jew's Body* (New York: Routledge, 1991), especially chap. 4, "The Jewish Murderer: Jack the Ripper, Race, and Gender." For a fuller discussion of East End immigration history, see Anne J. Kershen's *Strangers, Aliens and Asians: Huguenots, Jews and Bangladeshis in Spitalfields, 1660–2000* (London: Routledge, 2005), which demonstrates the long history of a diverse population within the East End. Other noteworthy events simultaneously played a part in the sensationalism that culminated with the Whitechapel murders: the cholera epidemics of 1832 and 1866, the birth of William Booth's Salvation Army, and the rise of trade unionism led by prominent New Women such as Annie Besant, Beatrice Potter Webb, and Eleanor Marx. Such narratives bolstered ideas about the East End as a place where left-leaning social activities took root and where residents were in need of being saved by outsiders. Similarly, the publication of Walter Besant's *All Sorts and Conditions of Men* (1882) inspired the creation of the People's Palace, a cultural center in Mile End that opened in 1887 and provided cultural activities for the East End working poor.

5. Cecil Roth, *The Evolution of Anglo-Jewish Literature* (London: Edward Goldstein, 1937), 4. Identifying the very first Anglo-Jewish novelist is complicated by a number of factors. Several earlier writers converted to Christianity or ceased identifying publicly as Jewish. Roth's claim seems to suggest that in the period when their work appeared in print, these writers did outwardly identify as Jews. The King sisters were born to a Jewish man who did not associate with the Jewish community. His daughters married Christians and remained separated from the Jewish community throughout their lives. Benjamin Disraeli's novels appeared before Polack's *Fiction without Romance;* however, Disraeli was baptized as a child and remained Anglican throughout his adult life. Therefore, Roth and others don't always consider Disraeli a Jewish writer. Polack appears to be the first known Anglo-Jewish novelist who published while identifying as Jewish. For important discussions that challenge or complicate Roth's view, see Michael Scrivener, *Jewish Representation in British Literature, 1780–1840: After Shylock* (New York: Palgrave Macmillan, 2011), especially chap. 5; and Diane Long Hoeveler, "Charlotte Dacre's *Zofloya:* The Gothic Demonization of the Jew," in *The Jews and British Romanticism: Politics, Religion, Culture,* ed. Sheila A. Spector (New York: Palgrave, 2005), 165–78.
6. Christopher Reynolds, "London's East End, an Olympics Alternative," *Los Angeles Times,* December 4, 2011, https://www.latimes.com/travel/la-xpm-2011-dec-04-la-tr-eastlondon4-20111204-story.html.
7. This trend is beginning to change with Diana Maltz's edition of Morrison's *Child of the Jago* (Peterborough, Ontario: Broadview Press, 2013) and Meri-Jane Rochelson's edition of Israel Zangwill's *Children of the Ghetto: A Study of a Peculiar People* (Detroit: Wayne State University Press, 1998). Both texts mark a welcome shift toward greater attention to East End writers. East End literature from earlier decades has not received the same kind of attention.
8. Ellen Ross, *Love and Toil: Motherhood in Outcast London, 1870–1918* (Oxford: Oxford University Press, 1993), 22.
9. For further details see Heidi Kaufman, "1800–1900: Inside and Outside the Nineteenth-Century East End," BRANCH: Britain, Representation, and Nineteenth-Century History, January 2016, http://www.branchcollective.org/?ps_articles=heidi-kaufman-1800-1900-inside-and-outside-the-nineteenth-century-east-end.
10. Paul Newland, *The Cultural Construction of London's East End: Urban Iconography, Modernity and the Spatialisation of Englishness* (Amsterdam: Rodopi, 2008). Newland includes a helpful discussion of East End ethnic, national, and religious diversity in this period. He notes, "East London's population is, and has been, one of the most ethnically diverse in

England" (25). See especially the introduction and chapter 1 for further details on East End demographics. See also Kershen, *Strangers.*

11. Charles Dickens, *Oliver Twist,* ed. Kathleen Tillotson and intro. Stephen Gill (Oxford: Oxford University Press, 1999; originally published 1837–38), 147.
12. While Polack does not name the exact street of the sukkah, her narrative takes place in the East End and neighboring streets of Aldgate.
13. Maria Polack, *Fiction without Romance, or The Locket-Watch* (London: Effingham Wilson, 1830), 2 vols., 2:24–25.
14. Julia Brauch, Anna Lipphardt, and Alexandra Nocke, "Exploring Jewish Space: An Approach," in *Jewish Topographies: Visions of Space, Traditions of Place,* ed. Julia Brauch, Anna Lipphardt, and Alexandra Nocke (Burlington, VT: Ashgate, 2008), 1–23, 3.
15. Patrick Brantlinger, *Dark Vanishings: Discourse on the Extinction of Primitive Races, 1800–1930* (Ithaca, NY: Cornell University Press, 2003), 2.
16. David B. Ruderman, *Jewish Enlightenment in an English Key: Anglo-Jewry's Construction of Modern Jewish Thought* (Princeton, NJ: Princeton University Press, 2000), 242.
17. A number of excellent studies have traced this development. See, for example, Susan David Bernstein, ed., *Reuben Sachs,* by Amy Levy (Peterborough, Ontario: Broadview Press, 2006), and *The Romance of a Shop,* by Amy Levy (Peterborough, Ontario: Broadview Press, 2006); Michael Galchinsky, *The Origin of the Modern Jewish Woman Writer: Romance and Reform in Victorian England* (Detroit: Wayne State University Press, 1996); Michael Galchinsky, ed., *Grace Aquilar: Selected Writings,* by Grace Aquilar (Peterborough, Ontario: Broadview Press, 2003); Cynthia Scheinberg, *Women's Poetry and Religion in Victorian England: Jewish Identity and Christian Culture* (Cambridge: Cambridge University Press, 2002); and Nadia Valman, *The Jewess in Nineteenth-Century British Literary Culture* (Cambridge: Cambridge University Press, 2007), especially chap. 4.
18. Todd Endelman, in *Radical Assimilation in English Jewish History, 1656–1945* (Bloomington and Indianapolis: Indiana University Press, 1990), notes that although John King was "known popularly as 'Jew King,'" he was not a practicing Jew for much of his adult life. While enrolled as a charity student in school, he attended synagogue services regularly; later in life he abandoned religious observance entirely, only to return again later in his life (151–52, 178–80). See also Scrivener, *Jewish Representation,* especially chaps. 4 and 5. Scrivener considers the King sisters to be Anglo-Jewish writers. It's important to note that there is no standard definition of what constitutes the category "Jewish writer." Roth was unclear in this delineation.
19. According to Diane Long Hoeveler, Charlotte King's embarrassment over her father's scandalous public identity, combined with her desire to

become "a newly purified British matron-mother" upon her marriage to her "respectable WASP and Tory husband Nicholas Byrne," was partly responsible for her inclusion of anti-Semitic representations in her published work ("Charlotte Dacre's *Zofloya*," 166). Hoeveler refers to *Zofloya, or The Moor: A Romance of the Fifteenth Century,* which Charlotte King published under the pseudonym Charlotte Dacre. See also Duncan Wu, *Romantic Women Poets* (Oxford: Blackwell, 1997), 358–63; Todd M. Endelman, "The Checkered Career of 'Jew' King: A Study in Anglo-Jewish Social History," in *From East and West: Jews in a Changing Europe, 1750–1870,* ed. Frances Malino and David Sorkin (Oxford: Basil Blackwell, 1990), 151–81; Paul Baines, "Byrne, Charlotte (1782–1825)," in *Oxford Dictionary of National Biography* (Oxford: Oxford University Press, 2004); online ed., January 2015.

20. Galchinsky, *Origin,* 10. Galchinsky adds, "Anglo-Jewish women writing in the 1830s preceded women elsewhere in Europe and the United States into print by fifteen years. Even in Germany, where Jewish salonières like Rahel Varnhagen were entertaining German literati, or the United States and France, where the movement for religious reform was likewise taking hold and offering women more of a public role—even in these places, Jewish women in the 1830s and 1840s were not publishing books. But Anglo-Jewish women became active as novelists, poets, polemicists, and speakers in the modernizing Victorian community in these decades" (19).

21. Heidi Kaufman, "England's Jewish Renaissance: Maria Polack's *Fiction without Romance* (1830) in Context," in *Romanticism/Judaica: A Convergence of Cultures,* ed. Sheila A. Spector (Farnham, Surrey, UK: Ashgate, 2011), 69–84; and Heidi Kaufman, "Romance in Maria Polack's *Fiction without Romance,*" *Romantic Circles Praxis Series,* November 2020, https://romantic-circles.org/praxis/sundryfaces/praxis.2020.sundry.kaufman.html.

22. David Feldman, *Englishman and Jews: Social Relations and Political Culture, 1840–1914* (New Haven, CT: Yale University Press, 1994), 1.

23. James Shapiro, *Shakespeare and the Jews* (New York: Columbia University Press, 1995), 199.

24. London Metropolitan Archives Record LMA/4046/A/01/001, containing records of the Jews' Free School, p. 181.

25. According to the website Measuring Worth (https://www.measuringworth.com/calculators/ppoweruk), this amount holds a relative value today at £9,474, or according to OANDA's currency converter (https://www1.oanda.com/currency/converter), US $12,819 in 2020.

26. London Metropolitan Archives Record LMA/4046/A/01/001, containing records of the Jews' Free School, p. 182.

27. Emma Lyon, *Miscellaneous Poems* (Oxford: printed by J. Bartlett for the author, 1812). Emma Lyon is the first known Anglo-Jew to publish a book of poetry while identifying outwardly as a Jew.

28. London Metropolitan Archives Record LMA/4046/A/01/001, containing records of the Jews' Free School, p. 285.
29. Ann Laura Stoler, *Along the Archival Grain: Epistemic Anxieties and Colonial Common Sense* (Princeton, NJ: Princeton University Press, 2009), 48, 47.
30. Stoler, *Along the Archival Grain*, 47.
31. Hal Foster, *Vision and Visuality* (Seattle: Bay Press, 1988), ix.
32. W. J. T. Mitchell, *What Do Pictures Want? The Lives and Loves of Images* (Chicago: University of Chicago Press, 2005), 2.
33. Hilda Kean, *London Stories: Personal Lives Public Histories* (London: Rivers Oram Press, 2004), 7.
34. I am indebted to Nancy K. Miller's impressive story of a family archive, *What They Saved: Pieces of a Jewish Past* (Lincoln: University of Nebraska Press, 2011), which helped me to process my own searching acts. Miller notes two important lessons that guided me: "The hardest thing to find is what you think you are looking for" and "You don't necessarily know what it is you'll want to know" (22).
35. Claire Battershill, Helen Southworth, Alice Staveley, Michael Widner, Elizabeth Willson Gordon, and Nicola Wilson, *Scholarly Adventures in Digital Humanities: Making the Modernist Archives Publishing Project* (New York: Palgrave, 2017); Arlette Farge, *The Allure of the Archives*, trans. Thomas Scott-Railton (New Haven, CT: Yale University Press, 2015); Saidiya Hartman, *Lose Your Mother* (New York: Farrar, Straus & Giroux, 2008); Carolyn Steedman, *Dust: The Archive and Cultural History* (New Brunswick, NJ: Rutgers University Press, 2002).
36. Richard Altick, *Scholar Adventurers* (Columbus: Ohio State University Press, 1987); Farge, *Allure of Archives;* Antoinette Burton, ed., *Archive Stories: Facts, Fictions, and the Writing of History* (Durham, NC: Duke University Press, 2006); and *Dwelling in the Archive: Women Writing House, Home and History in Late Colonial India* (Oxford: Oxford University Press, 2003); Seth Koven, *The Match Girl and the Heiress* (Princeton, NJ: Princeton University Press, 2015); Hartman, *Lose Your Mother;* Steedman, *Dust;* and Miller, *What They Saved.*
37. Eric Ketelaar, "Tacit Narratives: The Meaning of Archives," *Archival Science* 1 (2001): 131–41, 138.
38. Michelle Caswell, *Archiving the Unspeakable: Silence, Memory, and the Photographic Record in Cambodia* (Madison: University of Wisconsin Press, 2014), 17.
39. Walkowitz, *City of Dreadful Delight*, 26.
40. I've created two linked digital archives that correspond to chapters 2 and 3 of this study. These archives demonstrate how repositories do more than merely save and store artifacts.
41. As Foucault has noted, the archive "is not that which, despite its immediate escape, safeguards the event of the statement, and preserves, for future

memories, its status as an escapee; it is that which . . . defines at the outset the *system of enunciability*" (Michel Foucault, *The Archeology of Knowledge: And the Discourse on Language.* trans. A. M. Sheridan Smith. [New York: Pantheon, 1972], 129).

42. The Multigraph Collective, *Interacting with Print: Elements of Reading in the Era of Print Saturation* (Chicago: University of Chicago Press, 2018), xv.

43. Michelle Allen, *Cleansing the City: Sanitary Geographies in Victorian London* (Athens: Ohio University Press, 2008); William A. Cohen and Ryan Johnson, eds., *Filth: Dirt, Disgust, and Modern Life* (Minneapolis: University of Minnesota Press, 2005); Pamela K. Gilbert, *Mapping the Victorian Social Body* (Albany: State University of New York Press, 2004), and *Cholera and Nation: Doctoring the Social Body in Victorian England* (Albany: State University of New York Press, 2008); Stephen Halliday, *The Great Stink of London: Sir Joseph Bazalgette and the Cleansing of the Victorian Metropolis* (Stroud, Gloucestershire, UK: History Press, 2008; originally published 1999); Steven Johnson, *The Ghost Map* (New York: Penguin, 2006); Mary Poovey, *Making a Social Body: British Cultural Formation, 1830–1864* (Chicago: University of Chicago Press, 1995). For important discussions of class, class conflict, and poverty, see Gareth Stedman Jones, *Outcast London: A Study in the Relationship between Classes in Victorian Society* (Oxford: Oxford University Press, 1971).

44. The nineteenth-century East End was flooded by social reformers who wanted both to make social problems in that area visible to a broader audience and to work toward improving the lives of the poor. For important discussions of reformers, see William Fishman, *East End 1888* (Nottingham, UK: Five Leaves, 2005; first published 1988); Peter Keating, ed., *Into Unknown England, 1866–1913: Selections from Social Explorers* (Manchester: Manchester University Press, 1976, by arrangement with Fontana); Margaret Harkness, *In Darkest London: A Social Documentary of the East End in the 1880s* (London: Black Apollo Press, 2003; originally published 1889); William Booth, *In Darkest England and The Way Out* (Cambridge: Cambridge University Press, 2014; originally published 1890); Ross, *Love and Toil;* and Ellen Ross, ed., *Slum Travelers* (Berkeley: University of California Press, 2007).

45. Gretchen Holbrook Gerzina, *Black London: Life before Emancipation* (New Brunswick, NJ: Rutgers University Press, 1995).

46. Coll Thrush, *Indigenous London: Native Travelers at the Heart of Empire* (New Haven, CT: Yale University Press, 2016), 3.

47. Joseph McLaughlin, *Writing the Urban Jungle: Reading Empire in London from Doyle to Eliot* (Charlottesville: University of Virginia Press, 2000).

48. Tanya Agathocleous, *Urban Realism and the Cosmopolitan Imagination in the Nineteenth Century: Visible City, Invisible World* (Cambridge: Cambridge University Press, 2011), xvi.

49. Paul Fyfe, *By Accident or Design: Writing the Victorian Metropolis* (Oxford: Oxford University Press, 2015).
50. Pamela K. Gilbert, ed., *Imagined Londons* (Albany: State University of New York Press, 2002).
51. Bernstein, ed., *Romance of a Shop* and *Reuben Sachs;* William J. Fishman, *The Streets of East London* (London: Gerald Duckworth, 1979); Galchinsky, ed., *Grace Aguilar;* Meri-Jane Rochelson, *A Jew in the Public Arena: The Career of Israel Zangwill* (Detroit: Wayne State University Press, 2010); Rochelson, ed., *Children of the Ghetto;* Nadia Valman and Emma Francis, "Introduction: Revisiting the Victorian East End," *19: Interdisciplinary Studies in the Long Nineteenth Century* (2011), https://19.bbk.ac.uk/article/id/1518; and Sharon Aronofsky Weltman, "Melodrama, Purimspiel, and Jewish Emancipation," *Victorian Literature and Culture* 47, no. 2 (2019): 305–45.
52. Lynda Nead, *Victorian Babylon: People, Streets and Images in Nineteenth-Century London* (New Haven, CT: Yale University Press, 2000), 8.
53. Gerard Genette, *Paratexts: Thresholds of Interpretation* (Cambridge: Cambridge University Press, 1997).
54. Shalini Puri, "Finding the Field: Notes on Caribbean Cultural Criticism, Area Studies, and the Form of Engagement," *Small Axe* 17, no. 2 (July 2013): 58–73, 59.
55. Davis, *Fiction in the Archives,* 2.

1. Before the Archive

1. Oliver Strand, "An Oasis Off London's Beaten Path," *New York Times,* September 5, 2010, Travel.
2. I want to acknowledge Paul Newland's powerful discussion of the way London identities emerge through one another, in *The Cultural Construction of London's East End: Urban Iconography, Modernity and the Spatialisation of Englishness* (Amsterdam: Rodopi, 2008). His study shaped my thinking about spatial narratives in London and the related identities of the people who live there and define themselves through and against one another.
3. Gareth Stedman Jones, *Outcast London: A Study in the Relationship between Classes in Victorian Society* (Harmondsworth, UK: Penguin, 1986; originally published 1971), 1.
4. Jones, *Outcast London,* 1.
5. Deborah Epstein Nord, *Walking the Victorian Streets: Women, Representation, and the City* (Ithaca, NY: Cornell University Press, 1995), 1.
6. Seth Koven, *Slumming: Sexual and Social Politics in Victorian London* (Princeton, NJ: Princeton University Press, 2004), 1.
7. Henri Lefebvre, *The Production of Space,* trans. Donald Nicholson-Smith (Oxford: Blackwell Publishers, English translation, 1991), 17–18.

8. Jacques Derrida, *Archive Fever: A Freudian Impression,* trans. Eric Prenowitz (Chicago: University of Chicago Press, 1995), 36.
9. Pamela K. Gilbert, introduction to *Imagined Londons,* ed. Pamela K. Gilbert (Albany: State University of New York Press, 2002), 1–3, 1.
10. Alan Palmer, preface to *The East End: Four Centuries of London Life* (London: John Murray, 2004), xvii–xix, xvii.
11. Palmer, preface to *East End,* xvii.
12. Newland, *Cultural Construction,* 17.
13. Judith R. Walkowitz, *City of Dreadful Delight: Narratives of Sexual Danger in Late-Victorian London* (Chicago: University of Chicago Press, 1992), 17.
14. Alex Goody, "Murder in Mile End: Amy Levy, Jewishness, and the City," *Victorian Literature and Culture* 34, no. 2 (2006): 461–79, 463.
15. Peter Ackroyd, introduction to *The East End: Four Centuries of London Life,* by Alan Palmer (London: John Murray, 2004), xi–xvi, xv.
16. Nils Roemer, "London and the East End as Spectacles of Urban Tourism," *Jewish Quarterly Review* 99, no. 3 (2009): 419–20.
17. For an important discussion of the way maps worked to identify and define space, see Pamela K. Gilbert, *Mapping the Victorian Social Body* (Albany: State University of New York Press, 2004), especially chap. 1.
18. *A New and Accurate Description of the Present Great Roads and the Principal Cross Roads of England and Wales, Commencing at London, and Continued to the Farthest Parts of the Kingdom, with the Several Branches Leading out of Them; and a Description of the Several Towns That Stand Thereon.* [. . .] (London: printed for R. and J. Dodsley, 1756), 129.
19. *The London Guide, Describing the Public and Private Buildings of London, Westminster, & Southwark* (London: printed for J. Fielding, [1782?]), 25.
20. Charles Dickens, *Oliver Twist,* ed. Kathleen Tillotson, intro. Stephen Gill (Oxford: Oxford University Press, 1999), 163.
21. Johann Wilhelm von Archenholz, *A Picture of England: Containing a Description of the Laws, Customs, and Manners of England, trans. from the Original German of W. de Archenholtz. Formerly a Captain in the Prussian Service. A New Translation* (London, 1797), 119.
22. Archenholz, *Picture of England,* 119.
23. Members of the Cruikshank family were successful satirists and caricaturists in this period. Isaac Cruikshank (1764–1811) was a well-known political satirist. His sons Isaac Robert Cruikshank (1789–1856) and George Cruikshank (1792–1878) followed in their father's footsteps. George Cruikshank would not only illustrate Egan's novel with his brother, but developed a working relationship with Dickens and later created the illustrations for *Oliver Twist.*
24. Pierce Egan, *Life in London* (New York: D. Appleton), 1904; repr. from *Life in London; Day and Night Scenes of Jerry Hawthorn, Esq. and His Elegant Friend Corinthian Tom, Accompanied by Bob Logic, the Oxonian, in Their*

Rambles and Sprees through the Metropolis (London: printed for Sherwood, Neely, and Jones, 1821), 226.

25. Isaac Robert and George Cruikshank, "Lowest Life in London," in Egan, *Life in London*, n.p.
26. Joseph McLaughlin, *Writing the Urban Jungle: Reading Empire in London from Doyle to Eliot* (Charlottesville: University of Virginia Press, 2000), 1.
27. John Marriott, *Beyond the Tower: A History of East London* (New Haven, CT: Yale University Press, 2011), 331.
28. Rodreguez King-Dorset, *Black Dance in London, 1730–1850: Innovation, Tradition and Resistance* (Jefferson, NC: McFarland, 2008), 83.
29. Efraim Sicher, "The 'Attraction of Repulsion': Dickens, Modernity, and Representation," in *A Mighty Mass of Brick and Smoke: Victorian and Edwardian Representations of London*, ed. Lawrence Phillips, 2nd ed. (New York: AMS Press, 2015), 25–50, 27.
30. Sicher, "'Attraction of Repulsion,'" 28.
31. Dickens, *Oliver Twist*, 54.
32. Dickens, *Oliver Twist*, 147.
33. Dickens, *Oliver Twist*, 120.
34. Dickens, *Oliver Twist*, 139.
35. Dickens, *Oliver Twist*, 139.
36. Dickens, *Oliver Twist*, 163.
37. Dickens, *Oliver Twist*, 163.
38. Dickens, *Oliver Twist*, 163.
39. Dickens, *Oliver Twist*, 163.
40. Dickens, *Oliver Twist*, 206.
41. Clive Bloom, "Jack the Ripper—A Legacy in Pictures," in *Jack the Ripper and The East End*, ed. Alex Werner, intro. Peter Ackroyd (London: Chatto & Windus, 2008), 239–67, 239.
42. George Eliot, *Daniel Deronda*, ed. Terence Cave (New York: Penguin, 1995), 380.
43. See Heidi Kaufman, "Jewish Space and the English Foreigner in George Eliot's *Daniel Deronda*," in *Fear, Loathing, and Victorian Xenophobia*, ed. Marlene Tromp, Maria K. Bachman, and Heidi Kaufman (Columbus: Ohio State University Press, 2013), 249–66.
44. Jones, *Outcast London*, 100–101.
45. Jones, *Outcast London*, 101.
46. Palmer, *East End*, 55.
47. John Fisher Murray, *The World of London* (Edinburgh and London: William Blackwood and Sons, 1843), 2 vols., 1:252.
48. Murray, *World of London*, 1:252.
49. John Hollingshead, *Ragged London in 1861*, intro. Anthony S. Wohl (London: Everyman's Library, 1986), 58.
50. Hollingshead, *Ragged London*, 112.

51. Albert Fried and Richard M. Elman, introduction to *Charles Booth's London: A Portrait of the Poor at the Turn of the Century, Drawn from His "Life and Labour of the People in London,"* sel. and ed. Albert Fried and Richard M. Elman (New York: Pantheon Books, 1968), xvii.
52. Fried and Elman, introduction to *Charles Booth's London*, xvii.
53. Charles Booth also wrote and hired a team of others to compose journal entries depicting the lives of the poor. These records have been digitized by the London School of Economics: http://booth.lse.ac.uk.
54. Peter Keating makes a similar point, explaining that the results of Booth's study showed that "35.2 per cent of the East London population lived in poverty, and, what was even more disturbing considering that the East End was supposed to be a special case, later investigation gave the corresponding figure for London as a whole as 30.7 per cent" (introduction to *Into Unknown England, 1866–1913*, ed. Peter Keating [Manchester, UK: Manchester University Press, 1976], 11–32, 25).
55. William Fishman, *East End 1888* (London: Gerald Duckworth, 1988; repr., Nottingham, UK: Five Leaves Press, 2005), 50.
56. Marriott, *Beyond the Tower*, 199.
57. Marriott, *Beyond the Tower*, 151.
58. Drew D. Gray, *London's Shadows: The Dark Side of the Victorian City* (London: Bloomsbury, 2010).
59. Peter Cunningham, *Hand-book of London: Past and Present* (London: John Murray, 1850), 441.
60. Sander Gilman, *The Jew's Body* (New York: Routledge, 1991), see chap. 4.
61. Heidi J. Holder, "The East-End Theatre," in *The Cambridge Companion to Victorian and Edwardian Theatre*, ed. K. Powell (Cambridge: Cambridge University Press, 2004), 257–76, 265.
62. Arthur Morrison, "A Street," *Macmillan's Magazine* 64 (1891): 460–63, 460.
63. W. T. Stead, *The Maiden Tribute of Modern Babylon*, ed. Antony E. Simpson (Lambertville, NJ: True Bill Press, 2007), 67.
64. Stead, *Maiden Tribute*, 69.
65. Stead, *Maiden Tribute*, 74.
66. Stead, *Maiden Tribute*, 74.
67. Stead, *Maiden Tribute*, 192.
68. Stead, *Maiden Tribute*, 120.
69. Stead, *Maiden Tribute*, 120.
70. Saidiya Hartman, *Lose Your Mother: A Journey along the Atlantic Slave Route* (New York: Farrar, Straus & Giroux, 2007), 174–75.
71. *In Darkest London* was originally published in 1889 as *Captain Lobe: A Story of the Salvation Army* under Harkness's pseudonym, John Law. The text was based upon a publication from 1888 in the *British Weekly*. Harkness republished this work with a new title in 1891 following the success of books by Stanley and Booth.

72. Joseph Conrad, *Heart of Darkness,* ed. Ross C. Murfin, 2nd ed. (Boston: Bedford Books of St. Martin's Press, 1996), 19.
73. See Suzanne Keen, *Romances of the Archive in Contemporary British Fiction* (Toronto: University of Toronto Press, 2001).

2. Archive Models

1. Felicia R. Lee, "New Novel of Harlem Renaissance Is Found," *New York Times,* September 15, 2012.
2. Lee, "New Novel."
3. For discussions of the seduction of recovery, see Ann Laura Stoler, *Along the Archival Grain: Epistemic Anxieties and Colonial Common Sense* (Princeton, NJ: Princeton University Press, 2009); Carolyn Steedman, *Dust: The Archive and Cultural History* (New Brunswick, NJ: Rutgers University Press, 2001); and Anjali Arondekar, *For the Record: On Sexuality and the Colonial Archive in India* (Durham, NC: Duke University Press, 2009). Suzanne Keen's *Romances of the Archive in Contemporary British Fiction* (Toronto: University of Toronto Press, 2001) lays important groundwork for considering how novels have prepared us to think of archives and archival records as a site of discovery and/or recovery.
4. Michael Galchinsky, *The Origin of the Modern Jewish Woman Writer: Romance and Reform in Victorian England* (Detroit: Wayne State University Press, 1996), 17.
5. I used a copy of the novel owned by the Corvey Collection of Women's Writing. Gale/Cengage digitized the Belser Wissenschaftlicher Dienst copy (an imprint on one of the title pages indicates that Gale used the Belser copy) and included it on the Nineteenth Century Collections Online database (NCCO). Gale's copy was reprinted in 2017 in paper and is now available as an Amazon.com reprint. According to the Sheffield Hallam Corvey project site, "The Corvey library, near Höxter in Germany, houses one of the largest collections of Romantic-era literature in the world. Thanks to the eccentric buying policy of the original owner, it also contains the best collection of popular fiction in English between 1798 and 1834 to be found anywhere. There are many rare works; several are unique. Novels which were generally treated as ephemera were here preserved virtually untouched for two centuries. It was only in the 1980s that the scholarly importance of Corvey was recognised. In 1987 the publisher Belser Wissenshaftlicher Dienst produced the first section of the Corvey Microfiche Edition, including facsimiles of more than 3,000 works of fiction, drama, and poetry in English" (https://extra.shu.ac.uk/corvey).
6. *The English Catalogue of Books, 1801–1836,* ed. and compiled by Robert Alexander Peddie and Quinton Waddington (repr., New York: Kraus Reprint, 2005). https://www.nationalarchives.gov.uk/currency-converter.

7. Known copies of the novel can be found at the University of Glasgow, Cambridge University, the University of St. Andrews, the University of Toronto (volume 2 only), and the British Library. One additional copy is known to exist in a German library.
8. Unknown employee of the Museum of London, email discussion, August 21, 2012.
9. Gérard Genette, *Paratexts: Thresholds of Interpretation,* trans. Jane E. Lewin, foreword by Richard Macksey (Cambridge: Cambridge University Press, 1997), 1.
10. Genette, *Paratexts,* 1–2.
11. Giorgio Agamben, *Remnants of Auschwitz: The Witness and the Archive,* trans. Daniel Heller-Roazen (New York: Zone Books, 2002), 144, my emphasis.
12. Michel-Rolph Trouillot, *Silencing the Past: Power and the Production of History* (Boston: Beacon Press, 1995), 26.
13. Maria Polack, "To Subscribers," in *Fiction without Romance, or The Locket-Watch* (printed in London by J. Wertheimer, 1830), n.p.
14. Johanna Drucker, "Humanities Approaches to Graphical Display," *Digital Humanities Quarterly* 5, no. 1 (2011): para. 1. Lisa Gitelman, *Raw Data Is an Oxymoron* (Cambridge, MA: MIT Press, 2013).
15. Gitelman, *Raw Data,* 3.
16. Lauren F. Klein, "The Image of Absence: Archival Silence, Data Visualization, and James Hemings," *American Literature* 85, no. 4 (December 2013): 661–88, 684.
17. According to Cecil Roth, "The earliest records of the Great Synagogue have been lost. Until the year 1722, all that we have to go upon are stray references in scattered sources in a bewildering variety of languages: a couple of old deeds: the casual statements, sometimes contradictory, of the protagonists in a forgotten quarrel: and (a document now studied for the first time) the oldest account-book of the congregation, with sporadic entries referring to the first decade of the eighteenth century" (*History of the Great Synagogue, 1690–1940* [London: E. Goldston, 1950], online ed. reproduced by Susser Archive, http://www.jewishgen.org/jcr-uk/susser/roth/index.htm [chap. 2, para. 1]).
18. Chancery Record for The Goodmans [*sic*] Field Estate, October 4, 1804, pp. 1–2, manuscript copy. Confirmation of this address also appears in the following source: Ancestry.com, *London and Country Directory, 1811* (Provo, UT: Ancestry.com Operations, 2004). Original data: *Holden's Annual London and Country Directory, of the United Kingdoms, and Wales, in Three Volumes, for the Year 1811. Vol. I–III* (London: W. Holden, 1811), http://search.ancestrylibrary.com/cgi-bin/sse.dll?h=380&db=London-1811&indiv=try.

19. James Picciotto, *Sketches of Anglo-Jewish History* (London: Trübner, 1875), 231–32.
20. From *Great Synagogue Marriage Records, 1791–1830,* introduction, notes, and indexes by Angela Shire (Crediton, Devon, UK: Frank J. Gent, 1999), 54. "Privileged" synagogue members were those who made larger donations to the synagogue for its upkeep and charity efforts. This record indicates that at the time neither Polack nor her husband was privileged, as they are listed as "Desc from privileged."
21. Burial Book, 1838–1853, Archives of the United Synagogue and Predecessors, London Metropolitan Archives MS ACC/2712/GTS/383, p. 308.
22. Nineteenth-century sources are inconsistent in their spelling of "Goodman's Fields." Some do not include an apostrophe, while others hyphenate the location (Goodman's-fields). I defer to the original spelling used in quoted passages.
23. Great Synagogue Burial Register, 1850–1860, Archives of the United Synagogue and Predecessors, London Metropolitan Archives MS ACC/2712/GTS/384, p. 5.
24. The novel and the British Library copy of the book suggest that Polack may have spent a portion of her life prior to writing the novel in Newton Abbot near Plymouth where a home mentioned in the novel—Greenwood Cottage—may recall an actual home built in the seventeenth century and renovated in 1800. The house is a grade 2 listed building. Visit the listing for further details: https://britishlistedbuildings.co.uk/101256908-greenwood-cottage-newton-abbot.
25. Ancestry Library ed., 1841 England Census, https://www.familysearch.org/ark:/61903/1:1:MQVT-M3Y. The English census listed ages in five-year increments. Hence, the ages listed for Lipman and Maria Polack are not exact. I've used official death certificates to find more accurate birth and death records.
26. I would like to acknowledge that this point came from Nicholas Hatton, a volunteer at the Woodhams Stone Collection.
27. It's likely that the Elizabeth Polack listed here is not the same one who wrote the plays *Esther, the Royal Jewess: An Historical Drama, in Three Acts* (1835) and *St. Clair of the Isles; or the Outlaw of Barra: A Scottish Historical Melodrama, in Three Acts* (1840). Chapter 4 discusses family relations in greater detail. For further information on Elizabeth Polack's plays, see Sharon A. Weltman, "Melodrama, *Purimspiel,* and Jewish Emancipation," *Victorian Literature and Culture* 47, no. 2 (Summer 2019): 305–45. On Picciotto's claim, see Picciotto, *Sketches of Anglo-Jewish History,* 31–33.
28. Ancestry.com, *London, England, Deaths and Burials, 1813–1980* (Provo, UT: Ancestry.com Operations, 2010). This record comes from original data: Board of Guardian Records, 1834–1906, and Church of England

Parish Registers, 1813–1906. London Metropolitan Archives, London. London Metropolitan Archives, Saint Mary, Whitechapel, Register of Burials, P93/MRY1, Item 069, P93/MRY1/069.

29. Ancestry.com record: BSGSBUR 329/2475.
30. Ancestry.com, *UK, Register of Duties Paid for Apprentices' Indentures, 1710–1811* (Provo, UT: Ancestry.com Operations). This collection was indexed by Ancestry World Archives Project contributors. Original data: *Board of Stamps: Apprenticeship Books,* Series IR 1; The National Archives of the UK (TNA), Kew, Surrey, England, http://search.ancestrylibrary.com/cgi-bin/sse.dll?h=336893&db=ApprenticeDutyIR1&indiv=try.
31. *Old Bailey Proceedings Online* (www.oldbaileyonline.org, version 8.0), May 1819, trial of William Dawes (t18190526–135). The transcript spells Maria Polack's husband's name with an "e": Lepman Polack. Extant records are inconsistent in the spelling. At other times the name appears as Lipman Polack.
32. *Old Bailey Proceedings Online* (www.oldbaileyonline.org, version 6.0), May 1819, trial of William Dawes (t18190526–135).
33. English efforts to convert Jewish children to Christianity posed a threat and challenge to London's Jewish community. See Todd M. Endelman, *The Jews of Britain, 1656 to 2000* (Berkeley: University of California Press, 2002), and *Radical Assimilation in English Jewish History, 1656–1945* (Bloomington: Indiana University Press, 1990). See also Gerry Black, *J.F.S.: The History of the Jews' Free School, London, since 1732* (London: Tymsder, 1998); and Michael Ragussis, *Figures of Conversion: "The Jewish Question" and English National Identity* (Durham, NC: Duke University Press, 1995).
34. For a discussion of Polack's interest in literary debates, see Heidi Kaufman, "Romance in Maria Polack's *Fiction without Romance,*" *Romantic Circles Praxis Series,* November 2020, https://romantic-circles.org/praxis/sundryfaces/praxis.2020.sundry.kaufman.html; and Heidi Kaufman, "England's Jewish Renaissance: Maria Polack's *Fiction without Romance* (1830) in Context," in *Romanticism/Judaica: A Convergence of Cultures,* ed. Sheila A. Spector (Surrey, UK: Ashgate, 2011), 69–84.
35. Polack, *Fiction without Romance,* 1:3.
36. Polack, *Fiction without Romance,* 1:164.
37. Polack, *Fiction without Romance,* 1:177.
38. Polack, *Fiction without Romance,* 1:210.
39. Keith Pearce, *The Jews of Cornwall: A History* (Somerset, UK: Halsgrove, 2014); Bernard Susser, *The Jews of South-West England: The Rise and Decline of their Medieval and Modern Communities* (Exeter, UK: University of Exeter Press, 1993); and Bernard Susser, *The Jews of Devon and Cornwall: Essays and Exhibition Catalogue* (Bristol, UK: Redcliffe Press, 2000).
40. Gary Kelly, *Women, Writing, and Revolution, 1790–1827* (Oxford: Clarendon Press, 1993), 10.

41. Linda H. Peterson, *Becoming a Woman of Letters: Myths of Authorship and Facts of the Victorian Market* (Princeton, NJ: Princeton University Press, 2009), 4.
42. According to the *English Catalogue of Books, Fiction without Romance* was published on May 30, 1830, for 16 shillings (*The English Catalogue of Books, 1801–1836,* ed. and compiled by Robert Alexander Peddie and Quinton Waddington [repr., New York: Kraus Reprint, 2005]). According to William St. Clair, by the 1820s, the cost of the three-volume novel was between 24 and 31.5 shillings. *Fiction without Romance* was only two volumes, but its price seems low when we consider that Mary Shelley's *Frankenstein* was published in 1818 for 16.5 shillings, and Jane Austen's *Sense and Sensibility* appeared even earlier, in 1811, for 15 shillings (William St. Clair, *The Reading Nation in the Romantic Period* [Cambridge: Cambridge University Press, 2004]), 203.
43. Michael Scrivener, "Following the Muse: Inspiration, Prophecy, and Deference in the Poetry of Emma Lyon (1788–1870), Anglo-Jewish Poet," in *The Jews and British Romanticism: Politics, Religion, Culture,* ed. Sheila A. Spector (New York: Palgrave, 2005), 106.
44. Polack, *Fiction without Romance,* 1:i.
45. Polack, *Fiction without Romance,* 1:i.
46. Two reviews mention *Fiction without Romance:* the *Literary Gazette* and *Edinburgh Review.* Both include only the title and author of the novel with no further commentary.
47. Unsigned review, "*Fiction without Romance; or, the Locket-watch.* By Mrs. Maria Pollack" [*sic*], *London Literary Gazette and Journal of Belles Lettres, Arts, Sciences, Etc.,* May 8, 1830, 303.
48. St. Clair, *Reading Nation,* 166. Lee Erickson notes that in the early decades of the nineteenth century readers did not typically purchase the books they read, for "the high price of novels prohibited most individuals from purchasing them and . . . encouraged the establishment of circulating or subscription libraries that would lend books to a borrower for an annual fee of two guineas a year, which would allow a member of a library to borrow two volumes at a time" (*The Economy of Literary Form: English Literature and the Industrialization of Publishing, 1800–1850* [Baltimore: Johns Hopkins University Press, 1996], 143).
49. Solveig Robinson, *The Book in Society: An Introduction to Print Culture* (Peterborough, Ontario: Broadview Press, 2014), 157–58.
50. St. Clair, *Reading Nation,* 165.
51. "Van Oven Family," in *The Palgrave Dictionary of Anglo-Jewish History,* ed. William D. Rubinstein, Michael A. Jolles, and Hilary L. Rubinstein (New York: Palgrave, 2011), 999.
52. Arthur Kiron, "An Atlantic Jewish Republic of Letters," *Jewish History* 20 (2006): 171–211, 172–73.

53. See Nicholas Draper, *The Price of Emancipation: Slave Ownership, Compensation, and British Society at the End of Slavery* (Cambridge: Cambridge University Press, 2013).
54. Wai Chee Dimock, *Through Other Continents: American Literature across Deep Time* (Princeton, NJ: Princeton University Press, 2006), 3.
55. See Keith Pearce, Bernard Susser, and Helen P. Fry, *Jews of North Devon* (Somerset, UK: Halsgrove, 2005).
56. Obituary of Mary Hart, October 24, 1852, *Gentleman's Magazine* 38 (July–December 1852): 659.
57. "Lemon Hart," in *Palgrave Dictionary of Anglo-Jewish History*, ed. William D. Rubinstein, Michael A. Jolles, and Hilary L. Rubinstein (New York: Palgrave, 2011), 403.
58. Emanuel Baruh (or Barrow) lived from 1783 to 1854. He was a member of a Sephardic family with roots in England dating back to the seventeenth century. The entry in the *Palgrave Dictionary of Anglo-Jewish History* explains that "Emanuel was the son of Isaac Baruh Lousada (1748–30 May 1831) whose family were prominent planters and merchants in Jamaica. Emanuel settled in London, where he was a successful West India merchant. He later lived at Peak House, Sidmouth, Devon, and he is credited with developing Sidmouth as a popular resort. In 1842–3 he served as High Sheriff of Devon, the first provincial Jew to hold that office. . . . He was related to many other notable Sephardi families, including the Montefiores" (618).
59. While the novel does not directly mention Atlantic slavery, it does still include metaphoric references to the institution of slavery. For example, characters mention being "enslaved" by ideas. In another passage a women victimized by a man who took advantage of her is compared to an enslaved woman. Such allusions suggest that Polack was well versed with the language of slavery, even though she doesn't make explicit reference to the Atlantic contexts evoked by the word.
60. Marisa J. Fuentes, *Dispossessed Lives: Enslaved Women, Violence, and the Archive* (Philadelphia: University of Pennsylvania Press, 2016), 4.
61. Priya Joshi, "Globalizing Victorian Studies," *Yearbook of English Studies* 41, no. 2 (2011): 20–40, 21.
62. Wolfgang Ernst, *Digital Memory and the Archive*, ed. and intro. Jussi Parikka (Minneapolis: University of Minnesota Press, 2013), 83.
63. Richard Jean So, "All Models Are Wrong," *PMLA* 132, no. 3 (2017): 668–73, 668.
64. So, "All Models Are Wrong," 671.
65. Andrew Piper, *Enumerations: Data and Literary Study* (Chicago: University of Chicago Press, 2018), 9.
66. Piper, *Enumerations*, 12.

67. Andrew Piper, "Think Small: On Literary Modeling," *PMLA* 132, no. 3 (2017): 651–58.
68. Ted Underwood, *Distant Horizons: Digital Evidence and Literary Change* (Chicago: University of Chicago Press, 2019), 17.
69. I collaborated with R. Benjamin Gorham on the data curations and creation of this graph. The Gephi graph was produced by R. Benjamin Gorham, PhD, the Research Data and GIS Specialist at the Freedman Center for Digital Scholarship, Kelvin Smith Library, Case Western Reserve University.
70. Belisario is the granddaughter of the well-known Jamaican artist Isaac Mendes Belisario. Her family connections may explain some of the West Indian ties on the lists.
71. See David Cesarani, *The Jewish Chronicle and Anglo-Jewry, 1841–1991* (Cambridge: Cambridge University Press, 1994).
72. I collaborated with R. Benjamin Gorham on the data curations and creation of this graph. The Gephi graph was produced by R. Benjamin Gorham, PhD, the Research Data and GIS Specialist at the Freedman Center for Digital Scholarship, Kelvin Smith Library, Case Western Reserve University.
73. Piper, "Think Small," 652.
74. Marlene Manoff, "Archive and Database as Metaphor: Theorizing the Historical Record," *Portal: Libraries and the Academy* 10, no. 4 (October 2010): 385–98, 386.
75. I collaborated with R. Benjamin Gorham on the data curations and creation of this graph. The Gephi graph was produced by R. Benjamin Gorham, PhD, the Research Data and GIS Specialist at the Freedman Center for Digital Scholarship, Kelvin Smith Library, Case Western Reserve University.
76. N. Katherine Hayles, *How We Think: Digital Media and Contemporary Technogenesis* (Chicago: University of Chicago Press, 2012), 178.
77. Hayles, *How We Think,* 178.
78. Anjali Arondekar, "Without a Trace: Sexuality and the Colonial Archive," *Journal of the History of Sexuality* 14 (2005): 10–27, 12.

3. The Noisy Archive

1. See note 5 in the introduction to this study for a fuller discussion of the first Jewish writers in England. Emma Lyon and Maria Polack are the first writers of poetry and a novel who identified outwardly as Jewish. Other earlier writers, such as the Dacre sisters and Benjamin Disraeli, had Jewish parents but did not identify outwardly as Jews, nor were they affiliated with Jewish institutions or cultural life. Isaac D'Israeli published essays

and books. In 1813 he broke from the Sephardi synagogue, Bevis Marks. A few years later he had all four of his children, including Benjamin, baptized.

2. Until very recently, both Polack and Lyon have been mostly neglected in critical discussions of early nineteenth-century women writers and Anglo-Jewish literary history. For recent key discussions of their work, see Karen A. Weisman, *Singing in a Foreign Land: Anglo-Jewish Poetry, 1812–1847* (Philadelphia: University of Pennsylvania Press, 2018), especially chap. 1; Michael Scrivener, "Following the Muse: Inspiration, Prophecy, and Deference in the Poetry of Emma Lyon (1788–1870), Anglo-Jewish Poet," in *The Jews and British Romanticism: Politics, Religion, Culture,* ed. Sheila A. Spector (New York: Palgrave, 2005), 105–26; and Naomi Cream, "Revd Solomon Lyon of Cambridge, 1755–1820," *Jewish Historical Studies* 36 (1999–2000): 31–69.
3. Cream, "Revd Solomon Lyon," 31–32.
4. Cream, "Revd Solomon Lyon," 41.
5. Over the course of his lifetime Solomon Lyon published three books: *A Compendious Hebrew Grammar* (1799); *Explanation of and Observations on an Antique Medal* (1810); and *A Theological Hebrew Grammar and Lexicon Entitled "A Key to the Holy Tongue"* (1815). See the Lyon Archive's "About the Project" page for further details.
6. Cream, "Revd Solomon Lyon," 66.
7. Scrivener, "Following the Muse," 105.
8. For important discussions of Anglo-Jewish women's literary culture in the nineteenth century, see Michael Galchinsky, *The Origin of the Modern Jewish Woman Writer: Romance and Reform in Victorian England* (Detroit: Wayne State University Press, 1996); Nadia Valman, *The Jewess in Nineteenth-Century British Literary Culture* (Cambridge: Cambridge University Press, 2007); and Weisman, *Singing.*
9. Galchinsky, *Origin,* 10. "A Daughter of Israel," in *The Jewish Preceptress; or, Elementary Lessons: Written Chiefly for the Use of the Female Children, Educated at the Jews Hospital* (London: printed by N. Archer, 1818), xi.
10. Heidi Kaufman, "Romance in Maria Polack's *Fiction without Romance,*" *Romantic Circles Praxis Series,* November 2020, https://romantic-circles.org/praxis/sundryfaces/praxis.2020.sundry.kaufman.html.
11. Emma Lyon did not live in the East End. However, she had family and social connections with many who did, including Maria Polack.
12. The unnamed author of *The Jewish Preceptress* produced a text for classroom use rather than a work of literature, such as a novel or poetry collection. *The Jewish Preceptress; or, Elementary Lessons: Written Chiefly for the Use of the Female Children, Educated at the Jews Hospital,* by a daughter of Israel, was printed two years before the admission of girls to the Jews Hospital, which was subsequently renamed the Jews' Free School. Gerry Black

notes that Mrs. Leah Barnett was the first elected governess of the Girls' School (*J.F.S.: The History of the Jews' Free School, London, since 1732* [London: Tymsder, 1998], 39), which opened in 1820. Some believe that Barnett may be the author of *The Jewish Preceptress,* although the fact that the book appeared two years earlier than her appointment, combined with the author's dedication—which states, "To Samuel Joseph, ESQ. President of this excellent institution, this work is respectfully inscribed, by his grateful and obliged servant, The Author"—might suggest another author. Anglo-Jewish girls would have had difficulty acquiring a formal education prior to 1820, when they were admitted to the Jews' Free School. As Karen A. Weisman observes, "As a Jewish woman, Emma Lyon's access to formal higher education was severely limited. There is anecdotal evidence that she became well read all the same, and her poetry is obtrusively dense with allusions to canonical ancient and modern English culture whose authority she putatively cannot appropriate, indeed whose contents her poetry laments not knowing. She was herself a Hebrew teacher, and it is certainly clear that her father would have taught her Hebrew as well" (*Singing,* 17).

13. Scrivener, "Following the Muse," 105–26.
14. Scrivener, "Following the Muse," 105–26.
15. Scrivener, "Following the Muse," 122.
16. Scrivener, "Following the Muse," 122.
17. Scrivener, "Following the Muse," 122–23.
18. It's worth noting that a few wealthier patrons, such as the Montefiores and Rothschilds, purchased multiple copies of *Fiction without Romance.* The identities of these families, Jewish philanthropists who famously supported Jewish causes, are represented on a single line, with a single name followed by the number of copies they purchased. In contrast, two other families, the Goldsmids and the Lyons, have multiple listings—one line for each member of the family. The difference in presentation of families suggests that each name on the list might have been known to Polack personally.
19. Original copies of the diaries are part of a private family collection. Digital copies can be found under the "editions" tab on the Lyon Archive (http://lyon.eastendarchives.net). A. S. Lyon used inconsistent pagination in his diaries. The earlier 1823 diary includes some page numbers, which I've included in quotes from those pages. When diary page numbers are missing in the diary, I include a reference to "n.p." The second diary, kept from 1826 to 1839, does not include page numbers, and hence I have not listed them in my citation notes.
20. From 1625 to 1966, Barbados was a British colony. The British controlled Jamaica from 1655 to 1962. Sarah Phillips Casteel notes, "The story of Caribbean Jewry dates back to the earliest moments of New World colonialism,

when the expulsions from the Iberian Peninsula in the 1490s propelled some Sephardic Jews and Conversos to resettle in the Americas. Jewish settlement in the Caribbean occurred over a period of more than three hundred years, establishing itself in the seventeenth century and peaking in the latter half of the eighteenth century. As a result, Dutch and British Caribbean colonies such as Curaçao, Suriname, Jamaica, and Barbados have had significant and long-standing Jewish populations" Lyon was part of an Ashkenazi migration that emerged in the late eighteenth and early nineteenth centuries. Casteel is right in noting that this Jewish presence "complicates master narratives of race and empire" as we see with Lyon's journey across the Atlantic (*Calypso Jews: Jewishness in the Caribbean Literary Imagination* [New York: Columbia University Press, 2016], 3, 4–5).

21. Arlette Farge, *The Allure of the Archives* (New Haven, CT: Yale University Press, 2013), 42.
22. Society of American Archivists Terminology, s.v. "provenance," https://dictionary.archivists.org/entry/provenance.html.
23. Steven L. Hensen, "The First Shall Be First: APPM and Its Impacts on American Archival Description," *Archivaria* 35 (Spring 1993): 64–70, 67.
24. Bethany Nowviskie, "Speculative Collections," nowviskie.org (blog), October 2016, nowviskie.org/2016/speculative-collections.
25. Nowviskie, "Speculative Collections."
26. Alan Galey and Stan Ruecker, "How a Prototype Argues," *Literary and Linguistic Computing: Journal of the Association for Literary and Linguistic Computing and the Association for Computers and the Humanities* 25, no. 4 (2010): 405–24, 407.
27. Jarrett M. Drake, "Liberatory Archives: Towards Belonging and Believing (Part 1)," *On Archivy* (blog), October 2016, medium.com/on-archivy/liberatory-archives-towards-belonging-and-believing-part-1-d26aaeboedd1.
28. Ann Laura Stoler, *Along the Archival Grain: Epistemic Anxieties and Colonial Common Sense* (Princeton, NJ: Princeton University Press, 2010), 21.
29. Diane Lyon Wead (great-great-granddaughter of A. S. Lyon), personal interview, January 2014.
30. A. S. Lyon, August 3, 1823, *1823 Diary,* digital edition, Lyon Archive, http://lyon.eastendarchives.net/editions, p. 96.
31. A. S. Lyon, November 3, 1823, *1823 Diary,* digital edition, Lyon Archive, n.p.
32. A. S. Lyon, December 10, 1823, *1823 Diary,* digital edition, Lyon Archive, p. 142.
33. A. S. Lyon, May 4, 1823, *1823 Diary,* digital edition, Lyon Archive, p. 30.
34. A. S. Lyon, January 24, 1826, *1826–1839 Diary,* digital edition, Lyon Archive, n.p.
35. As a formal category, the early nineteenth-century "private diary" is difficult to categorize. For some it represented a space to recount a day's

activities. For others it served the purpose of analysis and processing of events. Some diaries were private while others were meant to be public and shared among family members. Lyon's first diary begins with the word "Private." The second diary begins on the first day, leaving no clue about whether audiences were invited to read the diary. Both remained part of a family archive alongside diaries by family members. It's unclear if Lyon expected others to read his diaries, although he held on to them, carried them from England to Jamaica, and passed them down to the next generation, thereby enabling their survival to the present day. It was not uncommon for someone in Lyon's position in England to keep a diary. Martin Hewett explains, "The popularity of the early versions of the diaries of John Evelyn and Samuel Pepys which first appeared in the 1810s and 1820s prompted a flood of diary publications which peaked in the 1860s but ebbed thereafter only slowly" ("Diary, Autobiography and the Practice of Life History," in *Life Writing and Victorian Culture,* ed. David Amigoni [London: Routledge, 2006], 21–39, 26). Martin A. Danahay adds that "for the Victorian male the boundary between 'public' and 'private' was crucial to identity formation" ("Male Masochism: A Model of Victorian Masculine Identity Formation," in *Life Writing and Victorian Culture,* ed. David Amigoni [London: Routledge, 2006], 87–104, 88). Lyon's choice to include the word "Private" on the title page of the earlier diary might be a sign of his desire for privacy during the period of composition. If he wanted the diary to remain unread after his death, he might have made the decision to destroy the diary. His choice to preserve it suggests, perhaps, that later in life Lyon was willing to share the pages of his earlier diary with future generations.

36. Andrew Piper, *Dreaming in Books: The Making of the Bibliographic Imagination in the Romantic Age* (Chicago: University of Chicago Press, 2009), 4.
37. Carolyn Steedman, *An Everyday Life of the English Working Class: Work, Self and Sociability in the Early Nineteenth Century* (Cambridge: Cambridge University Press, 2013), 29.
38. A. S. Lyon, May 9, 1826, *1826–1839 Diary,* digital edition, Lyon Archive, n.p.
39. Michael Lobban, "'Private Law' and the Laissez-Faire State," in *The Victorian World,* ed. Martin Hewitt (New York: Routledge, 2012), 398–414, 405.
40. A. S. Lyon, May 10, 1826, *1826–1839 Diary,* digital edition, Lyon Archive, n.p.
41. A. S. Lyon, May 13, 1826, *1826–1839 Diary,* digital edition, Lyon Archive, n.p.
42. A. S. Lyon, June 15, 1826, *1826–1839 Diary,* digital edition, Lyon Archive, n.p.
43. Debates concerning the place of Jews in England continued throughout the nineteenth century. Lyon never mentions Jewish emancipation in his diary, or the extent to which British national identity could expand to include Jews. This passage in the diary suggests something more akin to what Ian Baucom describes as a proclivity to "identify oneself with

Britishness" that emerges as "an affective condition" rather than a legal stipulation (*Out of Place: Englishness, Empire, and the Locations of Identity* [Princeton, NJ: Princeton University Press, 1999], 11–12).

44. Anne-Marie Millim, *The Victorian Diary: Authorship and Emotional Labour* (Surrey, UK: Ashgate Publishing, 2013), 28.
45. A. S. Lyon, July 12, 1826, *1826–1839 Diary*, digital edition, Lyon Archive, n.p.
46. Miles Ogborn, *Spaces of Modernity: London's Geographies, 1680–1780* (New York: Guilford Press, 1998), 35.
47. By the 1880s, East End writers published with increasing frequently. Accounts from outsiders gazing upon the East End continued to be published, but at the same time literary culture witnessed a rise of published novels by East End writers, including Arthur Morrison and Israel Zangwill.
48. Barbara E. Mann calls "diaspora" a "loan word—from the Greek dia [through] and spora [to scatter or sow], and usually indicates an involuntary dispersed condition. First found in the Septuagint, it gained currency among Jewish communities to describe their dispersal and scattering away from the mythic centers. We have seen how the power of this spatial model predicated on center and margins has informed Jewish culture and history from its inception. Indeed, the idea of diaspora has persisted in Jewish consciousness and informed Jewish cultures in a variety of settings, often beyond any relation to physical or logistical conditions" (*Space and Place in Jewish Studies* [New Brunswick, NJ: Rutgers University Press, 2012], 98).
49. Anne McClintock, *Imperial Leather: Race, Gender and Sexuality in the Colonial Contest* (New York: Routledge, 1995), especially chaps. 1 and 6.
50. A. S. Lyon, May 15, 1826, *1826–1839 Diary*, digital edition, Lyon Archive, n.p.
51. Barbara E. Mann notes that "the idea of diaspora has persisted in Jewish consciousness and informed Jewish cultures in a variety of settings" (*Space and Place*, 98), and while A. S. Lyon never uses this word, it's difficult not to see his migration and his family's patterns of emigration in light of this context.
52. See Heidi Kaufman, "Jamaican Tricksters: Philip Cohen Labatt's (1823–54) Literary Crossings," in *Caribbean-Jewish Crossings: Atlantic Literature and Theory*, ed. Sarah Philips Casteel and Heidi Kaufman (Charlottesville: University of Virginia Press, 2019), 66–88; and Tim Barringer, Gillian Forrester, and Barbara Martinez-Ruiz, eds., *Art and Emancipation in Jamaica: Isaac Mendes Belisario and His Worlds* (New Haven, CT: Yale University Press, 2007).
53. Jane S. Gerber, introduction to *The Jews in the Caribbean*, ed. Jane S. Gerber (Oxford: Littman Library of Jewish Civilization, 2014), 11.
54. Kay Dian Kriz, "Belisario's 'Kingston's Cried' and the Refinement of Jewish Identity in the Late 1830s," in *Art and Emancipation in Jamaica: Isaac Mendes Belisario and His Worlds*, ed. Tim Barringer, Gillian Forrester, and

Barbara Martinez-Ruiz (New Haven, CT: Yale University Press, 2007), 163–78, 165.

55. Holly Snyder, "Customs of an Unruly Race," 151. It's important to note that recent scholarship has brought into focus the diversity of ethnic, religious, and racial groups living in nineteenth-century Jamaica. See Tim Barringer and Wayne Modest, eds., *Victorian Jamaica* (Durham, NC: Duke University Press, 2018). Nicholas Mirzoeff notes the existence in British colonies of "Creole anti-Semitism," which "led to discriminatory taxation, limits on Jewish slave ownership and compulsory militia service on the Sabbath. Local British Assemblies justified their actions because of the 'great ease and indolence' of the Jews, by which they meant their failure to plant and trade in slaves. In 1739, white Barbadians burnt down the Bridgetown synagogue during an anti-Semitic riot. In short, having failed to 'Europeanize' the Jews, the planters sought to 'Africanize' them, a task finally accomplished by nineteenth-century race science" ("Pissarro's Passage: The Sensation of Caribbean Jewishness in Diaspora," in *Diaspora and Visual Culture: Representing Africans and Jews,* ed. Nicholas Mirzoeff [London: Routledge, 2000], 57–75, 58).

56. Podcast interview with Annabel Foster-Davis, July 2017, Lyon Archive. In her podcast A. S. Lyon's great-great-granddaughter Annabel Foster-Davis frames her own experience of migration around her reading of A. S. Lyon's diary entry. Upon leaving Jamaica in the 1970s, she notes, "In some ways I regret leaving Jamaica," and says that she recalled A. S. Lyon's similar feelings: "He did say in one of his diaries, 'I shall always leave England with regrets.' And this is how I feel about Jamaica. I just have this strong connection."

57. N. Katherine Hayles, "Literary Texts and Cognitive Assemblages: The Case of Electronic Literature," *Electronic Book Review,* August 5, 2018, http://electronicbookreview.com/essay/literary-texts-as-cognitive-assemblages-the-case-of-electronic-literature.

58. My reading is indebted to Amy Earhart's helpful comparison on digital archives with new historicism. She explains, "The digital archive seems designed to meet the needs of the scholar interested in producing the 'thick description' criticism central to new historicist work. Derived from anthropologist Clifford Geertz, thick description was the practice of 'giving the act its place in a network of framing intentions and cultural meanings.' Thick description necessitated the examination of a broad selection of materials including literature, political documents, art, newspapers, material objects, and more" (*Traces of the Old Uses of the New: The Emergence of Digital Literary Studies* [Ann Arbor: University of Michigan Press, 2015], 45). In more ways than one, the Lyon Archive engages with forms of thick description to acknowledge the broad cultural meanings of the objects it houses, including responses to those objects.

59. Heidi Kaufman, transcription of a portion of the interview with Naomi Cream, August 2017. Full recording of this interview can be found on the Lyon Archive.
60. Podcast interview with Diane Lyon Wead, July 2017, Lyon Archive.
61. Jacques Derrida, *Archive Fever: A Freudian Impression,* trans. Eric Prenowitz (Chicago: University of Chicago Press, 1995), 11.
62. *Oxford English Dictionary Online,* s.v. "blue devils."
63. All passages taken from A. S. Lyon's *1826–1839 Diary:* digital edition, Lyon Archive, n.p.
64. Mai-Ling Maas, "A Lyon's Share of Sickness: One Man's Battle against the Blue Devils," Lyon Archive, December 2016.
65. For a more detailed study of working-class autobiographies of Victorians with disabilities, see Martha Stoddard Holmes, *Fictions of Affliction: Physical Disability in Victorian Culture* (Ann Arbor: University of Michigan Press, 2010); and for a fuller discussion of working-class self-representation, see Reginia Gagnier, *A History of Self-Representation in Britain, 1832–1920* (Oxford: Oxford University Press, 1991). Although A. S. Lyon is not writing in a traditional autobiographical form, many of Gagnier's observations and methodologies are tremendously useful for thinking about features of Lyon's diary writing.
66. The diaries had not been digitized at the point when I taught the course. I distributed copies of the diary we studied in the course on Canvas, our university's course management system. Digital surrogates of the diaries were made available to the public in 2017, once I received signed consent forms from Diane, Naomi, and Annabel.
67. The language from the revised consent form appears below.

> I understand that the purpose of the TLADP [The Lyon Archive Digital Project] is to gather, disseminate, and study the Lyon family's cultural activities. I understand that Professor Heidi Kaufman may include student work on TLADP, including, for example, student exhibit essays, mapping projects, and archival items. Student work will only be visible on TLADP once students have turned in signed release forms. I hereby donate the digital objects identified above to TLADP which may be displayed for educational purposes as part of TLADP or may be enfolded into the library's archive in the future. If requested, names of persons mentioned may be changed to protect the privacy of those mentioned.
>
> I hereby grant to Professor Heidi Kaufman property rights to the digital files (digital copies of the diaries, podcasts, photographs, etc.). By giving this permission, I understand that I retain all intellectual copyright and related rights that I may hold. Anyone who wishes to reproduce this material (the digital files displayed on TLADP)

must abide by the terms of a Creative Commons Attribution, Noncommercial License (Share Alike 4.0). This means that the digital objects listed above may be copied or distributed only for noncommercial, educational purposes *provided that I am given credit as owner of the originals.*

Use of or reproduction of the digital objects listed above or their content for *commercial use of any kind* requires my permission.

68. Bryan Cheyette, *Diasporas of the Mind: Jewish and Postcolonial Writing and the Nightmare of History* (New Haven, CT: Yale University Press, 2013), 6.
69. A. S. Lyon, September 14, 1823, *1823 Diary*, digital edition, Lyon Archive, p. 145.
70. Anat Rubinstein, "The Majesty and the Mystery of Kol Nidre," *Jerusalem Post*, September 17, 2018, https://www.jpost.com/israel-news/culture/the-majesty-and-the-mystery-of-kol-nidre-567366.
71. David J. Bodenhamer, John Corrigan, and Trevor M. Harris, "Introduction: Between Matter and Meaning: Deep Maps and the Spatial Humanities," *Deep Maps and Spatial Narratives*, ed. David J. Bodenhamer, John Corrigan, and Trevor M. Harris (Bloomington: Indiana University Press, 2015), 3.
72. The diary, in fact, seldom mentions his journey from one place to the next, only the final stopping point for each errand or event.
73. I draw from Julia Kristeva's notion of abjection in *Powers of Horror: An Essay on Abjection* (New York: Columbia University Press, 1982).
74. Derrida, *Archive Fever*, 36.
75. This epitaph appears on the grave of the Honorable Alexandre Joseph Lindo, located in Orange Street Cemetery, Kingston, Jamaica.
76. Mendelsohn, "Tongue Ties," 196.
77. Qtd. in James Stevens Curl, *The Victorian Celebration of Death* (Cheltenham, UK: Sutton, 2001), 11.
78. Curl, *Victorian Celebration*, 13–14.
79. James Robertson, Professor of History, University of the West Indies, Mona, personal conversation, January 2014; personal email, February 2021.
80. Colette Colligan and Michelle Levy have written an insightful article titled "Fieldwork" (in *Digital Pedagogy in Humanities: Concepts, Models, and Experiments*, MLA Commons, https://digitalpedagogy.mla.hcommons.org/keywords/fieldwork) that has helped me to think through the scope and aims of fieldwork's potential in humanities work. Summarizing Clifford, they note, "Fieldwork as a pedagogical practice has two central components: learning by doing through an immersive encounter, and learning by traveling and dwelling in a spatially-demarcated field (Clifford). We think that digital culture, and the new methods and tools it introduces, are transforming the practice of fieldwork, for scholars and students alike."

Particularly helpful is the point they make about the intersection of digital technology and fieldwork: "Fieldwork is undergoing a remediation of form, pushing the boundaries of academic inquiry and communication. As digital technology frees fieldwork from the traditional confines of a spatially demarcated 'field,' it introduces new immersive and expressive forms of fieldwork practice and pedagogy."

81. Shalini Puri, "Finding the Field: Notes on Caribbean Cultural Criticism, Area Studies, and the Form of Engagement," *Small Axe* 17, no. 2 (July 2013): 58–73, 59.
82. Henry Ware Jr., *The Works of Henry Ware, Jr., D.D.* (Boston: James Munroe, 1846), 1:206.
83. Mark Taylor and Dietrich Christian Lammerts, *Grave Matters* (London: Reaktion Books, 2002), 18.
84. This poem appears on the tombstone of Sarah Lyon, located in Elletson Road Cemetery, Kingston, Jamaica.
85. Mrs. Robert T. Dory, "In Memory of Dennis Conners," *Railroad Trainman*, 8, no. 83 (1891): 323.
86. From Mrs. M. G. Bruton, "The Beautiful," *Happy Home and Parlor Magazine*, ed. Rev. A. R. Baker, vol. 5–6 (Boston: C. Stone, 1857), 99. The periodical's editor, Baker, includes a statement on the last page of the magazine titled "Prospectus of The Happy Home and Parlor Magazine and of The Mother's Assistant and the Child's friend for 1858" in which he notes, "These Magazines have been published long enough to secure an established reputation for exerting a healthful, intellectual, moral, and religious influence upon the family," adding, "The publisher will spare neither labor nor expense to render these the best Magazines for the Christian family in the land" (no page number listed).
87. Jonathan Boyarin and Daniel Boyarin, *Powers of Diaspora* (Minneapolis: University of Minnesota Press, 2002), 4.
88. Antoinette Burton, "Introduction: Archive Fever, Archive Stories," in *Archive Stories: Facts, Fictions, and the Writing of History* (Durham, NC: Duke University Press, 2005), 1–24, 6.

4. An Archive of Lies

1. James Picciotto, *Sketches of Anglo-Jewish History* (London: Trübner, 1875), 232.
2. Maria Polack, *Fiction without Romance, or The Locket-Watch* (London: Effingham Wilson, 1830), 2 vols., 1:42.
3. Polack, *Fiction without Romance*, 1:51–52, 53.
4. David Conway notes, "Two if these careers, that of Lyon and his nephew John Braham, developed under the aegis of Isaac Polack, *chazan* [cantor] of the Great Synagogue," also known as the German synagogue located in

London's East End (*Jewry in Music: Entry to the Profession from the Enlightenment to Richard Wagner* [Cambridge: Cambridge University Press, 2012], 75). It's not clear whether Isaac Polack is related to Maria Polack; her father, Ephraim Polack; or her husband, Lipman Polack. The name "Polack" was common in the East End in this period. For good discussions of this collaboration and its significance within Anglo-Jewish culture in this period, see Sheila A. Spector, "The Liturgical Context of the Byron-Nathan Hebrew Melodies," *Studies in Romanticism* 47 (Fall 2008): 393–412; and David Ben-Merre, "Reading Hebrew Melodies," *Shofar: An Interdisciplinary Journal* 24, no. 2 (2006): 11–32.

5. James Picciotto, *Sketches of Anglo-Jewish History* (London: Trübner, 1875), 232.
6. Report of the Subcommittee, May 13, 1856, Norwood Archives, 1678–1951, Archives of the Jews' Orphan Asylum, University of Southampton, Hartley Library MS 127, AJ/19/C/76/1.
7. *House,* created by David Shore (Heel and Toe Films, Shore Z Productions, Bad Hat Harry Productions, NBC Universal Television Studio), 2004–2012.
8. Natalie Zemon Davis, *Fiction in the Archives: Pardon Tales and Their Tellers in Sixteenth-Century France* (Stanford, CA: Stanford University Press, 1987), vii, 2.
9. Davis, *Fiction in the Archives,* 3.
10. Davis, *Fiction in the Archives,* 4.
11. Arlette Farge, *The Allure of the Archives,* foreword by Natalie Zemon Davis (New Haven, CT: Yale University Press, 2013), 29–30.
12. I use the term "digital archive" to refer to archives created on digital platforms. Digital archives are composed of digital objects, such as databases, digital recordings of podcast interviews, or multimedia maps. The term "physical archives" refers, in contrast, to archives made of physical, material objects. Those physical objects would include, for example, papers, photographs, and headstones.
13. Nancy K. Miller, *What They Saved: Pieces of a Jewish Past* (Lincoln: University of Nebraska Press, 2011), 126.
14. Picciotto, *Sketches,* 257.
15. Picciotto, *Sketches,* 257, 259.
16. P. Colquhoun, LL.D., *A Treatise on the Police of the Metropolis; Containing a Detail of the Various Crimes and Misdemeanors by which Public and Private Property and Security Are, at Present, Injured and Endangered: and Suggesting Remedies for their Prevention,* 6th ed. (London: H. Baldwin and Son, printers, 1800), 120–21.
17. Colquhoun, *Treatise,* 120–21.
18. Dr. Gerry Black, *J.F.S.: The History of the Jews' Free School, London, since 1732* (London: Tymsder, 1998), 14.

19. See Heidi Kaufman, *English Origins, Jewish Discourse, and the Nineteenth-Century British Novel* (University Park: Pennsylvania State University Press, 2009), especially chap. 1.
20. Qtd. in Picciotto, *Sketches*, 259.
21. John Marriott, *Beyond the Tower: A History of East London* (New Haven, CT: Yale University Press, 2011), 157. See chap. 1 for further examples.
22. Marriott, *Beyond the Tower*, 156.
23. Michael Ragussis, *Figures of Conversion: "The Jewish Question" and English National Identity* (Durham, NC: Duke University Press, 1995), 3.
24. Ragussis, *Figures*, 4.
25. Black, *J.F.S.*, 15.
26. Todd Endelman, *The Jews of Britain, 1656 to 2000* (Berkeley: University of California Press, 2002), 86–87.
27. Edward S. Conway, "The Origins of the Jewish Orphanage," *Transactions & Miscellanies* (Jewish Historical Society of England) 22 (1968–69): 53–66, 57.
28. Norwood Archives, 1678–1951, Archives of the Jews' Orphan Asylum, University of Southampton, Hartley Library MS 127 AJ/19/C/76/1.
29. Report of Education Committee, September 5613 [1853], Norwood Archives, 1678–1951, Archives of the Jews' Orphan Asylum, University of Southampton, Hartley Library MS 127, AJ 19/C/76/1.
30. Simon Phillips, statement, January Examinations, appendix F, 1853. Norwood Archives, 1678–1951, Archives of the Jews' Orphan Asylum, University of Southampton, Hartley Library MS 127, AJ/19/C/76/1.
31. January Examinations, 1856. Norwood Archives, 1678–1951, Archives of the Jews' Orphan Asylum, University of Southampton, Hartley Library MS 127, AJ/19/C/76/1.
32. January Examinations, 1856. Norwood Archives, 1678–1951, Archives of the Jews' Orphan Asylum, University of Southampton, Hartley Library MS 127, AJ/19/C/76/1.
33. Myer Levy, January Examinations, appendix F, 1853. Norwood Archives, 1678–1951, Archives of the Jews' Orphan Asylum, University of Southampton, Hartley Library MS 127, AJ/19/C/76/1.
34. Myer Levy, January Examinations, appendix F, 1853. Norwood Archives, 1678–1951, Archives of the Jews' Orphan Asylum, University of Southampton, Hartley Library MS 127, AJ/19/C/76/1. I've added punctuation in this and subsequent quoted passages only where it aids in clarity. I have not otherwise corrected typographical errors from the original documents.
35. Myer Levy, January Examinations, appendix F, 1853. Norwood Archives, 1678–1951, Archives of the Jews' Orphan Asylum, University of Southampton, Hartley Library MS 127, AJ/19/C/76/1.

36. Myer Levy, January Examinations, appendix F, 1853. Norwood Archives, 1678–1951, Archives of the Jews' Orphan Asylum, University of Southampton, Hartley Library MS 127, AJ/19/C/76/1.
37. Myer Levy, January Examinations, appendix F, 1853. Norwood Archives, 1678–1951, Archives of the Jews' Orphan Asylum, University of Southampton, Hartley Library MS 127, AJ/19/C/76/1.
38. Cheryl L. Nixon, *The Orphan in Eighteenth-Century Law and Literature: Estate, Blood, and Body* (Surrey, UK: Ashgate, 2011), 15.
39. January Examinations, appendix F, 1853. Norwood Archives, 1678–1951, Archives of the Jews' Orphan Asylum, University of Southampton, Hartley Library MS 127, AJ/19/C/76/1.
40. P. Abrahams, letter to the President and Committee of Enquiry of the Jews' Orphan Asylum, February 11, 1857. Norwood Archives, 1678–1951, Archives of the Jews' Orphan Asylum, University of Southampton, Hartley Library MS 127, AJ/19/C/76/1.
41. P. Abrahams, letter to the President and Committee of Enquiry of the Jews' Orphan Asylum, February 11, 1857. Norwood Archives, 1678–1951, Archives of the Jews' Orphan Asylum, University of Southampton, Hartley Library MS 127, AJ/19/C/76/1.
42. Simon Phillips, letter, February 19, 1857. Norwood Archives, 1678–1951, Archives of the Jews' Orphan Asylum, University of Southampton, Hartley Library MS 127, AJ/19/C/76/1.
43. Simon Phillips, partial letter, February 19, 1857. Norwood Archives, 1678–1951, Archives of the Jews' Orphan Asylum, University of Southampton, Hartley Library MS 127, AJ/19/C/76/1.
44. Simon Phillips, statement, 12 o'clock February 19, 1857. Norwood Archives, 1678–1951, Archives of the Jews' Orphan Asylum, University of Southampton, Hartley Library MS 127, AJ/19/C/76/1.
45. Ann Laura Stoler, *Along the Archival Grain: Epistemic Anxieties and Colonial Common Sense* (Princeton, NJ: Princeton University Press, 2009); Antoinette Burton, ed., *Archive Stories: Facts, Fictions, and the Writing of History* (Durham, NC: Duke University Press, 2005); and Anjali Arondekar, *For the Record: On Sexuality and the Colonial Archive in India* (Durham, NC: Duke University Press, 2009).
46. Montague Leverson, cover letter, February 16, 1857. Norwood Archives, 1678–1951, Archives of the Jews' Orphan Asylum, University of Southampton, Hartley Library MS 127, AJ/19/C/76/1.
47. Montague Leverson, cover letter, February 16, 1857. Norwood Archives, 1678–1951, Archives of the Jews' Orphan Asylum, University of Southampton, Hartley Library MS 127, AJ/19/C/76/1.
48. Report of Education Committee, September 5613 [1853]. Jews' Orphan Asylum Papers, University of Southampton, Hartley Library MS 127, AJ/19/C/76/1.

49. Appendix C, statement offered by Moses Angel, 1853. Jews' Orphan Asylum Papers, University of Southampton, Hartley Library MS 127, AJ/19/C/76/1.
50. Myer Davis, statement, January 28, 1857. Norwood Archives, 1678–1951, Archives of the Jews' Orphan Asylum, University of Southampton, Hartley Library MS 127, AJ/19/C/76/1.
51. Myer D. Davis, letter to the Chairman and Members of the Education Committee, January 14, 1856. Jews' Orphan Asylum Papers, University of Southampton, Hartley Library MS 127, AJ/19/C/76/1.
52. Myer D. Davis, letter to the Chairman and Members of the Education Committee, January 16, 1856. Jews' Orphan Asylum Papers, University of Southampton, Hartley Library MS 127, AJ/19/C/76/1.
53. Transcription of testimony of Mr. Myer Davis by Subcommittee of Jews' Orphan Asylum, April 17, 1856. Jews' Orphan Asylum Papers, University of Southampton, Hartley Library MS 127, AJ/19/C/76/1.
54. Myer D. Davis, letter to the President of the Jews' Orphan Asylum, May 20, 5616 1856. Jews' Orphan Asylum Papers, University of Southampton, Hartley Library MS 127, AJ/19/C/76/1.
55. Myer D. Davis, statement to the President and Members of the Com^{ee} of Investigation of the Jews' Orphan Asylum, January 28, 1857. Jews' Orphan Asylum Papers, University of Southampton, Hartley Library MS 127, AJ/19/C/76/1.
56. Myer D. Davis, statement to the President and Members of the Com^{ee} of Investigation of the Jews' Orphan Asylum, January 28, 1857. Jews' Orphan Asylum Papers, University of Southampton, Hartley Library MS 127, AJ/19/C/76/1, p. 1; Davis's letters did not include page numbers. Most were only one page. However, he did include page numbers on the longer ninety-two-page statement. I have therefore included page numbers when referring to passages from this statement.
57. Myer D. Davis, statement to the President and Members of the Com^{ee} of Investigation of the Jews' Orphan Asylum, January 28, 1857. Jews' Orphan Asylum Papers, University of Southampton, Hartley Library MS 127, AJ/19/C/76/1, pp.1–2.
58. Myer D. Davis, statement to the President and Members of the Com^{ee} of Investigation of the Jews' Orphan Asylum, January 28, 1857. Jews' Orphan Asylum Papers, University of Southampton, Hartley Library MS 127, AJ/19/C/76/1, p. 48.
59. Myer D. Davis, statement to the President and Members of the Com^{ee} of Investigation of the Jews' Orphan Asylum, January 28, 1857. Jews' Orphan Asylum Papers, University of Southampton, Hartley Library MS 127, AJ/19/C/76/1, p.53.
60. Myer D. Davis, statement to the President and Members of the Com^{ee} of Investigation of the Jews' Orphan Asylum, January 28, 1857. Jews' Orphan

Asylum Papers, University of Southampton, Hartley Library MS 127, AJ/19/C/76/1, p.54.

61. Myer D. Davis, statement to the President and Members of the Com^{ee} of Investigation of the Jews' Orphan Asylum, January 28, 1857. Jews' Orphan Asylum Papers, University of Southampton, Hartley Library MS 127, AJ/19/C/76/1, p.86.
62. Myer D. Davis, statement to the President and Members of the Com^{ee} of Investigation of the Jews' Orphan Asylum, January 28, 1857. Jews' Orphan Asylum Papers, University of Southampton, Hartley Library MS 127, AJ/19/C/76/1, p. 2.
63. Myer D. Davis, statement to the President and Members of the Com^{ee} of Investigation of the Jews' Orphan Asylum, January 28, 1857. Jews' Orphan Asylum Papers, University of Southampton, Hartley Library MS 127, AJ/19/C/76/1, p. 2.
64. H. S. Jones, *Intellect and Character in Victorian England: Mark Pattison and the Invention of the Don* (Cambridge: Cambridge University Press, 2007), 129.
65. Samuel Smiles, *Character* (London: John Murray, 1876), 1.
66. "Myer David Davis," in *The Palgrave Dictionary of Anglo-Jewish History*, ed. William D. Rubinstein, Michael A. Jolles, and Hilary L. Rubinstein (Houndmills, Basingstone, UK: Palgrave Macmillan, 2011), 204.
67. *Palgrave Dictionary*, 204.
68. *Palgrave Dictionary*, 204.
69. *Palgrave Dictionary*, 204.
70. Myer D. Davis, letter to the President of the Jews' Orphan Asylum, May 21, 5616 1856. Jews' Orphan Asylum Papers, University of Southampton, Hartley Library MS 127, AJ/19/C/76/1.
71. The Rev. John Mills, *The British Jews* (London: Houlston & Stoneman, 1853), 206.
72. Archivist's note, n.d. Jews' Orphan Asylum Papers, University of Southampton, Hartley Library MS 127, AJ/19/C/76/1.
73. No author, no title, *Jewish Chronicle* 5, no. 14 (January 12, 1849): 116. The spelling of Lipman Polack's name changes frequently, alternating between Lipman and Lepman.
74. No author, "Lecture at Malton," *Jewish Chronicle* 10, no. 21 (February 24, 1854): 181.
75. No author, "Malton.—Musical Lecture," *Jewish Chronicle* 12, no. 20 (May 4, 1855): 156.
76. No author, "Our Synagogal Music," *Jewish Chronicle* 14, no. 111 (January 30, 1857): 886.
77. "Our Synagogal Music," 886.
78. "Our Synagogal Music," 886.

79. References in the following conversation stem from my email correspondence with Nicholas Hatton, Woodhams Stone Collection (Registered Charity Number 1177312), Malton & Norton Heritage Centre, Malton, England YO17 9HX, personal email March 2021. I am extremely grateful for Nicholas's generous help and expert guidance in tracking down and interpreting records about the Polack family.
80. Ephraim purchased a "Consolidated Loan Annuity," listed in *The Unclaimed Dividend Books of the Bank of England* (London: W. Strange, 1851). See also the Bank of England, *The Names and Descriptions of the Proprietors of Unclaimed Dividends on Bank Stock, and on All Government Funds and Securities, Transferable at the Bank of England. By Order of the Court of Directors* (London: Teape and Jones, 1823).
81. "Dreams," originally published in the *New Monthly Belle Assemblée* (London: Joseph Robertson, 1834), 194. It appeared again in the *Dudley Castle Miscellany* (Wolverhampton: W. Parke, 1860), 98.
82. Jacques Derrida, *Archive Fever: A Freudian Impression* (Chicago: University of Chicago Press, 1995), 1.

Conclusion

1. I borrow the term "understory" from Nancy Miller, *What They Saved: Pieces of a Jewish Past* (Lincoln: University of Nebraska Press, 2011).
2. Lady's Visitor's Book, Norwood Archives, 1678–1951, Archives of the Jews' Orphan Asylum, University of Southampton, Hartley Library MS 127, AJ/19/C/76/1.
3. Maria Polack, preface to *Fiction without Romance, or The Locket-Watch* (London: Effingham Wilson, 1830), 1:i-ii.
4. Suzanne L. Barnett and Katherine Bennett Gustafson, "Introduction: The Radical Aesop: William Godwin and the Juvenile Library, 1805–1825," *Romantic Circles,* July 2014, https://romantic-circles.org/editions/godwin_fables/editions.2014.godwin_fables.introduction.html.
5. Minute Book of the Jews' Free School, Norwood Archives, 1678–1951, University of Southampton, Hartley Library MS 127, AJ/19/C/76/1.
6. Abigail Lindo was a relative of Benjamin Disraeli. Her father, David Abarbanel Lindo, had close ties with Disraeli's family. Abigail learned Hebrew and biblical studies from her mother's brother, Moses Mocatta. This choice of subject was unusual for the education of girls in this period. Abigail Lindo is one of the earliest women to become a philologist.
7. Michal Shahaf, "Charlotte Montefiore's Secret: The Cheap Jewish Library—An Educational Philanthropic Mission," *Nashim: A Journal of Jewish Women's Studies & Gender Issues* 30 (Spring 2016): 48–73.

8. For a relevant and helpful study of writing and reading from below, see Jonathan Rose, *The Intellectual Life of the British Working Classes* (New Haven, CT: Yale University Press, 2008).
9. Kenneth Rose, *Elusive Rothschild, The Life of Victor, Third Baron* (London: Wiedenfield and Nicholson, 2003), 293–94.
10. From Thomas Burke, *The Real East End* (London: Constable, 1932). A copy of the original from Burke's book has been reproduced here by permission of Pearl Binder's children.
11. Hugh Meller and Brian Parsons, *London Cemeteries: An Illustrated Guide and Gazetteer* (Amersham, UK: Avebury, 1981), 172–73.

INDEX

Page numbers in italics refer to illustrations.

RECENT BOOKS IN THE

Victorian Literature and Culture Series

Evangelical Gothic: The English Novel and the Religious War on Virtue from Wesley to "Dracula"
Christopher Herbert

Reading with the Senses in Victorian Literature and Science
David Sweeney Coombs

Parting Words: Victorian Poetry and Public Address
Justin A. Sider

The Physics of Possibility: Victorian Fiction, Science, and Gender
Michael Tondre

Willful Submission: Sado-Erotics and Heavenly Marriage in Victorian Poetry
Amanda Paxton

Pirating Fictions: Ownership and Creativity in Nineteenth-Century Popular Culture
Monica F. Cohen

Mathilde Blind: Late-Victorian Culture and the Woman of Letters
James Diedrick

Poetry and the Thought of Song in Nineteenth-Century Britain
Elizabeth K. Helsinger

The Antagonist Principle: John Henry Newman and the Paradox of Personality
Lawrence Poston

Personal Business: Character and Commerce in Victorian Literature and Culture
Aeron Hunt

Second Person Singular: Late Victorian Women Poets and the Bonds of Verse
Emily Harrington

The Ghost behind the Masks: The Victorian Poets and Shakespeare
W. David Shaw

Victorian Poets and the Changing Bible
Charles LaPorte

Liberal Epic: The Victorian Practice of History from Gibbon to Churchill
Edward Adams

Supposing "Bleak House"
John O. Jordan

Feeling for the Poor: Bourgeois Compassion, Social Action, and the Victorian Novel
Carolyn Betensky

The Science of Religion in Britain, 1860–1915
Marjorie Wheeler-Barclay

Reading for the Law: British Literary History and Gender Advocacy
Christine L. Krueger

The Dynamics of Genre: Journalism and the Practice of Literature in Mid-Victorian Britain
Dallas Liddle

The Fowl and the Pussycat: Love Letters of Michael Field, 1876–1909
Edited by Sharon Bickle

Victorian Prism: Refractions of the Crystal Palace
Edited by James Buzard, Joseph W. Childers, and Eileen Gillooly

Nostalgia in Transition, 1780–1917
Linda M. Austin

The English Cult of Literature: Devoted Readers, 1774–1880
William R. McKelvy

Artist of Wonderland: The Life, Political Cartoons, and Illustrations of Tenniel
Frankie Morris

The Material Interests of the Victorian Novel
Daniel Hack

Behind Her Times: Transition England in the Novels of Mary Arnold Ward
Judith Wilt

The Circus and Victorian Society
Brenda Assael

Christina Rossetti: The Patience of Style
Constance W. Hassett

Frances Power Cobbe: Victorian Feminist, Journalist, Reformer
Sally Mitchell

Acting Naturally: Victorian Theatricality and Authenticity
Lynn M. Voskuil

Manufacturing Culture: Vindications of Early Victorian Industry
Joseph Bizup